Net Results:
Web Marketing That Works

USWeb and Rick E. Bruner

Hayden
Books

Hayden Publishing, Indianapolis, Indiana

Net Results: Web Marketing That Works

Library of Congress Catalog Number: 97-072165
ISBN: 1-56830-414-5

Copyright © 1998 by USWeb Corporation

Printed in the United States of America 1 2 3 4 5 6 7 8 9 0

Warning and Disclaimer

Trademark Acknowledgments

Publisher *Jordan Gold*

Executive Editor *Mark Taber*

Managing Editor *Patrick Kanouse*

Acquisitions Editor
Patty Guyer
Randi Roger

Development Editor
Scott D. Meyers

Project Editor
Dayna Isley

Copy Editor
Sean Medlock

Team Coordinator
Lorraine Schaffer

Cover Designer
Gary Adair
Jean Bisesi

Book Designer
Ann Jones

Production Team
Marcia Deboy
Michael Dietsch
Cynthia Fields
Maureen West

Indexer
Christine Nelsen

Visit Macmillan Computer Publishing's Web site at
http://www.mcp.com

About the Authors

USWeb Corporation was founded in 1995 and is a leading Internet professional services firm helping clients develop Internet strategies and improve business processes by using Internet-based technologies. USWeb offices nationwide provide clients with Internet business strategy consulting, needs analysis, architecture planning, Internet, Intranet, and Extranet solution design and development, audience development, hosting, professional education, and Internet certification services. The company works with a diverse range of clients, from Fortune 500 corporations to medium-size organizations. USWeb's strategic alliances with technology leaders such as Hewlett-Packard, Intel, Microsoft, SAP, and Sun Microsystems enable the company to assess how Internet technologies can be leveraged to transform a business. The company is headquartered at the USWeb Internet Strategy & Solutions Center in Santa Clara, California. Go to **http://www.usweb.com/** for company news and information.

Starting in a windowless 300 square foot office in Sausalito's "online shoreline," Cybernautics pioneered the disciplines of Web site awareness, online PR, and online direct marketing for such clients as Standard & Poors', Paramount Television, Women's Wire, and Silicon Graphics. In late 1996, the company added online media buying and planning to its range of services.

Bob Heyman, an entertainment attorney with an expertise in marketing music, and Leland Harden, a telecom veteran who helped found MediaLink, the video news release network, co-founded Cybernautics in the fall of 1994. From the beginning, the company concentrated not only on Web site design, but also on helping clients make a return from their Internet investment by developing targeted audiences for their Web offerings. Keith Schaefer, a legendary Silicon Valley marketer whose background includes success at Atari, NEC, and Viacom joined the company in 1996 as president.

USWeb Corporation acquired Cybernautics in September of 1997. Cybernautics has now become the Audience Development Group at USWeb.

Rick E. Bruner received a degree in writing from Columbia University and has worked as a journalist and publicist for nine years. In 1990, he joined "generation expat" in Eastern Europe and co-founded *Budapest Week* newspaper, Hungary's first independent English-language newspaper, serving as its editor-in-chief for two and a half years. In 1993, he began freelancing as a roving correspondent around Central Europe, writing regularly on social, business, and technology issues for *The Boston Globe* and *European Computer Sources*, as well as *The San Francisco Examiner*, *Cosmopolitan*, *Wired*, and other publications. He first ventured into online publishing in early 1995 with "The Hungary Report," a newsletter and Web site updated with weekly events of the region, reaching more than 3,000 email subscribers. In 1996, he moved to San Francisco and joined Niehaus Ryan Group Public Relations where he managed the PR launch for Marimba, Inc. and other firms. In 1997, he founded Bruner Communications, a strategic Web marketing consultancy. He also writes regularly about the Internet for *Advertising Age* magazine and other media. Visit **http://www.bruner.net** for more information.

Dedication and Acknowledgments

From USWeb

Leland Harden, Bob Heyman, and Keith Schaefer would like to dedicate this book:

To Elise & Verity Harden, Jill Cagan & Sean Heyman, and Larry Lucchesi, for their patience and support.

To our Employees, for their energy and enthusiasm. To our Shareholders for making all things possible.

To Bruce Gilpin, Joe Firmage, and Toby Corey, among others at USWeb, for embracing our vision.

And especially to our Clients, for allowing us to explore the cutting-edge of Cyber Marketing on their behalf.

From Rick E. Bruner

To Adrienne, with much love.

Like all books, this one could not have been written without lots of help and support from many sources. I wish to thank some here.

First and foremost, the folks from USWeb Marin, who envisaged, shaped, and managed the whole project: Keith Schaefer, Leland Harden, and especially Bob Heyman. The whole USWeb Marin crew contributed greatly to every chapter, but special credit is due for Alex Guerrero, Doug Moody, Rebecca Gilson, George Lawson, Priti Choksi, and Guy Hill, as well as Kristin Copper, Pete Everett, Michael Sheehan, Molly Parsley, Chris Frey, Jody Holman, and Steve Peace.

Very big thanks also to our faithful agent M.T. Caen for tremendous support, as well as the wonderful Macmillan editors Jim Chalex, Scott Meyers, Patty Guyer, Dayna Isley, Sean Medlock, and Randi Roger.

Special thanks to good friend Carla Schlemminger for superb networking.

Thanks also to my editors at *Advertising Age*, Kate Maddox, Pat Riedman, and Debbie Williamson, for patience, good cheer, and insight.

My mentors in understanding the wild, wooly Internet: Steve Carlson, Dave Del Torto, Ed Niehaus, and Bill Ryan. Good friends for lots of favors: Smitty, Tara, Strick, LeBor, Nick and Laci (a great guy, but a hell of a house guest, who drove me to the brink of insanity in the book's final weeks).

Plus, thanks to many industry insiders who shared generously of their expertise, including Marissa Verson Harrison, Ed Anuff, Bills Bass & Doyle, Evan Neufeld, Marc Johnson, Mark Mandle, Richard Hoy, Paul Grand, Neil Monnens, Kent Valandra, Rich LeFurgy, Ken McCarthy, Bill Miltenberg, and Andrew de Vries, among many others.

Contents at a Glance

Table of Contents

3 Design Optimization 71

4 Domain Brand 87

Foreword

The most tired cliché on the Web holds that no one's making any money. This book stands as an emphatic, real-world refutation of that fallacy.

At the root of this cliché is a reluctance to see the enormous creativity resident in global business. It's a testament to the ability of talented technologists and marketers—make that talented business people—to understand the online medium, to understand business, and then to devise fresh and effective vehicles that marry the two. Marketing is always the nexus between the business—any business—and the customer. Since the advent of the Web, we've just made it up as we've gone along.

I'm only half-kidding. The beauty of the new medium is that it has let a thousand ideas bloom; the reality of the new medium is that so many of these ideas have withered. The ideas that have flourished uniformly interpret time-honored principles in productive new ways.

To the extent the cliché is historically accurate, it's due to the uncanny ability of some to repeat past mistakes, to fail to re-think old norms and assumptions, or to hold fast to the belief that business must somehow be re-molded to fit a new paradigm. It doesn't, but the new technological environment must be understood, respected, and ultimately made malleable to serve business strategies.

To the extent the cliché has been shredded, it reflects an acceptance of the medium on its merits and a deftness in applying the medium to proven merchandising and marketing models. There is, indeed, a timeless quality to the lessons enumerated here: Whether online or off, you market in the same way. You still must connect one-to-one; only the techniques have changed.

As this book demonstrates with ringing clarity, the Internet is already on the way to becoming the preferred medium for a new generation of buyers, sellers, and creators. Clearly, some products and some business models are better suited to living online than others. For now, the Internet supplements, but does not replace, other media. But the migration to it is inexorable, and from high-tech wares to packaged goods and beyond, it will permeate every realm where people do business. Over time, the Internet will be the primary medium for information, communications, and education.

Best practices are elusive when basic practices are still evolving and learning is both instant and incremental. This book aims to articulate, share, and ultimately codify best practices; to showcase the strategies and tactics that work (and work powerfully) in Web marketing; and to place in bold relief the notion that "cultivating quality relationships with customers is the foremost value proposition of the Internet."

Indeed, the Internet is entirely about a new (pardon the expression) web of relationships. From our perspective, the most critical relationship exists between the Web professional services firm and its client. Together, we take the tabula rasa and make choices that determine all of the other relationships online—especially the bond between the business and its customers, its audience.

USWeb Marin—our Audience Development Group, which began life as Cybernautics—hasn't merely contributed to the evolution of best practices. It invented many of them and continues to serve as a beacon of common sense—technical sense, marketing sense, business sense—for those seeking to mine this medium.

The very notion of Audience Development on the Internet was spawned there and now ranks as a vital and growing Web discipline. "Audience Development" is another way of describing techniques that help people form new habits around participation in the Internet. So many of these techniques are by now familiar—linking with other sites, optimizing traffic with search engines, sponsoring awards and contests, seeding newsgroups and mailing lists, convening forums, using chat, staging cyberevents—that they have in fact become habits online. Audience Development now engages established companies from the advertising, market research, and public relations spheres, and emerging organizations who have come to adopt the Web as their vernacular.

Our paradigm of Audience Development holds that the Internet is a constellation of micro communities. We find audiences who are interested in the value proposition, and then evangelize and recruit. We cannot always make them drink, but we've surely got the divining rod. As we work to make the Internet truly mainstream, we won't just be delivering eyeballs, but creating experiences and environments where existing businesses can thrive and new businesses can be launched.

For those who still insist that the payoff from the Internet is years away, we say: Marketing well is the best revenge. To all current and would-be Web marketers, let this volume be your playbook.

Toby Corey, President USWeb
Keith Schaefer, Managing Partner, USWeb Marin

Online Marketing 3.0

B elieve the hype. There is no question that within the span of about two years in the mid-'90s, the Internet and the World Wide Web have become the most important new communication media since television, and ones that are fundamentally reshaping contemporary understanding of sales and marketing.

As new as these media are, discovering how to harness their power for marketing purposes is still a work in progress. This book is merely an early chapter in that history. We are not foolish enough to try to predict how the Internet will affect consumers and marketers 25 years from now. Rather, this book simply shares the extensive experience of the authors, as well as many other successful Web marketers who are finding immediate rewards online today.

In our first draft of this introduction, before we had written any of the book, we began by saying, "Sites on the Web today can effectively be broken down into two categories: those that get it and those that don't." Having since completed the book, we realize that this is not only too cynical, but it ignores the importance of the learning process inherent in entering this new medium.

The marketers who supposedly "get it" didn't simply wake up one day with divine insight. They learned by doing. No book can substitute for experience. There are many lessons in online marketing, as with everything else in life, that can be learned only through firsthand challenges, practice, and mistakes.

The object of *Net Results* is to give you a substantial boost through that learning curve and hasten your journey along the road to "getting it." We draw on the experiences of our clients and other leading companies. We quote USWeb and competitors. We discuss mistakes and mastery with marketers at familiar companies such as Tower Records, Tide, Federal Express, and *The New York Times*, as well as leading online-only ventures including Yahoo!, Amazon.com, Women's Wire, Excite, and many others.

This book doesn't contain an introduction to the Internet and the Web. We assume that you already have some general familiarity with cyberspace and at least a modicum of faith in its potential for marketing. We take for granted that you receive at least as many emails as voice mails a day, know that "dub-dub-dub-whatever-dot-com" refers to a Web address, and have cursed the design department of *Wired* magazine at least once.

You may already have a Web site and be in the thick of Internet marketing right now, on the road to "getting it" on your own. *Net Results* aims to help you take your online business strategies to the next level.

If you're a "newbie," uninitiated to the Internet at large, but are nonetheless determined to commit to its commercial potential, consider *Net Results* an advanced course for which you've skipped a prerequisite or two. With a bit of catching-up on the side, you'll be better off jumping straight onto the fast track. In the Appendix, "Internet Resources," we list some introductory Internet resources, history of the Net, glossaries, and other tools that should ease your transition to the new medium.

NOTE

The Appendix also contains the URLs for all the sites and companies mentioned throughout the course of this book.

We should also note that *Net Results* doesn't dwell much on pure business-to-business uses of the Web or the application of Internet technologies to internal corporate information processes, also called *intranets*. Although USWeb has much experience creating intranets and online business-to-business plans for its clients, those strategies are distinct enough to require a separate book. *Net Results* concerns itself exclusively with using the Internet as a consumer sales and marketing channel.

Why Read This Book?

Although we realize *Net Results* isn't the first book dedicated to online marketing, we haven't seen a more comprehensive, authoritative approach to the subject.

USWeb Marin, whose executives first conceived of this book, have been in the business of developing online marketing strategies for clients since shortly after the Web first emerged into the public consciousness. Previously known as Cybernautics before being adopted into the prestigious national USWeb family of design and marketing subsidiary companies, USWeb Marin has developed winning online marketing strategies for America Online, American Airlines, Avon, Bristol Myers Squibb, Diamond Multimedia, Macromedia, Microsoft, MTV, Netscape, Paramount Digital Entertainment, ParentTime, REI, Silicon Graphics, Time Inc., US West, and Women's Wire, among many other satisfied clients. The Marin division heads USWeb's Audience Development strategies group.

Rick E. Bruner brings to *Net Results* a background of nearly 10 years in journalism, publishing, and publicity. He first ventured into online publishing in January 1995 with the *Hungary Report*, a newsletter and Web site devoted to news of Central Europe, where he lived at the time. After a year working for a Silicon Valley public relations agency, representing such clients as Marimba, the push technology software leader, he has spent the last year as a freelance writer reporting Internet news for *Advertising Age* and other media. His company, Bruner Communications, also consults on Web marketing for select clients.

What sets *Net Results* apart from other books on Web marketing is its balanced treatment of both strategy and tactics. Part I, "Get the Site Right: Web Marketing Fundamentals," focuses on the fundamental strategies behind successful online marketing. Although several guides describe how to "get hits" for a Web site, we realize that no matter how many hits a site gets, there's no point in promoting it at all if the business lacks clear marketing objectives and the content offers little value to consumers.

Chapters 1 and 2 get to the heart of online marketing strategy. In Chapter 1, "Return on Investment Goals," we discuss the six key ways in which companies are successfully leveraging the Net to realize marketing objectives: brand-building, direct marketing, online sales, customer support, market research, and content publishing/services.

In Chapter 2, "Web Value Propositions," we analyze the critical features of the Internet that produce the most profound benefits for both marketers and users. Namely, that the Net is interactive, personal, infocentric, instantaneous, measurable, flexible, interlinked, and economical.

Chapters 3 and 4 complete the fundamentals of getting your site right, with in-depth discussions of design and domain issues. Chapter 3, "Design Optimization" does not pretend to inform designers of artistic principles, but rather addresses some of the key methods for improving your users' experiences with your site, such as fast response times and easy navigation.

Chapter 4, "Domain Brand," takes a close look at what is probably the most neglected aspect of online marketing strategy, even by some of the biggest, most successful online marketers. It examines the important principles of naming a site, how to settle domain disputes, and why domains such as generalmotors.com, pepsicola.com, and camry.com don't point to the companies you'd expect.

Part II, "Audience Development," reveals USWeb's highly effective, holistic approach to creating and maintaining a site's audience and traffic through a broad range of free and paid media-placement methods. Chapter 5, "Find and Be Found: Search Engines and Directories," is a detailed guide to maximizing your site's ranking in search engine listings.

Chapter 6, "Word of Web: Online Communities," describes how to leverage online communities, such as newsgroups, mailing lists, and America Online discussion groups, for marketing purposes without offending the norms of Net culture. Chapter 7, "Era of Innovation: Contests, Sweepstakes, and Other Special Promotions," recounts many of the most creative contests and other special promotions that well-known marketers have used to increase their online traffic. Chapter 8, "Media Savior-Faire: Public Relations for a Digital Age," is a comprehensive primer on conducting effective PR, including online, print, and broadcast media, that could serve as a handbook for any public relations agency. And finally, Chapter 9, "Paid Media: The Many Faces of Web Advertising," is a thorough examination of the fast-evolving world of online advertising.

Goodbye Brochureware

By now, roughly five years into the Internet boom, marketers are speaking of second- and third-generation Web sites. The best definition we've seen for these stages of evolution among Web marketers comes from Jupiter Communications, a leading Internet research firm based in New York. Jupiter analysts describe three types of sites, from least-to-most effective Web marketing: *brochureware, show-biz,* and *utilitarian*.

Brochureware

Brochureware has long been recognized as the most basic, boring, and impotent type of marketing site. Although businesses aren't unwise to ease into their commitment to the Web gradually, brochureware sites—little more than static text and graphics "about our company"—largely miss the point of the Web's many inherent marketing benefits.

These benefits, discussed in detail in the first two chapters of this book, essentially boil down to interacting with consumers. No other communication medium gives a company the chance to relate so intimately with prospective and existing customers as the Web does. A static, non-interactive site is no more effective in seizing that opportunity than the paper brochures for which this type of site is named.

Show-Biz

The show-biz site is a misguided attempt by marketers to lure visitors to their brand with "infotainment": cereal makers featuring online computer games, car companies publishing lifestyle Webzines, soft drink vendors providing sports news and movie reviews, and so on.

For example, Lipton's margarine brand, I Can't Believe It's Not Butter, has devoted its site to a romance novel theme. Highlights of the site include a gallery of beefcake photos of Italian fashion model Fabio and a serialized romance novel updated weekly.

Matt Smith, senior brand manager for I Can't Believe It's Not Butter, explains the thinking behind the site: "We want to own the concept of 'romance' on the Web. America has a love affair with the taste of butter, but that romance is on the rocks because of cholesterol. But I Can't Believe It's Not Butter rekindles the romance, without the cholesterol."

Whether or not romance is the ideal image for a margarine product is something we'll leave up to Lipton's marketing experts. We would argue, however, that the product would achieve that online brand-building goal more successfully through ad sponsorship of professional online editorial content, such as Harlequin's Romance.net or some of the many other romance-themed Web sites.

The goal of most show-biz sites is brand-building, or "branding." The Web is indeed an excellent medium for achieving that goal, as we'll discuss in depth in Chapters 1 and 9. But marketers of real-world consumer products can generally achieve better branding through means other than infotainment destination sites. For products about which there isn't a lot to elaborate, such as margarine, breakfast cereal, soap, and the like, they would best achieve branding through banner ads and sponsorship of kindred online content produced by independent, professional publishers.

It's a question of credibility. Makers of soap, cereal, margarine, and the rest simply aren't publishers, and there's little value in trying to convince consumers they are. Inevitably, professional publishers will produce more compelling content. Marketers would be wise to affiliate themselves with the highest-quality independent content rather than creating mediocre material of their own.

Utilitarian

For brands that lend themselves better to product details or that evoke expert authority in a certain field, the utilitarian site model provides the ultimate online branding opportunity.

Utilitarian sites are those that offer Web surfers a genuine service—an interactive information utility. The classic example of this is Federal Express's site, with its package shipping and tracking features. Starting far ahead of the curve, FedEx started letting customers track the status of their deliveries through the Web in November 1994. In early 1996, it added shipment ordering services to the site, letting customers store basic account information, such as their pickup address and billing information, within the system for added convenience.

"By now, about two-thirds of all our customer contact is done electronically," said Greg Rossiter, managing director of public relations at Federal Express. "Rather than picking up the phone or arranging for shipments in person, more customers are tracking packages, arranging for shipping, and confirming deliveries via the Web site."

In addition to being a great customer convenience, FedEx's utilitarian Web service saves millions in customer service support costs.

The advice in Part I of the book, "Get the Site Right: Web Marketing Fundamentals," provides a strategic overview for preparing most marketing sites to evolve into the utilitarian model, offering solid value to users and ensuring high customer loyalty. Part II teaches hands-on promotional techniques for developing a sizable audience for your company's marketing messages online.

All or Nothing at All

Before proceeding with this book, however, readers expecting real results from their online marketing must embrace one commitment: settle in for a long haul.

Successful marketing on the Internet requires nothing as much as persistence. The following chapters describe not secrets but methodologies, nearly all of which are time-consuming. Unfortunately, there never will be a software application that automates the process of Internet marketing so that it can be done with the push of a button. The mantra of Internet marketing is "customer relationships." Relationships, unlike bits and bytes, can't be generated and processed on-the-fly. They require careful seeding, diligent nurturing, and constant attention.

If you are to achieve success, prepare to answer hundreds of email messages a day. Expect to spend many hours simply researching your opportunities. Securing the first 1,000 links from other sites pointing to yours may take several months. And if you let down your guard for even a few days, you'll see the immediate drop in traffic statistics on your server logs.

Of course, the easiest way to meet your marketing goals may be just to hire a company like USWeb to manage the process for you. But even so, understanding the strategies involved is key to your program's success.

Whether yours is a large company or a one-woman enterprise, a professional services firm or a packaged goods manufacturer, the Internet can be an invaluable, truly revolutionary marketing resource waiting for you to plug in. Think of it not as a mass medium, but as a universe with microcosms of potential customers. It is governed by the laws of very large numbers, and if you're creative enough, understand how to make its virtues work for you, and are among those who really get it, the results of your efforts can be out of this world.

Get the Site Right: Web Marketing Fundamentals

Return on Investment Goals

A bad Web site is bad marketing.

If you still aren't convinced that Net marketing will amount to a hill of beans, we'll try to save a place for you in the history books. But you'd do better to stay offline than slap together a site that only tells digerati that you're totally clueless.

A variety of online audience-development techniques may succeed in attracting visitors to your site, but if you lick the great lollipop of mediocrity, no one will return a second time. You'll just be wasting time and money online. With a million other interactive multimedia destinations to choose from, Net surfers don't bother much with second-rate sites.

The Six Online ROI Models

Before worrying about what users will think of your site, however, you're answerable first to yourself. The first step toward getting your site—along with the rest of your online marketing mix—right is to set clear objectives for a return on your company's investment online. In USWeb's experience, too many large companies spend substantial sums on the Web without a clear articulation of what it might do for their businesses.

"Well, everyone has a Web site these days," eager executives might tell us. Or, "Our competition is online." Or, "The CEO wants a URL on his business card." Or the ever-popular, "Because we'll make millions of dollars!" Conceivable, perhaps, but good luck.

Figure 1.1

It may be Spam-o-rific, but has anybody at Hormel's **Spam.com** asked themselves, "What the heck are we doing in cyberspace?" The homepage suggests probably not yet.

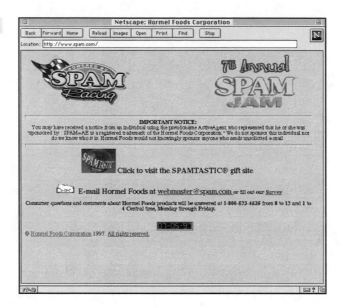

The Web can be a highly economical arm of a company's overall marketing program, but it can also be a colossal money pit if the company doesn't outline specific goals for using it. The precise objectives for each company depend on individual factors, of course, but most successful online ventures find that the Internet offers marketers a return on investment (ROI) in one or more of the following six models:

- Brand-Building

- Direct Marketing

- Online Sales

- Customer Support

- Market Research

- Content Publishing/Services

In the last category—which includes the majority of content destination sites, such as *The Wall Street Journal*, Suck.com, MSNBC, Yahoo!, Quote.com, and Preview Travel—the return on investment is revenue through advertising, subscriptions, syndication, transaction commissions, or other means. Similarly, the online sales model promises revenue through a new type of retail channel. For most real-world businesses that aren't publishers, however, the Web is primarily an expense in return for a competitive advantage in the form of promotion, customer support, or market research.

In practice, of course, companies overlap several of these six ROI models. Creative businesses are constantly pushing the boundaries of what's been tried before and interpreting these marketing objectives in myriad ways. To determine how each model might work best for any particular company requires insight into its unique corporate circumstances, as well as a full understanding of the Net's core marketing values, discussed in more detail in Chapter 2, "Web Value Propositions." In this chapter, however, we look at examples of how companies are realizing ROI today with these six models.

Brand-Building

The Web can play an important and cost-effective role, alongside television, print, billboards, and other advertising media, in building consumer awareness of an offline brand. Research by Millward Brown International, discussed in detail in Chapter 9, "Paid Media: The Many Faces of Web Advertising," argues that even standard ad banners can measurably increase brand awareness for advertisers.

In Part II, "Audience Development," we'll explore how to raise awareness of your site through advertising, public relations, online communities, and other means. All manner of Web marketing contributes to a positive brand image, however. Many companies, including Federal Express, Charles Schwab, Barnes & Noble, Sears Roebuck, Tower Records, *The New York Times*, Nike, Levi Strauss, and Harley-Davidson, have demonstrated that they are 21st-Century market leaders through their effective use of the Web.

Figure 1.2

Think Ragu on the Web and think Italian: trips to Italy, Italian recipes, or Italian language lessons.

Figure 1.2

Think Ragu on the Web and think Italian: trips to Italy, Italian recipes, or Italian language lessons.

The Net lets customers interact more intimately with brands than any other media. Unlike other media, which expect little of the consumer beyond passive attention, the Web invites netizens to get involved with the brand, learn details about the product, sign up for special services, return to the site regularly as a resource for a specific topic, and otherwise play an active role in the marketing experience, closely bonding with the brand along the way.

Even products like Crest, Ragu, and I Can't Believe It's Not Butter, with sites that are closer to show-biz than utilitarian, stand to impress the Web's demographically attractive consumers simply by having better sites than their traditional competitors.

Crest, for example, is unlikely to reach anyone online who's never heard of the product before. But if it provides a more engaging online experience than other toothpastes, the next time a netizen who's been to the site is looking at the supermarket shelves, Crest may stand out in her mind with a new positive brand association.

It's a bit like the joke about the two hikers in the woods who startle a grizzly bear. One guy drops his pack, yanks out a pair of running shoes, and frantically puts them on. The other guy says, "You're crazy, you'll never outrun that bear." "I don't have to outrun the bear," the first replies, sprinting off, "I just have to outrun you!"

Figure 1.3

You've been brushing all these years, but have you been doing it right? Crest's site is full of information for adults, kids, and dental professionals.

Which site do you want to be, the guy with the running shoes or the guy carrying the beef jerky?

Direct Marketing

Although the Web makes it easy to keep a product name in front of the right audience, many advertisers seek more immediate results than brand awareness. For such direct marketers, the Web is hog heaven. Its capability to deliver highly qualified sales leads with ease means that online mar keters can regularly outperform traditional direct mail, with none of the cost of paper, postage, and other associated expenses.

The Web audience is self-selecting by nature. According to Bruce Ryan, a VP and general manager at Media Metrix, a research firm that panels Web users for demographic characteristics, more than 80% of PC owners have at least one college degree, and the average household income of the same group is above $50,000 a year, well more than the $35,500 U.S. household average.

Figure 1.4

Using humor, Joe Boxer emphasizes the value of clean underwear throughout its hilarious site. Definitely a site worth bookmarking—you can't explore it all in under an hour, and it's good entertainment.

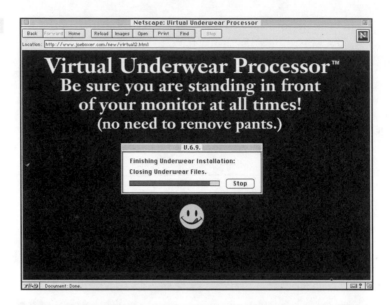

Figure 1.5

Joe Boxer's site is so successful, it's already attracted more than a billion visitors. ;-)

Those kinds of statistics make the online audience a more profitable market segment than TV viewers, who represent 95% of the households in the U.S. On the Web, marketers can easily find audience groups that are keenly defined by every kind of special interest. Add to that a wealth of techniques for further pinpointing user groups—with jargonistic names like *collaborative filtering* and *neural networks*, discussed further in later chapters—and the potential for target marketing online is tremendous.

Syed Madni, general sales manager of the JM Lexus dealer in Miami, raves about the results he got by targeting local residents on the Point-Cast push technology network. "We have already seen an amazing return on our advertising investment with the Miami Herald channel on Point-Cast," he said. "In just one month we scheduled 48 appointments because of our PointCast ad. From those appointments, we sold 16 cars."

PointCast offers users a variety of content programming "channels" that "push" information automatically to users' computers whenever they are connected to the Internet. The information is always ready on the users' desktop computers without requiring them to visit a traditional Web site and "pull" the information down themselves. (See further discussion of "push technology" in Chapter 7.)

As a charter advertiser on the Miami PointCast channel, JM Lexus spent only $700 for that month's advertising, according to PointCast officials. The rates for the same channel now range from $900–1,500 a month, depending on term of commitment. Considering the extraordinary return on investment JM Lexus found in its first month with the service, it's not surprising that PointCast reports the dealership just committed to another year's advertising on the channel.

As we will explore further in Chapter 9, several individual sites and networks, including DoubleClick and PointCast, allow advertisers to pay for ad banners on a performance basis, such as per clickthrough (that is, only for visitors who click on the ad banner and follow its link to the advertiser's site), per sales lead, or per completed sales transaction. Other services, such as BonusMail, Direct Value to You, and Netcentives, target users in various ways according to their known shopping interests and tempt them into action with discounts, coupons, and other promotional offers.

Smart marketers will exploit both direct and brand advertising possibilities online. For example, in most cases your banner ads should clearly state the product brand for the benefit of the 98% of surfers who won't click on them, even if driving site traffic with clickthroughs is your primary objective.

Figure 1.6

BonusMail offers the pâté de foie gras of spam services. Users can volunteer to receive email advertisements about products that interest them. Furthermore, it pays users incentive points for responding to promotions, redeemable for a variety of goods and services, such as airline miles and gift certificates.

As we will discuss further in Chapter 9, measuring the value of click-throughs is more complex than it may first appear. Your ad agency may help you achieve a higher-than-average clickthrough rate, and a publisher may charge you higher prices for them. But clickthroughs in and of themselves are meaningless if you can't relate them to clear objectives. Who exactly clicked through? A potential customer, or a randy teenager confused by a cryptic, teasing message? How many levels into your site did the visitor explore after clicking on the banner? How directly does a visit to the homepage translate into a sale or other marketing goal?

Marketers should rigorously demand from site publishers and agencies detailed accountability, cutting-edge software targeting, and generally a high measure of success. If your business partners have the creative will, there is certainly the technical infrastructure to deliver on all that. Yet those marketers must also be rigorous themselves in defining what results they are seeking.

Figure 1.7

Toyota understands the importance of presenting a strong brand identity in a simple animated ad banner, for the benefit of the vast majority of surfers who will see the ad but won't click on it.

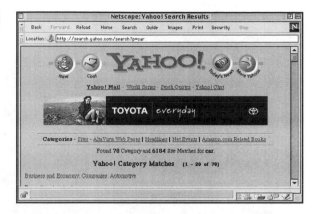

Online Sales

Occasionally, people ask us at USWeb when we think electronic commerce will become a reality. To which we reply, surprised to even hear the question still, that e-commerce already is a reality.

What do you want to buy? Whatever it is, you can get it online—cars, furniture, chocolate, computers, office supplies, hot sauce, houses, stereo equipment, books, maple syrup, plane tickets, CDs. You name it, it's for sale on the Net.

That's not to say every online vendor is making money—far from it. But some are. Already many of the biggest names in retail, such as Sears Roebuck, JC Penney, and L.L. Bean, have launched commerce sites offering vast arrays of products. Amazon.com sold $32 million in books from March 1996 to March 1997. Consumer products giant Sara Lee hopes women will want to shop in bulk for L'Eggs at **www.pantyhose.com**, while Peapod lets netizens in nine cities order their groceries online for home delivery. Fragrance Counter claims it's making a profit selling perfume online.

Forrester Research, a leading technology analysis group based in Cambridge, MA, predicts that online consumer-retail revenue will be $7.2 billion in the year 2000, almost twice their estimate of $4.5 billion that will be spent on Web advertising the same year.

Figure 1.8

Many retail giants, including L.L. Bean, are finding the Web a viable outlet.

One site that demonstrates how having clear objectives and planning well can pay off online is Andy's Garage Sale. A booming commerce site, Andy's motto is "New Stuff Dirt Cheap." The site sells a wide range of liquidation stock items at bargain prices, such as lamps, wet/dry vacuums, bird feeders, bathtub safety rails, hair clippers, bread boxes, jewelry, garage door openers, and much more.

Figure 1.9

Avuncular Andy and his lovable wife Gertie find the Web a downright hospitable place where ordinary folks want to shop ... with the help of a low-profile multimillion-dollar direct-marketing powerhouse.

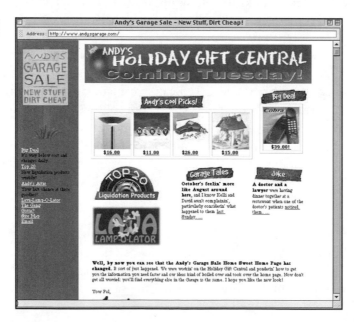

The site is far more entertaining than the infomercial tone you might expect based on the product line. This is thanks to the charming, folksy personality of your host Andy, his devoted wife Gertie, and a motley group of characters that keep the site running in a homespun, Midwestern style. Along with the Big Deal of the Day and the weekly top 20 bargains, Andy and crew serve up a groaner Joke of the Week, as well as Tales from the Garage, where Andy waxes sentimental about the amusing goings-on in his small hometown.

Andy has cultivated such a devoted following among his shoppers that when he asked for suggestions about where he and Gertie should go for their summer road-trip vacation, customers across the country wrote to invite the couple to stay in their spare bedrooms.

Although it would probably surprise most of the site's visitors, Andy and Gertie don't really exist. Like Mr. Whipple, Bartles and Jaymes, and other familiar commercial characters, Andy and crew are pure marketing personas. Andy's Garage Sale really belongs to Fingerhut Companies, Inc., one of the world's largest catalogue and direct-marketing businesses.

Jane Westlind, manager of electronic commerce for Andy's, explained that Fingerhut thought carefully about how to take advantage of the Web's strengths to add value for customers to what was already a thriving business. "We took a business challenge, excess inventory, and turned it into a business opportunity online," said Ms. Westlind.

The Web neatly complements aspects of Fingerhut's existing catalogue business, such as enabling the company to react instantly when items run out of stock or new merchandise becomes available.

"Foremost, I'd tell other marketers to take advantage of what the Web uniquely offers," said Ms. Westlind. "Don't just take your existing model from another medium and cut and paste it into this one. Really rethink it. There's got to be a reason for being online, some added value. If the only reason to get online is to have a Web presence, anyone can do that. It's got to be smarter or faster or better or cheaper or more fun or more informative. That's the bottom line for us."

Amen!

Figure 1.10

With the help of a team of writers emulating old-fashioned Midwestern charm, Fingerhut has found the Web to be a great place to liquidate excess inventory.

Customer Support

Customer support is truly one of the Web's killer apps. To date, few companies have realized the full potential of this opportunity. Analysts predict, however, that in the coming years many companies will shift significant portions of their existing telephone customer support to the Web.

Already customer support online is becoming more and more common, from simple FAQ (Frequently Asked Questions) Web pages to Federal Express's package-tracking system, discussed in the Introduction. In between those two ends of the spectrum, companies are aiding customers through staff replies to email inquiries, automated email responses, Web-based bulletin boards, newsgroups, AOL and CompuServe forums, complex searchable FAQ databases, live support chat, and more.

Specialized software products are making Web customer service a tempting alternative to traditional 1-800 and 1-900 telephone support, at potentially great savings in time, efficiency, and resources.

Figure 1.11

Microsoft, not one to do things halfway, offers every conceivable kind of online customer support, both for free and, if you want greater staff interaction, for a fee.

Aptex makes a product called SelectResponse that enables companies to automate email replies to customers, at least in part. Aptex's technology, an intelligent pattern-recognition *neural network*, can "understand" the context of most user questions sent in by email. According to Jane Leonard, Aptex's marketing manager, Charles Schwab uses the software to direct incoming emails to the appropriate internal analysts, who write personal replies to users' questions. Ms. Leonard also said that HomeShark, a Web-based realty service, uses SelectResponse to grab an appropriate answer to a user's email question from a FAQ database and forward it to a salesperson. The salesperson reviews the original question and the canned answer SelectCast supplies. If the match is appropriate, the salesperson personalizes the answer and forwards it to the consumer.

"Customer service on the Web has moved beyond nice-to-have to musthave," said Carter Lusher, VP and research director of Gartner Group's Customer Service & Support Strategies division. "It has true value by now. A lot of companies look at online customer support as a cost-saving opportunity."

Mr. Lusher cites three principal opportunities in online customer support: revenue enhancement, cost-avoidance, and "soft benefits."

In terms of revenue enhancement, he suggests that the added value of effective customer support for online commerce sites will build loyalty among repeat customers.

"It costs more than 10 times as much for a company to acquire new customers as it does to retain existing ones," he said. Furthermore, customer support representatives have the opportunity to up-sell and cross-sell customers by using chat technology or even email.

As for cost-avoidance, companies can eliminate staffing and large telecom expenses by automating answers to customer queries online, as Federal Express and others have discovered.

The "soft benefits" Mr. Luster describes are subtle but compelling, such as increased customer loyalty through the investment the user makes in learning the customer support system, making him less likely to go to a competitor and learn new systems from scratch. Mr. Luster reasons that training the customers to rely on themselves for support, using efficient, automated online services, also slows the demand for future customer service as the company grows.

Many times, customers won't want to wade through complex help applications online, however, which is where real-time customer-support chat is most promising.

P. V. Kannan, president of Business Evolution, maker of a sophisticated customer-support chat system called Interact Service, says his software is "the functional equivalent of dialing zero for a company's operator." If a customer is browsing at a large corporate site and has a quick question he can't find an answer to, he can chat with a live operator at the site.

The software, which works with most standard browsers that support Java, divides the user's screen horizontally into two panels. On top the staff and customers can chat, and on the bottom the staff can forward relevant answers to complex questions from a database of explanations, thus avoiding repeat answers.

Figure 1.12

Using customer-support chat software developed by Business Evolution, a Web site's visitors can ask questions of support staff in real-time, as in this simulation of a financial services company.

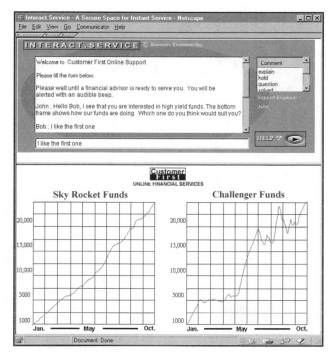

On the company side, a staff supervisor can monitor all the activities of the customer support representatives. And because a Web browser is the system's main interface, support staff and supervisors can work remotely, such as from home.

"Lots of merchants could encourage commerce with customer support," said Kate Doyle, an analyst in Jupiter Communication's Digital Commerce division. "Think of customers shopping at a site and wanting to ask, 'How big is the large size? Can I get a discount? Is the Web really safe to buy something on?' I often wish there were a way I could ask a question about a product on a site."

Besides Business Evolution, several companies produce Web-based customer-support software, including Smart Technologies and Silknet, and several makers of traditional telephone customer-support software are adapting their products for Web-based support, such as Vantive and Clarify.

Market Research

Increasingly, companies are recognizing the Net's awesome potential for market research. Market research consultants, of course, were quick to pick up on this.

Burke, Inc., an international market research firm that's been around for more than 65 years, conducts carefully controlled online focus groups for its clients in addition to its face-to-face and phone surveys. Using Web technology, the company brings together prescreened participants from different parts of the country for small, moderated real-time chat sessions. Clients can observe the chats from wherever in the country they happen to be.

Figure 1.13

Longtime market-research company Burke, Inc. got wise to the power of the Web quickly and now uses it to conduct research around the world.

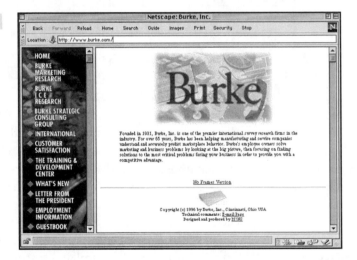

Market research in a variety of forms is an ROI available to most companies online. There is much information that users simply volunteer about themselves, if sites take the time to observe it.

Software by firms like Accrue, Andromedia, Aptex, Autonomy, Nestor, and Imgis enables sites to study patterns in anonymous users' behavior and use that information to improve the site, surmise visitor demographics, and personalize content for users on-the-fly.

Of course, sites can conduct their own research simply by surveying visitors. If it's well-planned, this can be effective. Unfortunately, many sites slap up user surveys or registration forms with little strategy for what data they need or what motivation users will have to comply. As a result, many users lie on these forms or just ignore them, and the companies don't know how to interpret the results they get.

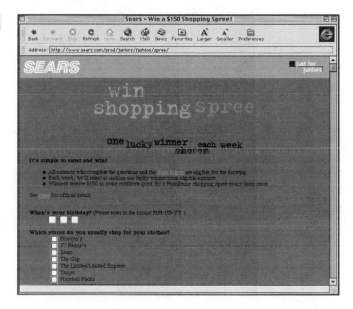

Figure 1.14

Sears Roebuck, amidst its extensive shopping site, offers Web surfers a chance to win prizes weekly in exchange for answering some questions about their shopping habits.

Beyond the inconvenience of surveys and registration forms, users fiercely guard their privacy online and fear their email addresses will be sold to reckless marketers. To overcome this, sites must earn users' trust and compensate them somehow for bothering to answer questions honestly for market research, ad targeting, or other purposes. (See more on privacy in Chapter 2.)

A few sites, such as *The New York Times*, offer such high-quality content that they can force all users to register for access to the site. Most sites, however, have found that 100% registration turns away too many users. Fortunately, there are several alternate ways to collect user information. Commerce sites can easily collect some demographic data as users enter their names and addresses for product delivery. Sweepstakes are a popular incentive to get users to fill out forms. Sites that personalize services can harvest loads of data as users reveal their likes and dislikes in exchange for a customized Web experience.

It boils down to trust and motivation: The more value a site offers its users and assurances that it will respect their personal data, the more information the users will reveal about themselves.

Content Publishing/Services

This last category is broad and includes many familiar online brands, such as Yahoo!, Excite, CNET, ESPN SportsZone, Microsoft Network, HotWired, Quote.com, Women's Wire, Disney.com, and so on. All of these sites produce or aggregate content or provide content services such as search engines, localized entertainment guides, or stock trackers.

The vast majority of these sites underwrite at least part of their costs by selling online advertising to sponsors. Many sites further subsidize their earnings with subscriptions, syndication agreements, transaction fees, sponsorships, special business services, and other revenue models. Few sites outside of the porno realm have been successful in charging a flat subscription price to all users, *The Wall Street Journal* being a notable exception.

Although few sites pursuing this ROI are profitable yet, many show the promise of success. But it's clearly not the model for everyone. Ad-Knowledge, a Palo Alto-based online ad services company, maintains a database called MarketMatch that lists details about commercial sites that accept advertising. The database is free for any site to sign up, but AdKnowledge counts just around 1,000 sites that are seriously pursuing advertising.

"As happens offline, advertising revenues online will aggregate among a small cluster of the top 20 or so publishers," predicts Marc Johnson, a Jupiter analyst. "It's happening now. The economies of scale, and the ability to brand across media properties and drive traffic that way just make it easier for big publishers. Smaller, niche-oriented players can certainly carve out nice profits, but as far as revenue goes, it is still going to be concentrated among a top few."

Figure 1.15

Jupiter Communications tracks who is spending and receiving the most online ad dollars in its monthly AdSpend newsletter. Topping the publisher list is software vendor Netscape's site, followed by familiar Web content brands such as Yahoo!, Excite, and CNET.

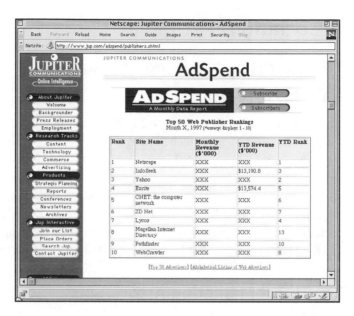

A few ad and content networks, including Aaddzz, DoubleClick, Value-Click, and PointCast, aim to help small- and medium-sized semiprofessional sites become ad revenue earners, too, by paying them for ad banners displayed on a per-clickthrough basis. Although the income may be a shot in the arm for many small-but-devoted publishers, few of them are likely to thrive on ads alone.

There are a handful of companies, such as Netscape, that aren't principally in the publishing business but do attract so much traffic to their sites that they can get into the ad revenue game. For most marketers of real-world products, however, this ROI model may be a fringe benefit at best and is unlikely to be a strong justification for online spending.

Resources

See other advertising-related resources in Chapter 9.

Associations

The Internet Advertising Bureau

http://www.iab.net/

The Internet Advertising Bureau (IAB) represents more than 100 members, including major publishers, large corporate advertisers, top agencies, and others. In mid-1997, the organization commissioned Millward Brown Interactive to complete a large study of online ad effectiveness with more than 16,000 respondents, which indicated that plain ad banners have a measurably positive effect on brand recognition amongst surfers. See the Resource section of Chapter 9 or the Appendix for the URL of the report, available for free on Millward Brown's Web site.

The Direct Marketing Association

http://www.the-dma.org/

The Direct Marketing Association doesn't have a particularly strong Web site yet, but it's a leading association for direct marketing in the real world, so maybe it will become a better resource with time.

Commerce.Net

http://www.commerce.net/

Commerce.Net is the largest association of e-commerce professionals, providing an excellent online resource. You'll find links to e-commerce news, legislation, survey results events, email discussion lists, and other useful information.

Professional News and Information Sites

NetMarketing

http://netb2b.com/

This is a sister publication to *Advertising Age* from Crain Communications, with news and research about Web marketing.

Direct Marketing News

http://www.dmnews.com/

This is the leading direct marketing magazine, with extensive (and free) industry news.

MediaCentral

http://www.mediacentral.com/

A product of Cowles Business Media, MediaCentral features extensive coverage of Web marketing activities, including direct and catalogue marketing, online publishing, e-commerce, and other topics covered in this chapter.

Who's Marketing Online?

http://www.wmo.com/

This site has excellent resources, including many other links, original articles, reviews of sites, and more.

American Demographic/Marketing Tools Bookstore

http://www.demographics.com/

Here you'll find research reports, books, and magazines for sale online, links to top-notch business resources, and other resources.

CommercePark

http://www.commercepark.com/

This site has lots of links to e-commerce sites.

Internet SourceBook

http://www.internetsourcebook.com/

You'll find lots of links to e-commerce sites.

MarketsResearch.com

http://www.marketsresearch.com/

This is an extensive directory of marketing research. Note the "s" in the middle of the domain name: market*s*research.com.

Internet Industry News

TechWeb & CMPnet

http://www.techweb.com/

http://www. cmpnet.com/

CMP is one of the largest publishers of computer industry trade publications. TechWeb and CMPnet are closely related domains offering a wide variety of news sources, including content from CMP's many print titles as well as original online news.

ZDNet

http://www.zdnet.com/

Ziff-Davis is CMP's main rival publisher of computer industry trades. ZDNet is a massive resource of news and information, with links to multitudes of other ZD resources.

Internet.com

http://www.internet.com

Mecklermedia, another high-tech publishing giant, launched this strong site in mid-1997. You'll find links to other Mecklermedia publications and much original, up-to-the-minute news.

Other Internet News Leaders

http://www.cnet.com/

http://www.news.com/

http://www.wirednews.com/

http://www.newspage.com/

http://www.newshub.com/

http://www.newslinx.com/

Leading Internet Research Groups

The following analyst groups and research firms are leading providers of industry information and influencers of opinion. Most offer some combination of subscription reports, custom research, and consulting. Many of their Web sites offer limited free resources, but more extensive information is available only to paying customers.

Cowles/Simba

http://www.simbanet.com/

CyberDialogue

http://www.cyberdialogue.com/

Find/SVP

http://www.findsvp.com/

Forrester Research

http://www.forrester.com/

Gartner Group

http://www.gartner.com/

Jupiter Communications

http://www.jup.com/

Media Metrix (formerly PC Meter)

http://www.mediametrix.com/

Millward Brown

http://www.millwardbrown.com/

NetRatings

http://www.netratings.com/

Relevant Knowledge

http://www.relevantknowledge.com/

YankeeGroup

http://www.yankeegroup.com/

Web Value Propositions

The most popular analogy for the development of the Web is the development of early television. If that's the case, the Web is no longer in the 1950s. It's already the mid- to late-'60s thanks to "Web years"—similar to "dog years." What seems like a year in the Web's maturation is really only about two months.

The explosive growth in new users follows a similar pace. According to data compiled by Morgan Stanley, it took radio 38 years to reach an audience of 50 million homes. Television took 13 years to reach the same number. Cable, from HBO's 1976 launch, took 10 years. The Web did it in four. Only four years between 1993, when 23-year-old Marc Andreesen wrote the first graphical Web browser, Mosaic, and the end of 1997, when even conservative estimates say the Web will have reached 50 million users worldwide.

Before the advent of the World Wide Web and a good graphical browser for experiencing it, the Internet had already existed for some 30 years, producing such earlier communication protocols as electronic mail, file transfers, discussion boards, and more arcane technologies like Telnet, Gopher, and IRC.

But then the Web came along and started a cultural revolution, leaving the Net's geekier features in the dust. At last, there was something compelling for the masses to do with a computer besides word processing that lived up to the hype "point and click." Anyone who can't get the hang of the Web in the first 10 minutes probably needs to repeat grade school.

What has made the Web's breakthrough so compelling? That's a question the whole industry needs to keep asking itself for years to come. Because the Web is currently going through the equivalent of 1960s TV, we have yet to see the likes of CNN, Court TV, cable, satellite, and other programming and technical innovations that redefined television from the '70s forward.

We can, however, identify a number of traits that combine uniquely on the Web and the Internet to offer both users and marketers exciting benefits in a way no other medium has done before. A strong site is likely to exploit many, if not all, of these features.

The Web is

- Interactive

- Personal

- Infocentric

- Instantaneous

- Measurable

- Flexible

- Interlinked

- Economical

These are the features we'll explore in this chapter.

Interactive

In the ceaselessly inventive lexicon of cyberslang, a *cobweb* is a site that never changes.

For the marketer, the Web's most important value is direct interaction with customers. Static brochure sites—product photos, lists of retail locations, recipe collections, and so on—miss a critical point. The Web offers more opportunities than most other media, in which you can only talk *at* your customers. Online it's about engaging with them, listening to them, and learning from them.

This may challenge traditional marketers who are accustomed to packaging flashy sound bites for mass delivery via television, publications, and billboards. Good.

Kotex

"What kind of conversation could a paper products company have with its customers?", you might ask. Kimberly & Clark turned that challenge into an excellent example of a brand community with its Kotex site.

The site's creators focused on a specific target audience: women. And in their GirlSpace section, they focus on junior high and high school girls in particular. The design of GirlSpace intimately reflects a typical teen girl's sensibilities with its style of artwork and language. The site contains frank discussions about the female anatomy, menstruation, gynecology, and other delicate topics without ever condescending to its audience.

Figure 2.1

In the GirlSpace section of the Kotex site, teens and preteens are encouraged to ask intimate questions and let off steam about whatever's on their minds.

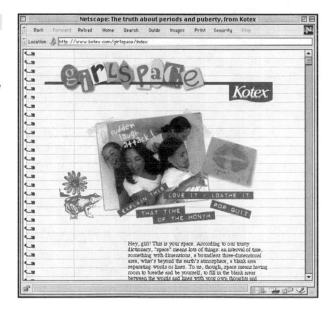

Most importantly, it invites girls to post questions that professionals answer online, as well as providing a dozen bulletin boards for girls to write each other about whatever they want. The site has clearly struck a chord. The forums are filled with regularly updated messages.

Coca-Cola

Okay, Kotex has a more obvious audience segment than other mass-market products. How do you create a community around a carbonated beverage?

So far, Coca-Cola's site has done little to invite user participation, compared to other marketers in its league. The few areas where users *can* contribute, however, enliven the site more than any amount of Java animation ever could.

In one section, the site simply asks visitors a silly question each week, such as, "Who, or what, were you in your past life?", and then posts 50 or so innocuous responses. Nothing too creative, but it's a better reason for bored teenagers to return to the site than the easily mastered Shockwave games.

Where Coke really scores online is with its free classifieds about Coke memorabilia. Despite the section's clunky design, hundreds of obsessed hobbyists post messages seeking to buy, trade, or sell novelty bottles, Olympic pins, neon signs, and everything else imaginable emblazoned with the Coke logo.

How could Coke take their online marketing to the next level? (Like they need free advice.) Of the several ideas we thought of, we'll give them this one, which both invites customers to interact *and* gives Coke free promotion: a logo button that says "This Site Fueled by Coca-Cola."

Webmasters are notorious for working all night and living on a diet of chips and caffeinated soda, right? So offer a coupon good for a free two-liter bottle of Coke to any site that posts the logo button with a link back to Coke's site. Geeks all over the Web would likely think it's funny and give Coke a free ad, just like they display "This Site Best Viewed with Netscape" and "This Site Made on a Macintosh" logos.

Figure 2.2

"Coke fiends" the world over now have an online trafficking center for their strange addictions.

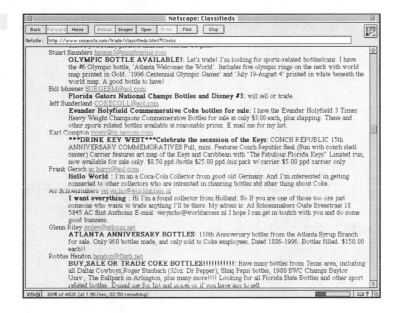

Coke could even raise the ante by offering reciprocal links back to any site that uses its icon. Small- and medium-sized sites Internet-wide would clamor for a link on the Coke site. For Coke's part, it could host a remote corner on its site with endless pages of links (monitored, of course, to guard against inappropriate content) that hardly any visitors would bother looking through extensively. In return, Coke would have its brand and site promoted for free on thousands of sites.

Participatory Marketing

The point is, people yearn to feel involved, and the Internet makes that easy. Simply providing an email address to the Webmaster isn't real interactivity, unless all your customers want to do is complain. People want to know their opinions are being heard. They want to make a difference. They love to see their name and words in print, even if only in the glow of their monitors.

Imagine two sites, each for a different food product. One takes the predictable route of listing a few recipes that incorporate its product. This requires no more than an afternoon's work by the in-house marketing team, which is exactly what it looks like to anyone surfing the site. The second site invites visitors to submit their own original recipes using the product, with the best ones posted the next week, along with a chance to win a T-shirt or the grand prize of a two-week cooking class.

Which site is a customer more likely to visit twice? Which product is she going to feel a closer loyalty to after seeing her name and recipe posted on the site?

Free Focus Groups

Interacting with your customers online is more than just a ploy to keep them coming back to your site, though. It's also a great way to learn from them how to better market your product, as discussed in the Market Research section of Chapter 1, "Return on Investment Goals."

That doesn't just mean having a link on the homepage saying "Survey: We want to hear what you think," like a quarter of a million sites do. Netizens don't like to give something for nothing. Besides, a simple survey is a small fraction of the customer research possible with two-way Web marketing.

Reading what customers say on discussion boards, such as Kotex's, can teach marketers volumes about what their customers really believe, good and bad, about the product and the market.

Taking it further, companies can conduct virtual focus groups on their sites. TV programs are already using their sites this way. Imagine a soap opera inviting audience input on what characters should sleep together, go to jail, die, and so on. Most other products could do the same.

Embrace the Net's interactivity and you'll be almost halfway to realizing its awesome marketing potential.

Figure 2.3

The official X-Files site offers an extensive fan forum, with a disclaimer that any contributions to the discussion boards automatically become the intellectual property of FOX.

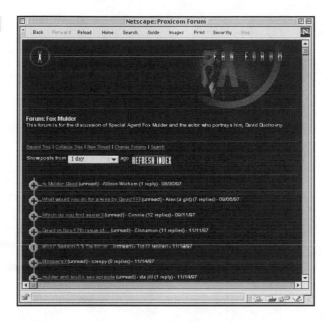

Personal

Every user has her own individual experience with the Web. Its randomness and vastness give the user much greater control than any other medium. Even the TV remote can't compare. We're not talking about 50 or 500 channels. We're talking about a million and a half Web sites as of November 1997, according to the count by Netcraft, a British networking company that regularly tabulates the number of unique Web sites. If you were to surf each one for 30 seconds, it would take almost a year and a half with no bathroom breaks. (That two-liter bottle from Coke might come in handy:—)

One way to stand out from the limitless choices in the consumer's mind is to personalize the site for each visitor. Some sites tailor the experience based on simple, observable information about each visitor (browser type, operating system, time of day, and so on). Others watch how a user interacts with the site and customize it accordingly, such as displaying sports up front for a reader who always hits those pages first. Still others let the visitors customize the sites themselves.

Technographics

CNET's site **Browser.com**, which specializes in browser information, tailors the site depending on whether the visitor is on a Mac or a PC.

Figure 2.4

CNET under-stands that we Mac diehards appreciate any favors we can get.

Site content personalized for Mac

In addition to revealing the visitor's operating system, every Web browser also automatically volunteers such technical data as the user's Internet domain (aol.com, npr.org, bruner.net, and so on), browser type (Navigator 3.0, Internet Explorer 4.0, WebTV), IP address (from which it is sometimes possible to deduce her geography), the time of the visit, and other data sometimes referred to as *technographics*.

For Web ventures specializing in non-technical content, such as a dog-fanciers' site, most technographic data may be irrelevant. Presumably, both Mac and PC users fancy dogs equally.

User-Driven Environments

For more intimate personalization, many sites let their users do the customization themselves.

Individual's NewsPage service, for example, lets the user choose from an array of business and technology topics to create a unique "My News-Page" section. With personalized news from more than 600 sources, NewsPage serves as a one-stop shop for business news, no matter what the visitor's industry. Many other sites, from Yahoo to CBS SportsLine to *The New York Times*, also let users identify their areas of interest to individually customize the site.

Figure 2.5

A Web page that knows my name and interests.

Personalization Software

A number of software companies specialize in personalization software using different flavors of artificial intelligence, such as *neural networks* and *collaborative filtering*.

Aptex, Autonomy, and Nestor make neural networking software. First developed for the military, police, and banks to scan volumes of data (such as fingerprints, credit habits, or terrorist cases) for recognizable patterns, the same software can be applied to recognize users' behavior patterns on the Web.

There are many applications for pattern-recognition technology in Web marketing, including ad targeting, customer service, and market research. Most important to many sites, though, is the capability to customize content and other site features on-the-fly to match each individual surfer's preferences.

Makers of neural network systems say their software can "understand" the gist of text a user is reading online and can distinguish contextual differences. For example, the word "breast" might appear on a magazine site in the context of cancer, chicken recipes, or erotica. If a reader surfs from a chicken recipe to a story about nutrition to a restaurant review, the system understands that the visitor has food on her mind and may recommend other appropriate content or links.

Collaborative filtering, from software companies including FireFly and Net Perspectives, is a somewhat simpler technology with more limited applications than neural networks, but its results can still be compelling when they're applied well. In a nutshell, collaborative filtering applications ask users to spend a few moments rating favorite examples within a well-defined category, such as movies, music, or books. As the collected sample grows, the system gets better and better at recommending items to new users based on the similar tastes of others.

MovieFinder.com is a good example of this technology. A component of E!Online, the Web incarnation of the cable network E!, MovieFinder.com offers users several movie-related services, including reviews, film industry news, local showings of current movies, and a virtual encyclopedia of films, stars, and directors.

The site's coolest feature, however, is its personalized film recommendations, using collaborative filtering from Net Perceptions. After having the visitor rank a series of films he's seen, the site recommends other films he'd probably like, too. For a film buff, the recommendations are fun and handy when it comes time to visit the video store. The personal recommendations definitely make the site worth bookmarking.

Privacy

A word of caution about the realm of personalized Web marketing: Online privacy is a bomb waiting to explode, so handle it with extreme care. Several studies show that the online public, fueled in part by alarmist press reports, feels strongly about privacy and security.

Figure 2.6

After I've ranked a few dozen movies from most to least favorite, MovieFinder predicts how I will like these recent video releases.

According to Boston Consulting Group researchers, more than 86% of respondents in a March 1997 poll were "somewhat" or "very" concerned about their online privacy. Of the more than 9,000 Web users who participated in the survey, 42% generally refused to fill out any registration forms online due to privacy concerns, and 27% reported sometimes lying on forms to protect their identity. The results did not vary much with regard to respondents' nationalities or how many years they had been online.

The survey's most encouraging findings indicated that users' willingness to reveal sensitive information about themselves went up dramatically when sites clearly explained how they treat users' personal data.

It's no coincidence that the organization TRUSTe, which commissioned the study from Boston Consulting Group, provides precisely this service, auditing sites' privacy ethics with a recognizable set of labels (just like the Good Housekeeping Seal of Approval). Their approach is a compelling solution to a problem that concerns almost every commercial Web site. We recommend that you investigate TRUSTe's model, or at least prominently publish your own privacy declaration on your site.

Figure 2.7

Lands' End takes online privacy seriously. A premier sponsor of TRUSTe, the merchant features the privacy group's logo on its homepage. It links to a page with detailed explanations of how customer data is used.

TRUSTe privacy logo

Infocentric

The hottest design and animation won't hold a user's attention for long without some substance to back it up. The Web is at heart a text-based medium, which is implicit in the names of its protocols: *hypertext transfer protocol (HTTP)* and *hypertext markup language (HTML)*. It's hyperized and otherwise jazzed up, but it's still good old text.

For marketers whose products entail a lot of details that need to be explained, such as cars, financial services, or travel, this feature of the Web is a great opportunity. For marketers of simpler products, such as soap, mayonnaise, and bubble gum, presenting the info may be more of a challenge. But that's why they pay the creative types so much.

Considered Purchases

The Web's provision of details is a golden opportunity for marketers to extol the virtues of many products whose complex features may not be done justice by a one-page magazine ad or 30-second TV commercial. These include big-ticket items and so-called "considered purchases," like cars, home computers, and vacations. Consumers are already using the

Web to research such products, seeking out both third-party write-ups and the official product sites.

Figure 2.8

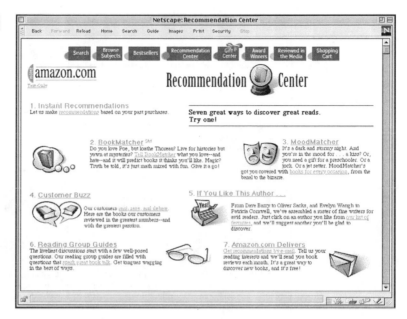

Amazon.com has book info coming out its ears, and users eat it up. You can find reviews from 14 top sources, including *The New York Times*, *The New Yorker*, and Oprah, as well as recommended reading lists, author interviews, reader discussion boards, and lots more.

All of the major car companies were quick to exploit the infocentric character of the Web. Take Ford Motor Company, for example. For its industry, Ford's site produces few surprises, but it certainly does an effective job of conveying a wealth of information about the company and its products. The site has easily thousands of pages, covering corporate history, environmental commitment, career opportunities, a company magazine, financial and investment services, and more.

The star attraction of the site, however, is the virtual showroom. With intuitive navigation and a simple design, Ford presents seemingly limitless details about dozens of models of cars from several brands, including Ford, Lincoln, Mercury, Jaguar, and Ford Heavy Trucks. For every model, the site offers exterior and interior photos, detailed technical and feature specifications, and even short video presentations. All of these pages also point to a dealer directory, pricing information, and a calculator for leasing and financing options.

Car buyers who are intimidated by salesmen can effectively make their purchasing decisions in the comfort of their living rooms, print out the site-generated financing terms, and walk into their nearest dealer with the confidence of knowing exactly what they want.

Figure 2.9

The Lease vs. Finance Calculator is one of the many strong information features on Ford's utilitarian site.

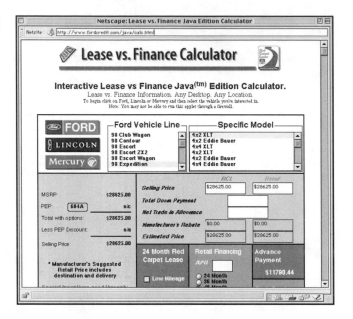

Consumer Staples

For consumer products deemed information-poor, such as gum, root beer, or light bulbs, the challenge is to find some hook by which to engage the visitor with the brand. Many such product sites have taken the show-biz approach, with goofy Shockwave games and other infotainment. The more successful sites, however, have either opted for heavy banner ad campaigns and sponsorship of content on real publishers' sites, or have found some aspect of their own expertise they can offer as utilitarian information to consumers.

Proctor & Gamble has quite a few sites for brands that aren't exactly information-rich. Its Tide "ClothesLine" site, however, is a decent example of a consumer brand offering valuable information.

Tide does its best to put a positive spin on what are essentially lessons about laundry soap. The homepage declares itself to be the "most comprehensive site on the Web dedicated to keeping your clothes looking their best. Hang around awhile and you'll find out everything your mother never told you about laundry and fabric care."

The quality of writing and presentation of the site is polished. Celebrating its 50th year in 1997, Tide makes a Web celebrity of P&G's chief archivist, Ed Rider, who has combed his files for an interesting tour of Tide's advertising images over the years. The site also plays to the online community, letting visitors vote for their favorite among some cute pictures for "America's Dirtiest Kid." And it features a monthly contest, effectively gleaning free market research by asking contestants to answer questions such as, "What Was Your Favorite Tide Commercial?"

However, according to Tide spokeswoman Tracy Long, the most popular feature of the site is "The Stain Detective." It's easy to see why. This is where Tide's expertise in one narrowly defined, if banal, field—stain removal—is offered as a useful, free consumer service. It's nothing more than a simple database that cross-references three user-selected stain variables—stain substance, fabric type, and fabric color—and returns the best stain removal remedy. The choices of stain types are wide-ranging, including all kinds of food, paint, makeup, bodily fluids, and other categories of smudges, smears, and soils.

Figure 2.10

"The Stain Detective" can find the solution to almost any stain scenario.

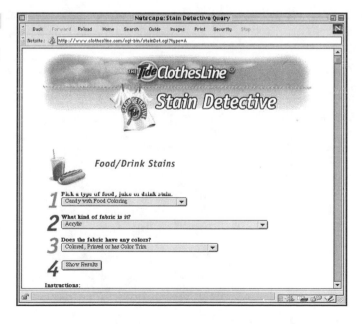

It's the kind of utility you may think is cute or dumb the first time you see it. But later, when you're in the throes of a stain emergency, such as your boss's blood on your white cotton shirt and blue corduroy jacket, it could be a lifesaver.

Instantaneous

The speed at which modern computers process and relay information makes the Web the most immediate mass communication medium. It's more timely than even live TV news because it's non-linear. You don't have to wait for a news anchor to finish his current boring story before getting to the topic you want. You just load the homepage and go straight to the headlines, weather, sports, or whatever else you're looking for.

How a news site benefits from this is obvious. The Web editions of *The New York Times* and other daily papers frequently scoop their print editions on breaking stories. They can post the stories on the Web long before the print editions, with their daylong production periods, can catch up. CNN goes into greater background detail on top stories, offering a multitude of links to the many topics its massive staff is always tracking.

Figure 2.11

The Web site of KPIX, San Francisco's CBS affiliate TV station, features popular up-to-the-moment traffic information, including photos of several Bay Area thoroughfares, so drivers can plan their routes home from work. Here, it's placed a camera atop the car dealership that sponsors the page.

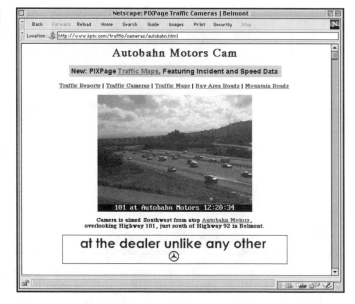

Real-Time Marketing

In computer jargon, there's a concept called *real-time*, meaning that data can bounce halfway around the world and back in a fraction of a second. The Web provides this. Its timeliness has been exploited by marketers in numerous creative ways: real-time audio concert broadcasts, celebrity chats, online customer service, time-sensitive promotional offers, and more.

Part of the benefit of FedEx's famous online package-tracking service is its immediacy, delivering up-to-the-minute package location information from FedEx's giant logistics communication system.

Providing current customer account information is another way to exploit the Web's immediacy, such as showing customers their records, business-to-business transactions, or retail shopping histories.

Certain industries, such as travel, have thrived online thanks to the Web's immediacy. Ever since American Airlines led the charge with its Net SAAver Fares program, most airlines have followed suit, providing short-notice email and Web alerts for heavily discounted tickets on flights that aren't sold out. Many entrepreneurs and established travel services are also doing booming business by selling up-to-the-minute fare discounts.

For online retailers, the Web's fast pace can mean quick response to inventory availability, as Fingerhut Companies, Inc. has learned with the Andy's Garage Sale site, discussed in Chapter 1.

Meanwhile, a marketer who studies the patterns of users' online behavior can immediately offer special promotions, modify the site's structure and content, or replace banner advertising that's performing poorly. Changes that could take weeks or longer to implement in magazine, billboard, and television advertising campaigns or national retail sales promotions can be programmed online to take effect on a user-by-user basis.

Measurable

The wonderful thing about computers is that they compute. This makes Web marketing a tremendously accountable medium.

Stats for Consumers

Many sites take the Web's bounty of numbers and offer it back to Web surfers as an added value to the sites' basic services. For example, at a glance a visitor may be able to see the size of files available for downloading, the number of visitors present in various chat rooms, or how many replies various subjects have generated on a discussion board.

The SF Bay MatchMaker, a local Web dating service, uses a more complex implementation of the Web's "numbers game." For a monthly fee, the service allows lonely singles to post information about themselves, browse the listings of other members, and trade messages with prospective mates.

When SurferBoy browses CyberGirl's introduction, the system reveals a variety of statistics about her. It tells him, for example, how many times she has logged on to check her account, how many others have browsed her listing, how many have written her messages, how many of those she's replied to, and so on.

Figure 2.12

SFPrincess617 isn't kissing any frogs these days. Her Royal Highness hasn't checked her messages since she first signed onto the system, although a few Prince Charmings have tried their luck.

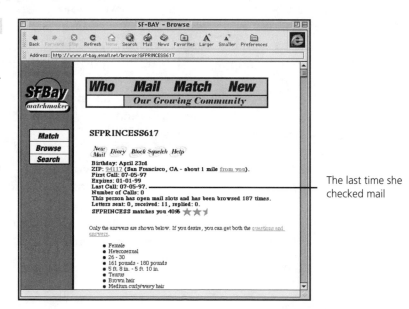

The last time she checked mail

Stats for Marketers

The real advantage of the Web's calculability, however, is not so much a benefit to users as to marketers. Philadelphia department store magnate John Wanamaker coined an axiom of marketing when he said, "I know half of my advertising is wasted. The trouble is, I don't know which half." On the Web, however, that no longer needs to be true.

If an advertiser uses the clickthrough rate on ad banners as a measure of success for direct response objectives, it will be clear in a matter of hours which creative material generates the strongest response. The proverbial "other half" that isn't performing can be readily identified and replaced with more effective advertising.

(As we discuss in Chapter 9, clickthrough is not always the best measure of a banner's success, such as when branding is the goal, despite click-through's near universal acceptance as the litmus test for performance. We use it here just to make a point. Millward Brown demonstrates that branding can also be measured effectively online, it's just more compli-cated—also discussed in Chapter 9)

Jonathan Nelson, CEO of Organic Online, a San Francisco-based design company whose clients include Nike, Kinko's, and McDonald's, offers this advice to marketers on the Web:

"Take your best guess in terms of strategic objectives and then measure the hell out of your responses. Experiment. Make mistakes. Learn. Inno-vate. Be Open. The Web is infinitely measurable. Every Web marketer should be poring over their logs to see what's working and what's not."

Room for Improvement

A word of caution, however: Measurement on the Web is not yet an exact science. Due to the decentralized nature of the Internet, originally designed by the U.S. military to withstand the disruption of a nuclear attack, data finds its way from sites to end users through circuitous and unpredictable routes.

The delivery of a banner ad, for example, is much more complex than one Web server displaying the ad onto one Web browser. That seemingly simple transaction may also involve a regional *mirror* server of the site, a *proxy* server behind a corporate firewall serving an untracked copy of the ad from a *cache* file, and any number of routing servers in between. Not to mention the chance that the Web surfer may hit the Stop button before the ad and page have loaded.

For such reasons, there is generally more activity going on behind a site's content than is reflected in a standard Web server log, leaving marketers with a less-than-perfect understanding of the surfers who may or may not have viewed the site.

Meanwhile, the very terminology of Web measurements remains vague. Web publishers use terms such as *hits, clicks, visits, page views, page requests*, and others to mean often different things. An advertiser may face difficulty comparing the performance of the same banner ad on different sites that use varying lingo in their reports.

Despite such imprecision, a business that's determined to make sense of the results of Web marketing has much better data at its disposal than the cloudy estimates about audience penetration that television, magazines, and other media can offer.

The good news for Web marketers is that lots of companies are constantly pushing the envelope on improving online measurements, including Accrue, Andromedia, MatchLogic, Sofres IMR, Internet Profiles (I/PRO), Media Metrix, Relevant Knowledge, and others.

Flexible

At Alice's trial in her *Adventures in Wonderland*, the King gives the White Rabbit these instructions on how to present some evidence: "Begin at the beginning… and go on till you come to the end: then stop."

It's perfectly sensible advice for how to relate most stories, and indeed it's how information is organized in most media. TV shows, books, magazines, letters, songs, radio traffic reports, and most other forms of communication have in common a beginning, a middle, and an end.

Web sites, however, break that mold. Online data is much more flexible and can be arranged and rearranged in a variety of ways, both by site designers and by surfers themselves.

Sure, a homepage can be seen as the beginning of a site, but from there a surfer can normally continue deeper into the material from a number of different directions.

Base Data on Databases

Moreover, moving beyond HTML's inherent hierarchical data structure, whereby pages branch out from the homepage into the levels of a directory tree, a Web site can take advantage of the true flexibility of electronic data by incorporating a database into its programming infrastructure. Using database functionality, a site can break entirely free from the linear beginning-middle-end format by letting visitors search out exactly the information they're seeking.

TV Guide's site is a good example of this flexibility. From the homepage, users have numerous options, including links to current entertainment industry stories, sports and news highlights provided by the FOX Network, movie listings, online shopping, and more.

Of course, the site also features the TV listings for which *TV Guide* is famous. The detail of those TV listings is remarkable. A user need only enter his ZIP code to receive comprehensive local listings of all programming on broadcast, cable, and pay-per-view television. Furthermore, he can customize the listings in a number of formats, such as to include only his favorite channels and viewing nights, laid out by day or by week, with favorite shows highlighted and so on.

Based on the flexibility of the database, the information is not static. Within two or three links from the homepage, the user can create a personalized version of the available information. After customizing the listings to his particular preference, he can bookmark the page and return thereafter directly to his one-of-a-kind TV directory, something the print edition could never hope to achieve.

Figure 2.13

At *TV Guide's* site, users can enter their zip codes and the massive database of TV listings returns their local daily listings. The site lets users further customize the data seven ways from Sunday.

Consumer Convenience

Enhanced consumer loyalty is a strong marketing benefit of the Web's flexibility of data. By letting users bookmark a customized service, *TV Guide* ensures a healthy percentage of regular return visitors.

Along with frequently updated content, warehoused data is a top feature for increasing repeat site traffic. The latest news is important to a user, but so is reliable access to quality archived information.

The convenience for consumers is readily apparent at many online shopping services. Compare, for example, two CD shopping experiences: looking for the latest album by the Squirrel Nut Zippers in a local Tower Records outlet versus looking for the same album on Tower's Web site.

In the store, the shopper must first consider what genre the album would be filed under: jazz or pop or swing or alternative? Perhaps if he can buttonhole a busy clerk, he can find out. Then he must stroll the aisles of alphabetized titles, inevitably taking a wrong turn or two before figuring out the various zigzags the alphabet takes, due to the store's floor plan.

When he finds the S section, he flips through several rows of CDs to discover that the Squirrel Nut Zippers don't have their own listing. So he has to wade through all of the S listings, only to find that due to the store's limited inventory space, they're all out of the current release. So he grabs their previous album and then stands in line at the cashier for 15 minutes.

Or he could type **www.towerrecords.com** into his browser, enter "Squirrel Nut Zippers" into the homepage's search field and, presto, there's the band's entire discography. After he enters a couple more pages of shopping info, the CD arrives in the next day's mail.

Figure 2.14

One mouse-click from the home-page, Tower's site shows all the Squirrel Nut Zippers titles it carries, both in and out of stock.

Mike Farrace, VP of publishing and electronic commerce at Tower, confirms that many users approach Tower's site exactly that way.

"Some stores tell us that customers come in to buy records they found in the Web database," he said. "We call this 'real instant gratification.'"

Interlinked

Obviously inherent in the Web experience are *hypertext links*, those words and images that the user clicks to go to a new page. These links give the Web its nonlinear structure, producing the effect of *browsing* pages in a seemingly random order.

Arguably, hypertext has its roots in centuries-old monastic texts and even experimental 18th-century literature. In the computer era, hypertext's roots go back to a visionary 1945 essay by Vannevar Bush, "As We May Think," published in *The Atlantic Monthly*. Mr. Bush's wide-ranging essay had a big impact on future technologies, providing not only a clear description of hypertext (which he referred to as "associative trails"), but also foretelling microfilm, digital photography, personal computers, and other modern technologies.

Ted Nelson coined the term "hypertext" as part of his ill-fated 1960s "docuverse" project called Xanadu. Later Apple, IBM, and others continued developing the hypertext concept through the '80s, but it wasn't until 1989 that a Brit named Tim Berners-Lee created the two protocols we know and love—HTTP and HTML. This laid the foundations for the grandest example yet of hypertext, today's World Wide Web.

Think Web, Not Strand

Look at the popular metaphors for the Web. The Oxford American Dictionary defines "web" as "a network of fine strands made by a spider, etc." So the "etc." in this case doesn't mention computer nerds, but otherwise the word depicts the HTML/HTTP universe vividly. In addition to "web," another persistent image is that of an "information superhighway" or "Infobahn." Both metaphors connote a sense of interconnectedness and travel, the way a spider traverses a Web or a driver travels the interstates.

At play on the Web is the phenomenon of "Metcalfe's Law": *The value of a network to its users is equal to the number of users squared*. That is, networks grow exponentially more valuable as they gain more users (and nodes, routers, and other communication points). As Bob Metcalfe, inventor of the Ethernet protocol, analogized in his *InfoWeek* magazine column, "If you had the only telephone in the world, who would you call?"

According to this principle, every Web site is expected to play some role as a hub. It's the same way the intersections of strands in a spider's web lead in multiple directions, and how roads into a city generally exit in at least one other direction. Sites without links are like loose strands on a web, leaving visitors stranded like dead flies. Or think of them as dead ends on the Infobahn.

Surprisingly, many Web marketers miss this point. A quick straw poll of well-known consumer brand sites, such as Coca-Cola, Pampers, Saturn, Nike, Staples, and others, reveals that they have almost no links to other sites on the Web.

Figure 2.15

Ragu is rare among con- sumer brand marketers online, seeing the value of linking to other sites. For some reason, Ragu's site has links to "family" sites— amateur fan sites devoted to famous TV fami- lies like the Brady Bunch, the Jetsons, and the Flintstones.

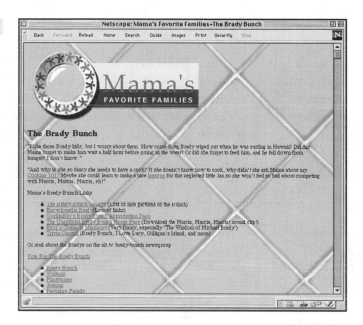

Presumably, these marketers fear that by providing "exit" links they will lose visitors to other sites. That view is naive. If visitors like your content enough, they'll stay a while and maybe even come back. But the Web is bigger than just your site, so eventually they're going to leave, with or without your help.

Gateway Content

Almost without exception, sites increase their value to users by linking to recommended content elsewhere on the Web. It's just as Metcalfe's Law describes, if we view one site as its own network. A site with no links is only as valuable as its original content, which, in the case of products such carbonated beverages or soap, could get old quick.

Links to other sites introduce the dimension of *gateway content*, opening up users to the vast resources of the Web without much extra effort on the referring site's part. Even after a user has seen everything there is to see at a marketing site, it may still be worth bookmarking if its links make it a portal to a unique collection of new material.

However, sites need not take Metcalfe's Law literally by amassing as many links as possible. For most sites, the *quality* of links is more important than the sheer *quantity*. That said, it's no surprise that search engines and directories, the largest aggregators of links, are among the most valuable Web networks in terms of advertising revenue.

Look at the other sites that feature abundant links to external resources. Netscape, CNET, *The New York Times*, CNN, HotWired, and other Web titans litter their content with links to other sites, and none of them seem to be losing traffic as a result.

Figure 2.16

The New York Times Web site routinely provides links at the ends of stories to relevant information elsewhere on the Web. Most users, glad for such service, are likely to come back again.

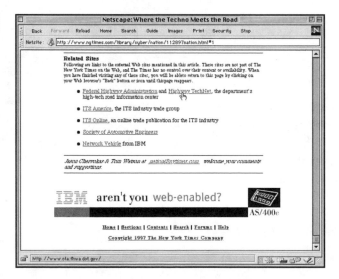

Link Partnerships

Not only can links serve as free, quality content, but for sites that generate substantial traffic, outbound links can earn money or other capital

TIP: LAUNCHING A NEW BROWSER WINDOW

Some sites employ a simple HTML trick in order to give their visitors the value of linking without losing them to other sites. When a user clicks on a link, the referred site opens in a new browser window while the referring site remains in the original window. When the user finishes looking at the new link, he can resume where he left off in the original site without having to use his Back button to get there.

You can do this by adding `target="new"` to a hypertext link's anchor (or "a") tag, like this:

```
<a href="http://www.usweb.com"
target="new">Visit USWeb</a>
```

This command creates a new browser window with USWeb's homepage when a user clicks the **Visit USWeb** hotlink.

Most site developers don't use this technique, some because they probably don't know about it, but many because they think users will find it annoying. Our view is that linking the standard way—sending users from your site to another one within the same browser window—expresses more confidence in the quality of your site. (Visitors can come back when they're ready.) It also respects basic Web standards. But creating a new target browser for links is a legitimate tool for Web designers that may be useful in some cases.

through partnerships with other Web ventures.

Many sites sell hypertext pointers, like banner ads, to other sites outright. Supposedly the highest-revenue example of this is Netscape's NetSearch page. The leading search engines reportedly pay as much as $5 million or more each per year to be included on the page.

Amazon.com pays sites to link to it not with ad dollars, but with sales commissions. Through their Associate program, sites that recommend and link to specific books for sale on Amazon.com can earn up to 15% of the transaction price if a surfer makes a purchase via the link.

Other sites work out mutual back-scratching arrangements along the lines of reciprocal traffic-building or other alliances. CNET's Snap! is an example of this. CNET launched the consumer service in mid-1997, aggregating content from other sites with the idea of rivaling America Online as a gateway for new Web users. Snap! struck deals with several ISPs, who provide new customers with browsers configured to open by default to Snap!'s homepage. The content on Snap! includes some original content by CNET staffers, but the service is mostly a well-organized directory of recommended links to other Web sites.

Figure 2.17

Home Depot is one of thousands of sites to join Amazon.com's Associate program, collecting a sales commission of up to 15% for every book sold via a link to Amazon.com. Users who click the "Home Improvements 1-2-3" icon on this page go directly to an Amazon.com page where they can buy the book.

At the top of the page within each topic "channel" (for example, Business, Sports, Entertainment), one Web site is featured as that category's leader. CNET insists that it isn't selling those premier positions, but that it's purely an editorial decision. You can be sure, however, that some serious behind-the-scenes power-brokering goes on for access to those link positions. Whether CNET is influenced by sites advertising heavily elsewhere within CNET's online empire is CNET's business. Either way, those links are clearly bargaining chips for CNET.

Linking Netiquette

Usually, sites will welcome a pointer to them from another site. In practice, many sites don't even bother notifying others when they've linked to them, although such a heads-up is generally a welcome courtesy.

This being the Web, of course, there have been some disputes over unwanted inbound links. One of the most notable battles is Ticketmaster's suit against Microsoft Sidewalk for unwelcome links.

As Microsoft prepared for the launch of its Sidewalk local entertainment listings service in early 1997, it negotiated with Ticketmaster about linking to its online ticket sales mechanism. At the last minute, however, Ticketmaster struck a deal with CitySearch, a competitor to Sidewalk. Microsoft decided to go with the flow of Web tradition and simply link its surfers to Ticketmaster anyway.

Ticketmaster—which, incidentally, is owned in majority by Paul Allen, a cofounder and remaining shareholder of Microsoft—cried foul and is taking its case to court. The ticket giant objects to Microsoft using Ticketmaster's brand to sell ads on Sidewalk pages. Originally, Microsoft linked to interior, ad-free Ticketmaster pages where Sidewalk users could make their ticket purchases, instead of linking to Ticketmaster's homepage where Ticketmaster could at least earn ad revenue from the new visitors.

Ticketmaster filed the suit in April 1997, and by that December the dispute had neither come to trial nor been resolved. Sidewalk continues to refer visitors to Ticketmaster for concert booking, and Ticketmaster intercepts the links with an access-denied message for anyone coming from Sidewalk.

Figure 2.18

Click this link on Microsoft's Sidewalk service to buy a concert ticket at Ticketmaster's site...

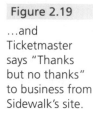

Figure 2.19

...and Ticketmaster says "Thanks but no thanks" to business from Sidewalk's site.

Many legal analysts expect Ticketmaster to lose its case. Meanwhile, Web advocates say a victory for the ticket company would undermine a fundamental principle of the Web: the freedom to link to other sites.

Another well-publicized linking dispute involved TotalNews, an aggregator of news headlines from other online media companies. Although several online news services, such as NewsHub and NewsLinx, also link to news stories on other sites, TotalNews raised the ire of some powerful media organizations for its practice of linking to their stories within HTML frames. That way TotalNews could continue to display banner ads over the content the other sites had produced.

In February 1997, the *Washington Post*, *Times Mirror*, Time Warner, CNN, Dow Jones, and Reuters New Media brought a lawsuit against TotalNews regarding the framed links. In June of that year, TotalNews, a five-person organization, relented and settled the suit out of court. As part of the settlement, the plaintiffs granted TotalNews a "linking license" to continue pointing to their stories, but without HTML frames.

Because the case didn't reach a court decision, it doesn't represent a proper legal precedent, but sites are advised to draw a lesson from the suit anyway. Use caution in linking to other sites within HTML frames,

TIP: GETTING INBOUND, AFFINITY LINKS TO YOUR SITE

Links go both ways, of course. If you're wondering how to encourage other sites to link to yours, see the section on affinity sites in Chapter 6, "Word of Web: Online Communities."

especially if your site is serving ads on top of the other sites' content.

Economical

Another tremendous benefit of the Web is that it's still a comparatively inexpensive marketing medium.

At one end of the spectrum is the individual with a good idea. On the Web, she can sit in her living room and run a publication, a mail-order business, a virtual porn parlor, or whatever else with practically no start-up costs or overhead. Self-publishing and micro-entrepreneurship was never so simple. Anyone with a computer and the determination to learn basic HTML coding can run a simple site for production costs of $50 per month in Web hosting fees.

At the other end of the spectrum is a large commercial site needing personalization, e-commerce, banner ad rotation, search facilities, dynamic page generation, good anti-hacker security, and a host of other special services common to sites of that size. After paying for specialized software, custom programming, design, and fast back-end bandwidth, you may be talking $1 million a year or more, not including staff salaries, marketing, and other expenses.

At $1 million and up, some may start to question the Web's supposed economical benefit. The key to remember is that it's *comparatively* inexpensive. Compared to a print magazine, where paper, printing, and distribution are enormous operating costs, the savings with Web publishing are huge. Compared to direct mail marketing, where paper, postage, and name acquisitions are expensive, target marketing on the Web is a steal. Compared to the cost of producing a high-production-value TV commercial and paying for extensive prime-time airing, Web advertising requires chump change.

Figure 2.20

A site like Disney's, featuring animation, video clips, secure e-commerce, personalization, push technology, and more, doesn't come free, but it's surely less than making a blockbuster movie.

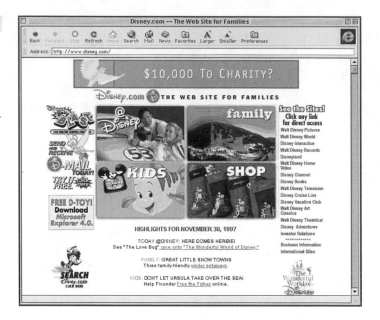

Contain Costs

Guy Hill, media planner at USWeb, said, "The Web is incredibly inexpensive if you do it right, with an eye on cost. What one of the fast food giants spends on the Web could be a rounding error compared to what they spend on TV and print. There's still no comparison."

Many marketers complain that advertising rates for Web banners are exorbitant, but as anyone who's been around the block can tell you, prices on most rate cards are very flexible.

Tower Record's Mike Farrace believes e-commerce on the Web offers savings over time to large retailers, after initial costs level out. In Tower's case, the site has borne extensive startup expenses to fully equip itself for secure commerce, in addition to extensive custom programming to put a Web interface on Tower's pre-existing computer system. "Nonetheless," Mr. Farrace said, "a little over a year since its launching, the site is already doing two-thirds the volume of business of Tower's biggest stores, which do $50–60 million a year." And the site's business is still growing fast. "The site could become the biggest and most profitable sales outlet in the chain," he said.

"For us, the startup costs of the Web enterprise are probably going to add up to more than it would cost to open a store, but my feeling is that economies of scale will start to show not too far down the road," said Mr. Farrace. "I think that the operating costs for the site will be a lower percentage of gross sales, when we get to where we want to be, than the 'brick and mortar' maintenance costs."

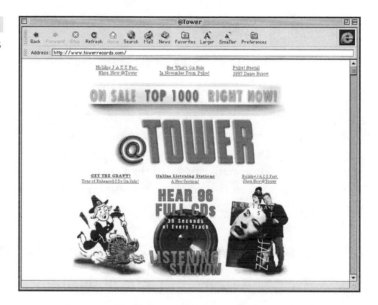

Figure 2.21

Tower Records is already doing tens of millions in sales after little more than a year in the game.

Mr. Farrace warns that even the ongoing costs of a site the size of Tower's aren't cheap. "You can hire a record store clerk for less than even an HTML coder, which is the entry-level Web guy. Also, when you have a Web site, you need specialized marketing people, too."

On the balance, however, the savings online are real as long as budgets are well-managed.

"To me, the whole thing is about containing costs. That's the number-one lesson in any business. It's so easy in this online world to take the bit in your teeth regarding a new technology or a certain type of Web exposure. But the longer you hang with it, you realize what you really need is the right kind of Web exposure."

Hear, hear!

Resources

See the Resource sections of Chapter 1, Chapter 9, and the Appendix for further online marketing references, as well as sources for demographic research, Internet history, and other related topics.

Web Demographics and Technical Research

Georgia Tech GVU's WWW User Survey

http://www-survey.cc.gatech.edu/

One of the most often cited surveys of Internet users, the Georgia Tech study is repeated once or twice a year and includes thousands of participants. Being a voluntary Web-based study, depending on users to learn of and volunteer for the study on their own, it represents clear statistical biases. Nonetheless, it is among the most comprehensive public surveys of Internet users available.

Morgan Stanley Internet Advertising Report

http://www.ms.com/misc/inetad/index.html

Compiled by Morgan Stanley analyst Mary Meeker, this 1996 document consists of the results of dozens of studies on Internet users and online trends.

Netcraft Web Server Survey

http://www.netcraft.com/survey/

This British networking company regularly runs a technical analysis of World Wide Web hosts to estimate the number of active Web sites.

TRUSTe/Boston Consulting Group Privacy Survey

http://www.truste.org/webpublishers/studies_BCG.html

The TRUSTe Internet privacy organization commissioned researchers at the Boston Consulting Group to conduct this extensive survey about Web users' views of online privacy.

Yahoo! on Netizen Demographics

http://www.yahoo.com/Computers_and_Internet/Internet/
World_Wide_Web/Statistics_and_Demographics/

You'll find links to other Web surveys.

Marketing Resources

Association for Interactive Media

http://www.interactivehq.org/

This site features various online marketing resources, including an excellent calendar of industry events.

Bruner Communications

http://www.bruner.net/

This site includes advice for online marketers and many up-to-date links to other resources and online marketing news.

A Clue

http://tbass.com/clue/

Here you'll find insider commentary about the Web industry, including evaluations of sites that either do or don't "have a clue."

USWeb's Resource Center

http://www.usweb.com/solutions/res_lib/whitepapers.html

This site contains white papers for Web marketers.

WilsonWeb

http://www.wilsonweb.com/

This site includes advice for online marketers, news, and links to other resources.

Other Related Resources

The Internet Society's Account of Internet History

http://www.isoc.org/internet-history/

Here you'll find detailed account of how the Internet came to be, written by many of those who made it happen.

Yahoo! on Internet history

http://www.yahoo.com/Computers_and_Internet/Internet/History/

This site features links to more accounts of Internet lore.

Vannevar Bush's "As We May Think"

http://www.bush.or.at/aswemaythink/

A seminal article in the annals of modern technology, originally published in *Atlantic Monthly* in 1945. If this link is dead, search for the author and article title on any search engine. Reproductions of it abound across the Web.

Metcalfe's Law

http://www.infoworld.com/cgi-bin/displayArchives.pl?dt_data40_25.htm

Bob Metcalfe, inventor of the Ethernet networking protocol and founder of 3Com, clarifies his principle of the exponentially increasing value of networks as they grow in this edition of his weekly *InfoWorld* column. This column was titled, "A Network Becomes More Valuable As It Reaches More Users," and appeared on October 2, 1995 (Vol. 17, Issue 40).

Design Optimization

L et's presume that you now have some ideas about what kind of strategic return on investment your company seeks from online marketing, and how you plan to leverage the Web's unique value propositions to attract users with your compelling content. The next priority in getting your site right is the presentation of the material. In addition to the critical issues of the quality and type of content required to interest the user, sites must be careful to optimize their network responsiveness and information architecture.

Although most users accept that they must tolerate ad banners on Web pages to finance free content, it is almost always solely their prerogative whether to interact with the marketer in any greater depth than that. A hint of slow response time, hokey graphics, or no obvious added value, and they'll be hitting the Back button faster than you can say "Transfer interrupted!"

Design for the Lowest Common Denominator

The Web tremendously complicates the traditional art of graphic design. In many ways it introduces new opportunities and design possibilities, but in at least as many more ways it limits artistic freedom.

Figure 3.1

No, they're
NOT... NOT...
NOT, when you
have to wait for
this GIF from
Hell to finish
downloading.

On the one hand, traditional four-color printing restricts graphic artists to creating all their shades of color from a mix of cyan, magenta, yellow, and black, while modern computer screens can display at least 256 basic colors, if not thousands or millions. On the other hand, incompatible color standards among different operating systems and browser types mean that designers must learn new techniques to strip color palettes down to the lowest common denominator and otherwise overcome new technical hurdles.

Because HTML is a *markup language*, it describes for a browser how certain elements should be displayed but leaves the specific implementation up to the end user's software. Fonts, for example, are a wild card on the Web. A designer can describe the type of font she wants, but the user's browser will substitute whatever is available on the local system. The user can also override the borrower's defaults and use whatever crazy font for headlines he darn well pleases, and the designer has to like it or lump it. Of course, sites can fix stylized fonts into graphic images, but that is costly in terms of download time.

On the plus side, designers can experiment with new media types such as animation, sound, and hyperlinks. On the minus side, there is great variance in how elements align themselves on the page, how big a user's monitor is, how fast his connection is, and so on.

Figure 3.2

Most browsers'
preferences let
users select their
own fonts for
Web pages,
much to the
grief of
designers.

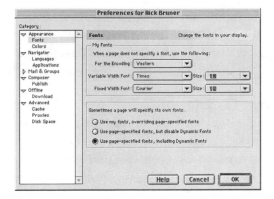

Design is a highly subjective area, of course. This book doesn't hope to
set down rules for artistic vision, but rather some general, practical suggestions that may improve users' overall experience at your site.

Know Your Audience

Just because your designers may be using 21" monitors, fast processors,
and a T1 line, not all the visitors to your site may be so lucky. Here are
some statistics to put that in perspective.

The Georgia Institute of Technology surveys Web users once or twice a
year. Drew Richardson, data manager at Find/SVP, an Internet research
group, points out that the Georgia Tech study's results are probably
more representative of technically savvy users than average netizens because it's a self-selected sample. The survey depends on respondents to
learn about the survey on their own and volunteer to fill it out during
the active two-week test period.

Bearing in mind this higher-than-average technology bias, the spring '97
survey found that nearly half of the respondents used 14" or 15" monitors, with a slow growth in upgrading over the years. (The complete
results of the November '97 survey weren't available at the time of this
writing.) Nearly two-thirds of those surveyed connected to the Web via
modems running at 33.3Kbps (33,300 bits per second) or slower.

In a separate study, Find/SVP found that in mid-'97, nearly 20% of surfers were still using the Windows 3.1 operating system to access the Web.

As a favor to the author, Wired Digital took a "snapshot" of its users on October 17, 1997 and found that approximately 41% of visitors to the HotWired site were using some version of Netscape Navigator, 22% were using Internet Explorer, and a healthy 37% were using "Other."

A page maintained by Ed Kubaitis, a student at the University of Illinois, gives some insight into that "Other" category. The page breaks down all the different browser types that surfers use to visit the university's thousands of student homepages. On a typical day, with nearly a quarter of a million page views, the system recorded dozens of browser types other than Internet Explorer or Netscape Navigator, including IBM Web-Explorer, Lotus Notes, Lynx (a stubbornly popular text-only browser for UNIX), NetAttache, NetCruser, NetJet, OmniWeb, PageWatch, Prodigy-WB, SearchPad, Slurp, StepToWord, WebChat, WebCompass, WebMogul, WebShades, WebWalker, WebWhacker, and others.

Figure 3.3

This industrious Czech software developer has spotted a growth market for a graphical browser for the DOS operating system. Might their users include some of your site's visitors?

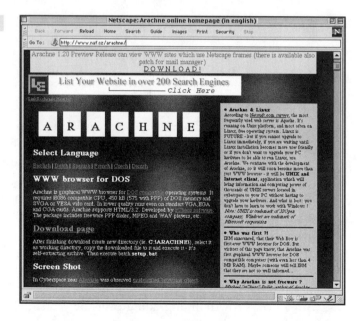

Site performance—how quickly pages can load in viewers' browsers—should be a chief consideration in every aspect of site design. Users are sick of the "World Wide Wait." Sites that are sloppy and don't carefully optimize performance for a variety of platforms will find that many users won't bother waiting around for them to load.

The users' technology threshold for any particular site depends to some extent on the site's target audience. A site aimed at corporate intranet administrators at Fortune 1000 companies, for example, may not care if they lose visitors from AOL who are using 28.8Kbps modems. The majority of general consumer sites, however, should be cautious not to overestimate the technical standards of their visitors.

Even sites courting a corporate audience, where it might be assumed that many users are on fast networks, shouldn't neglect traveling professionals connecting via notebook computers, small businesses with limited network resources, and corporate users checking in from home Internet accounts.

The 28.8Kbps Factor

Most sites, unless their audience is exceptional, should optimize performance for users of 28.8Kbps dial-up modems for the foreseeable future. The spring '97 Georgia Tech survey found that one-third of all users connect at that speed, which is the largest block at any connection speed. Competing protocol standards for the 56Kbps speed have kept that upgrade market from developing. Even when that debate is eventually settled (perhaps by the time this book is in print), a mass migration of surfers to the faster speed will likely take a year or more.

"I always keep the file sizes in mind when designing Web pages," said George Lawson, creative director of USWeb Marin. "Some clients don't mind making people wait for downloads if the visual experience is so powerful. I'd rarely advise that route myself."

Mr. Lawson is conservative in his numbers. "Forty-five K [kilobytes] should be the size limit for all the files that make up a Web page combined," he said. "That's a good rule of thumb, even generous. You could keep it lower."

Before the Web came along, computer designers generally had little reason to obsess about keeping graphic file sizes as small as possible. Graphics programs such as Photoshop are notorious for creating large files, easily taking up hundreds of kilobytes or even several megabytes. It's for files such as these that external storage devices like DAT and Zip drives were invented. But now designers are told to make powerful, exciting graphics, yet keep file sizes under 50KB, 25KB, or even 10KB.

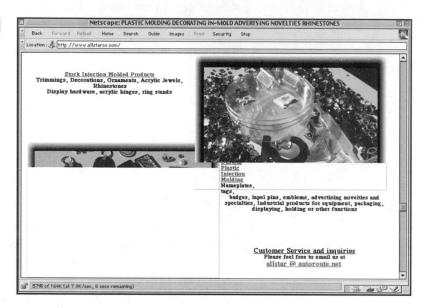

Figure 3.4

Ouch! Not only do these scintillating images of injection-molded plastic products weigh in at nearly 100KB each, their layout on this browser actually covers up navigational hyperlinks. Get a clue, boys.

Yahoo! demands that all standard banner ads running on its system be no larger than 10KB, including animation. HotWired has a policy to keep the combined elements of any page under 90KB, while they try to keep the homepage at no more than 60KB.

New software products—such as Equalibrium's graphics conversion program DeBabelizer, a staple in every serious Web designer's toolbox—help sites optimize their graphics for the Web's low-bandwidth restrictions. Yet, sadly, many less-sophisticated sites still feature individual graphics at upwards of 75KB, 100KB, and even 150KB and over. On an ISDN, this is okay, maybe. Otherwise … ouch!

A *bit*—a contraction of the phrase *binary digit*—is the most elemental unit of computer information, either a 1 or a 0. *Bit* is used mostly when speaking of transfer units, such as the transfer of information by modem. Eight bits make one *byte*, which is a data storage unit equal to one ASCII character. Therefore, a 75KB (75,000-byte) file would take 20.8 seconds to transfer at 28,800 bits per second.

This is if all other things on the network were neutral, which they never are. Imagine that the site's server is busy, it's during peak traffic hours on a workday, and the end user's ISP is a bit flaky and won't allow connection at maximum modem speed. That 75KB image is going to take the better part of a minute to download at 28.8Kbps. That's the same time it takes for two high-production-value television commercials to make their impact on viewers. That fat GIF sure better be worth the wait.

Figure 3.5

HotWired's WebMonkey site is a good place to start picking up the finer points of Web design. Practicing what they preach, the site's logo takes up only 3KB of disk space.

For more information on the latest graphics management techniques, consult some of the design and coding resource sites, such as Hot-Wired's WebMonkey, CNET's Builder.com, and others listed in the "Resources" section at end of this chapter.

The 14" and 15" Monitor Majority

There was a time—sure, it seems like eons ago to cutting-edge Web developers—when 14" monitors were all the rage. They were a big step up from what people were used to. Well, that was only about 2–3 years ago, and not every home PC owner who's since anteed up for a modem and monthly ISP service has also shelled out the $600+ for a new 17" monitor yet.

For these unlucky millions of Web users on 14″ and 15″ monitors, many Web pages appear to be cropped at least two inches short on the right and scroll downward for ages. Just imagine how such sites look to the business traveler checking in from a laptop.

Figure 3.6

This is what The Good Guys page looks like on a 14″ monitor. Now, what if someone was visiting the site because he was thinking of upgrading his monitor, but navigating the site was too much of a pain? He might just go off to CompuWorld's site instead…

For designers, keeping smaller monitors in mind is a matter of pixel resolution. *Pixels*, a contraction of *picture elements*, are the little spots of light that make up a computer screen's image. The bigger the monitor, the more pixels you can fit into it. A 14″ monitor, for example, generally uses 640×480 pixels to make up its screen. A 17″ monitor can comfortably fit 800×600 pixels or more.

"Even on a 14-inch monitor, you don't really have even 640×480 pixels to design with," said Mr. Lawson. "You have all the browser's toolbars and the operating system's menus, etc. So you really have something like 600×450, let's say. You should definitely try to get at least the most important elements of the page within that target."

Multiple Platforms Pervade

In order for a site to reach its biggest potential audience, its designers had better test it on as many different browser platforms as possible.

What may look dynamite on a Windows 95 PC running Internet Explorer 4.0 might be illegible on Netscape 2.0 and crash a Macintosh on IE 3.0. You can't know till you've looked at the site yourself on the various platforms.

America Online, don't forget, is the Web gateway for more than 10 million users, and sadly that service's Web browser tends to lag a few generations behind the latest standard browser features. Not anticipating how your site may appear to AOLers could deprive you of 30% of your potential visitors.

Another more vexing but potentially enormous type of Web platform to consider are television *set-top boxes*, such as WebTV.

"WebTV is going to be a huge force on the Web in the near future," predicts USWeb's Mr. Lawson. "At the moment, it poses tremendous design constraints. The available screen is much smaller than 640×480 [pixel resolution]. It flattens the text in a way that's hard to read. Certain colors, like reds, can vibrate violently on the screen. It generally wreaks havoc on design."

Sad but true. But with Microsoft's determination and gargantuan spending capacity now behind it, many analysts predict that WebTV and other TV set-top platforms like it may become the next big wave for the yet-unwired masses. Will your site weather the storm?

"Gratuitous Digitalization"

Tim Smith, CEO of Red Sky, a San Francisco-based Web design company whose clients include Land's End, Bank of America, and Sony, councils companies to avoid what he calls "gratuitous digitalization."

"The state of the art stinks," he said. "I tell all our clients to forget about the technology. It doesn't matter. When we sit down with clients, we clear the table of all the technical baggage—Java, CGI, back-end transactions—and ask them to concentrate on the experience they want for their users. Then we take it from there."

Animation, audio, video, 3D, and other whiz-bang features of the Web are wonderful and exciting in their place, but they come with a cost. Namely, large numbers of users are unable or unwilling to use such rich-media features.

Macromedia, maker of the immensely popular Shockwave and Flash animation standards, estimated in late 1997 that more than 20 million users had downloaded its Shockwave Player from its site. Even if every one of those downloads represented a unique user who had installed the plug-in to enable her to view Shockwave animation on sites, that represents only 40% of the 51 million adult Americans alone on the Web, according to a September '97 estimate by the IntelliQuest Information Group.

Figure 3.7

Apparently, Taco Bell's careful research indicates that anyone interested in learning about today's 99-cent junk-food special would naturally have all the latest browser plug-ins. If they don't, however, this is what the homepage looks like.

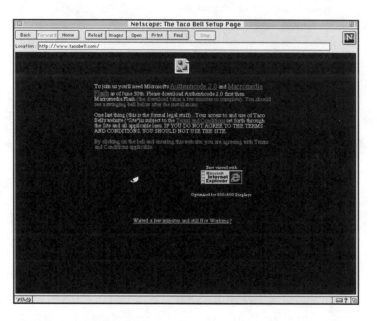

By no means are we recommending against exploiting the exciting multimedia features the Web offers. The point is, again, to know your audience and your objectives. If you believe your target audience, or at least a significant part of it, is *au courant* with the latest bells and whistles, and you believe such features strategically advance your marketing aims, push the envelope. If, however, your site blinks, wiggles, and sings Christmas carols just because your designers think it's neat-o, you should probably think twice.

Moreover, sites must avoid imposing so many limitations on surfers that they cannot appreciate the site's fundamental experience without a particular plug-in, platform type, browser version, monitor size, modem speed, or any other technical constraint. The Web was designed as an open-platform medium, and sites that fail to respect that simply don't get it.

Variable Interfaces Options

One option that many sites embrace is to provide alternative ways for viewers to interact with the site that respect their different network bandwidths, user platforms, and technical savvy. USWeb Marin's site, when the company was called Cybernautics, illustrated this by letting users choose either a Shockwave version of the entire site or a lower-tech version. The Shockwave version introduced a floating Shockwave navigation tool and other enhanced features, but the same basic content was available either way.

Figure 3.8

Name your bandwidth. USWeb Marin's old site didn't require lower-tech users to upgrade their systems in order to appreciate the message.

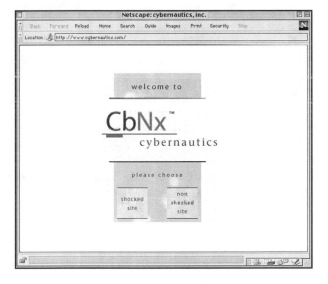

Many sites offer a text-only layout to accommodate the 10% or so of Web users who surf with graphics turned off on their browsers, or the few UNIX hardcores who still prefer the Lynx text-only browser. Other sites offer an alternate navigation system that's dumbed-down for AOL members (and, increasingly, WebTV users). And although HTML frames have done a lot for Web navigation since they were introduced with Netscape Navigator 2.0, there are still users who bristle at them. So some sites include a non-frames version.

Designing tandem versions of sites doesn't work for everyone, in part because it's no piece of cake to execute without sophisticated site-hosting software, such as Vignette's Story Server or Documentum's RightSite. It generally entails duplicating all the site's content and navigation architecture onto a separate Web server for each version of the site.

Thankfully, some Web software developers are building intelligence into their products that can determine which multimedia effects each user's browser can support, thereby giving each user exactly the level of experience they can support without having to ask.

Macromedia, for example, has developed Aftershock, a utility that sites can use to determine instantly whether a visitor's browser can support Shockwave, Java, GIF89s, or other animation file types and serve up the appropriate format. Likewise, InterVU introduced the V-Banner to insert full-motion video into advertising banners. InterVU's server sniffs out what type of video format each user can support and delivers a banner accordingly to give all visitors the best possible experience.

Consistent, Intuitive Navigation

In the behind-the-scenes battles at many sites for supremacy among artistic designers, programmers, and writers, the buck should ultimately stop with the business leaders who have defined the site's strategic objectives. In most cases, that means the site's design is secondary to its information.

Design in the online age, with the new Web dimension of hyperlink navigation, is fundamentally at the service of improving the user's interaction with the site's content. With some exceptions, most content boils down to text and occasional illustrations. A cool-looking site is nice, but not if it greatly slows things down and doesn't somehow advance the site's sacred marketing objectives.

Whether you use frames, a table of contents in the left-hand column, JavaScript-enriched pop-up buttons, or some other popular navigation convention, every page should contain elements to orient the user as to where he is within the site's architecture.

Every surfer has gotten stuck at some site whose navigation is so confusing—frames that seem like a hall of mirrors so the user roams in circles, sloppy "redirect" commands in the HTML code that prevent backing up, forms that deposit surfers on pages with no outbound links—that the easiest way to regain one's bearings is to visit another site altogether. At the other extreme, some sites make navigation cues so painfully obvious, embracing every cliché in the book—blue borders around every graphic link, left-hand margins always devoted to a list of site subsections, blinking "click here" signs—that the sites lack personality and stifle some of the fun of exploring a site, like a new neighborhood, for the first time.

Figure 3.9

A sloppy frames design, like this one, can make you feel like you're in the Hotel California: You can check out any time you like, but you can never leave.

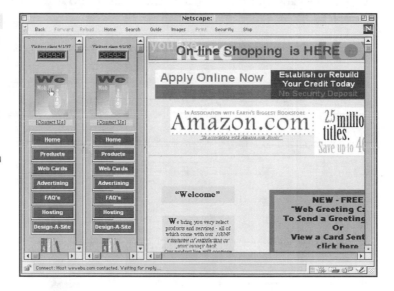

"A lot of sites overestimate users' learning curve for navigation cues," said Mr. Lawson. "Just because a link isn't bordered with a blue line doesn't mean users can't deduce where to go from other cues, like their cursor changing to a pointing finger. Idiot-proofing the navigation costs you in terms of design elegance and sophistication. It's a delicate balance."

Another popular navigation aid is the *site map*. Consisting of a complete index or outline of all the site's subsections, these maps are particularly useful for complex sites with lots of pages, where the breadth of material is not easily represented in just a few buttons across the top or down the side of the page.

Above all, navigation cues should be consistent and intuitive. Every Web site inevitably embodies a hierarchy, where users progress by layers deeper into a logical tree of content. Designers must not only plot this structure carefully, but they should generally signal users where they are within the hierarchy on every page.

Whether this is accomplished through buttons at the top or bottom of the page, lists down the left side, or amorphous blobs in the middle is up to the designers' creativity. What's important is that users can recognize the cues and quickly get where they want to go next, other than to new URLs.

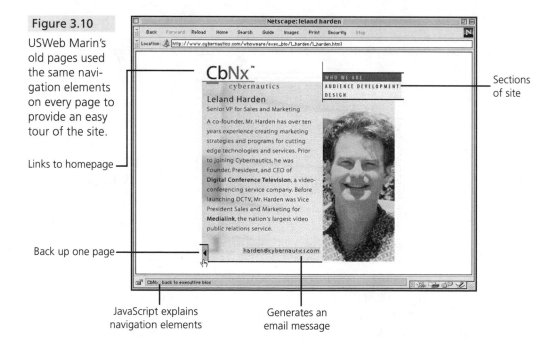

Figure 3.10

USWeb Marin's old pages used the same navigation elements on every page to provide an easy tour of the site.

Links to homepage

Back up one page

JavaScript explains navigation elements

Generates an email message

Sections of site

"Always give an exit," advises Mr. Lawson. "Many times creative types will design the look of pages and general site architecture, but then they'll hand off some of the more complex programming to subcontractors, like forms with CGI scripts. But the subcontractors drop the design conventions, so after a user fills out a form and hits Submit, he ends up at a dead-end page and has to use his Back button to find links to other parts of the site. That's weak."

Another reason to make sure every page clearly leads somewhere else on the site is to help orient visitors who arrive at an interior page through some outside link, such as a search engine. Although the user may enjoy the content he finds on that page, if it's not clear how to get to the homepage and other parts of the site, the new visitor will likely wander off again.

As we'll discuss in later chapters, you can always correct your mistakes if you pay attention to how visitors interact with your site. Careful analysis of traffic logs can reveal weaknesses in navigation and design, such as pages where large numbers of users reverse their steps due to unclear navigation design, or those where users abandon the site altogether because of slow-loading graphics or other problems. Several specialty software tools, such as Accrue Insight and Andromedia's ARIA Recorder Reporter, make the analysis of traffic patters easier when site traffic justifies their considerable expense.

Resources

Design and Navigation Aids

WebMonkey

http://www.hotwired.com/webmonkey/
Chockablock with reviews, news, an HTML 101 course, a searchable index of HTML techniques, and so on. A great resource for designers.

Builder.Com

http://www.builder.com

Part of the CNET family of sites, this is another serious Web publishing venture with a large staff churning out high-quality resources for designers, more than can be summarized here. A definite bookmark site for Web hackers.

Developer.Com

http://www.developer.com/

Another quality resource for site developers, with code samples, news, discussion boards, and so on.

High Five

http://www.highfive.com

Software and site reviews, plus interviews and profiles with top designers. The site's slick design showcases sponsor Vignette, maker of a dynamic site-hosting software system.

JavaScript.Com

http://www.javascripts.com/

A vast source of JavaScript tools and techniques, it's approaching one million registered users for its high-quality free resources.

WebCoder

http://www.webcoder.com/

Also specializing in JavaScript and Dynamic HTML issues. Includes a wonderful "scriptorium" archive of sample scripts in JavaScript and D-HTML.

Yahoo! on Design Guides

http://www.yahoo.com/Computers_and_Internet/Internet/World_Wide_Web/Page_Design_and_Layout/

An index of various other design guides and related resources.

4

Domain Brand

I f the three most important rules of retail are location, location, loca
tion, the online equivalent is domain, domain, domain, said Bob Hey
man, senior VP of audience development at USWeb. "Yet many sites
that should know better ignore this fundamental principle of getting the
site right."

A site's *domain* is a cross between a name and an address. It serves as
both an identifiable brand name and a pointer to the site's location. It's
the *uniform resource locator*, better known as the *URL*.

Technically, domain names are nothing more than mnemonic aids for the
IP (Internet protocol) numbers assigned to every host computer on the
Web. IP numbers come in four sets of digits divided by periods, such as
205.134.233.1. Because such number strings aren't particularly memorable to most humans, the architects of the Internet created a system of
domain name servers (DNS) that cross-reference the IP numbers with
alphanumeric domain names.

Routinely, companies fail to recognize important nuances when choosing
their domain names. Many companies that have been slow to get online
find that their trademarks are already claimed by shrewd Web startups,
traditional competitors, or others. Indeed, disputes over domains have
spawned a spate of legal actions and a new specialty among cyber-hip
intellectual property lawyers.

Other companies choose long, clunky domains that invite users to make mistakes when typing in the URLs, or cryptic abbreviations that surfers are unlikely to remember. One of the most common oversights of all is a site's settling on one domain name and then neglecting possible variations of the name that surfers are liable to try by mistake.

Figure 4.1

Amazon.com, where brand and domain are synonymous, is one of the best branded domains on the Web.

Get the Domain Right

"The domain is integral to a site's identity. To get the site right, you have to get the domain right," said USWeb's Mr. Heyman. "It is likely to be the first impression made on a netizen even before the homepage loads. Companies have to invest the same intensity of branding power in their domain names as in their corporate trademark. A weak domain name communicates to savvy surfers that a company isn't really hip to online culture."

For some companies, the corporate name and the domain are identical, like **Amazon.com**. The "dot-com" suffix, referred to as a *top-level domain (TLD)* (along with **.net**, **.org**, **.edu**, and other TLDs), immediately tells the consumer that it refers to a Web site, just as "Inc." or "Corp." convey an official corporate entity. When you say "Nike-dot-com," everybody knows that you're talking about the sports giant's Web site and not a new model of shoe or anything else. Like Nike's shoes, however, its site is a Nike product, recognizable by its unique brand. **Geocities.com/members/~hotsauce1/home.htm**, on the other hand, is not a brand.

Make It Catchy

The single most important point to remember when choosing a domain name is to keep it short and sweet. It should be easy to type and, above all, easy to remember. Think of a 1-800 number. If it's a good one, like 1-800 FLOWERS, a customer need hear it only once to remember it.

A good URL should be memorable enough that someone driving in her car could catch a glimpse of it advertised on the side of a bus and not think twice about remembering it. Moreover, it should be clear when spoken, so a commuter could hear it announced on drive-time radio and could type it into her browser when she got to work without writing it down. This means avoiding homonyms, such as **writestuff.com** for a literary services company, or cute spellings like **nitestories.com** or **litefoods.com**, which beg confusion for those who have only heard the domain name spoken.

For established companies, the domain should ideally be a short logical extension of the corporate name: **sun.com** for Sun Microsystems or **adage.com** for Advertising Age magazine. Companies attempting to secure their Internet domains for the first time today may find that the most obvious versions of their corporate names are already taken.

Figure 4.2

What other domain would you expect for Burger King? No search engine needed.

"For new companies, it is critical they consider what Web domain names are available before settling on a corporate name," Mr. Heyman advises.

Consider the company Autonomy, which develops personalization software for Web sites. According to Autonomy's president, Mike Lynch, **autonomy.com** was already taken by a guy who uses the domain as a personal vanity site and stubbornly won't sell it. So Autonomy has to use **agentware.com,** referring to Agentware, its main product. The confusion is a marketing headache, to say the least, for a Web-specialized company.

Figure 4.3

The InterNIC
WhoIs, where
one plays the
Domain Name
Game.

Picking Unique Domain Names

If the domain name you're seeking has already been taken, there are a few handy options available to you besides legal wrangling (for more discussion on disputes, see the "Domain Disputes" section later in this chapter).

One route is to alter the company name in some way, such as a contraction of two words. For example, Network Solutions, Inc. (a company that plays large in the Domain Name Game, as we'll see later in the chapter) uses the domain **netsol.com**. Public relations companies almost all tack -**pr** at the end of their names to get a unique domain, although many forget to register the hyphen, too. So **somethingpr.com** and **something-pr.com** are likely to turn up two different PR companies.

> ## TIP: USING INTERNIC WHOIS TO RESEARCH DOMAIN NAMES
>
> To search the main registrar of **.com**, **.net**, **.edu** and **.org** domain names and see what's available or who is leasing registered domains, navigate to the InterNIC WhoIs search page at **http://rs.internic.net/cgi-bin/ whois**. Find out more about the InterNIC and the WhoIs lookup service in "The InterNIC, Network Solutions, and Friends" section later in this chapter, as well as in the "Resources" section at the end of the chapter.

Another popular method along similar lines is to add a cyber-oriented prefix or suffix to a name, such as **netorange.com**, **orangeweb.com**, or **orangeonline.com**. Note that the popular suffix **net**, as in **orangenet.com**, may lead to some confusion because **.net** is a top-level alternative to **.com**. Some surfers might look for **orange.net** by mistake. The solution to that, of course, is to register both **orangenet.com** and **orange.net**.

Carl Oppedahl, a leading expert on Web law and a partner in the law firm Oppedahl & Larson, says that sites can best protect against domain disputes if they invent a "coined, unique name," like Xerox, and trademark it.

Another strategy is to pick a word or phrase different from but related to the company name. The Oppedahl & Larson law firm, for example, uses the domain **patents.com**. A company may pursue this strategy for one of several reasons. It may find that all basic forms of its name have already been claimed by others and have no choice but to look for alternatives. Or it may happen upon a word or phrase available as a domain that is more strategic than its own corporate name. Or it may opt to create a new online brand entirely.

Best Diamond Value, an online wholesaler of precious stones, secured as its domain the enviable **jeweler.com**. Its homepage prominently proclaims the service's name as Best Diamond Value, but the short, evocative domain name serves as a valuable mnemonic locator for the site.

Lipton's Ragu brand of Italian food products has claimed both **ragu.com** and **eat.com**. Its strategy is presumably to pick up traffic among any surfers who try **eat.com** out of blind curiosity.

An example of companies creating a new online brand is **sfgate.com**, the domain where *The San Francisco Chronicle* and *Examiner* newspapers and the local NBC affiliate television station, KRON, have joined forces to form "The Gate."

Figure 4.5

When you're
looking for the
best value on a
diamond online,
you need only
remember
jeweler.com.

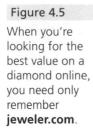

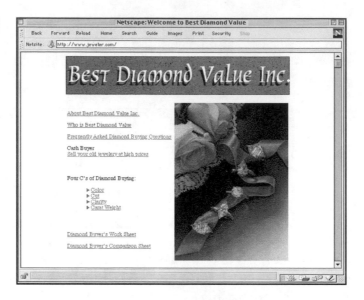

Figure 4.5

When you're looking for the best value on a diamond online, you need only remember **jeweler.com**.

Mecklermedia, a computer industry publisher and conference organizer, invested heavily in a new domain brand in the summer of 1997. The publisher, whose properties include a conference and magazine both called *Internet World*, ditched its established site brand of **iworld.com** in favor of **internet.com**, which it bought for upward of $100,000 from a failed ISP.

eschewobfuscation.com

The simple advice to make a domain memorable may seem obvious, but countless sites don't follow it. One popular way to screw up a Web brand is with an "alphabet soup" domain.

MetroMail, one of the world's largest catalogue merchants and direct mailers with more than 50 years of experience in consumer marketing, launched a Web site that offers discounts on a range of products through online promotions. Shortly before the site launch, the company changed the Web brand from CoolOffers (**cooloffers.com**) to Direct Value To You. The new URL is **www.dv2u.com**. Get it? Sure, but only after thinking about if for moment.

Put it to the drive-time radio test. Imagine the company president of MetroMail being interviewed on a talk show, promoting the site. What percentage of drivers are going to remember that cutesy domain when they arrive at the office 45 minutes later? "Was it **www.d2u.com?** **www.d2kv.com?** Something like that…" A certain percentage are going to make two failed attempts and then quit trying.

A tour of so-called Internet marketing consultants in Yahoo!'s directory is worth a laugh just to see what terrible domains some come up with for their own sites. GFJ Business Services claims to specialize in "Web site development, Internet advertising, and Internet consulting." It demonstrates its branding know-how with its catchy domain, **www.gfjbussvs.com**.

www.slash-tilde.com/~goblDgook/index.htm

The absolute worst kind of URL for a company's homepage is the extension of someone else's domain—the deadly "slash-tilde" approach. This may be fine for a teenager's personal homepage, but you won't be taken seriously as a business with a domain beginning **aol.com/~**, **geocities.com/~**, or **tripod.com/~**.

Consider D&T WWW Publishing and Network Solutions, also listed in Yahoo! as Internet marketing experts. Their homepage is at **www.bcpl.lib.md.us/~dflax/**. The site is hosted presumably for free by the Baltimore County Public Library (**bcpl.lib.md**). Imagine their radio ad: "We at D&T are Baltimore's premier Internet experts. Come see what we can do for your business online at aitch-tee-tee-pee, colon slash-slash, double-u double-u double-u, dot, bee-cee-pee-el, dot, el-aye-bee, dot, em-dee, dot, yew-ess, slash, tilde-dee-eff-el-ay-ex, slash."

Hmmmm. The phrase "Yeah, right!" comes to mind.

Using a slash-tilde extension of someone else's domain, besides making for an impossible-to-remember URL, says to your customers that you don't have enough faith in your business to invest the $100 it costs to register your own domain.

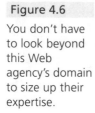

Figure 4.6

You don't have to look beyond this Web agency's domain to size up their expertise.

dontonly.net

Another inadvisable route some businesses choose when the **.com** domain they want has already been taken is to register the same name as a **.net** domain. "Dot-net" domains are supposedly reserved for companies that play some networking role in the Internet infrastructure, such as Internet service providers. But the InterNIC domain registrar service doesn't check too thoroughly, and it will normally provide a **.net** domain to anyone who gives some technical mumbo-jumbo explanation of how they intend to use the domain.

The problem with using a **.net** domain when the **.com** version is already taken is that surfers are likely to search for your homepage under the **.com** name and get someone else's site instead. Because **.com** is by far the dominant suffix for commercial sites, the confusion is inevitable. The wise marketer will register *both* extensions to avoid any confusion and prevent another service from accidentally or intentionally skimming off traffic intended for her site.

(At this point you may be saying, "A-ha!", noting that yours truly, Rick Bruner, has registered his Bruner Communications domain only as **bruner.net**. Yes, well, the short response is: Do as I say, not as I do. The situation is less than ideal and "under strategic review.")

www.avoid.com/CGI/ hiccup?boink*12345&aaahhh!!!!%etc.etc.html

Another pitfall to avoid is a long, unwieldy URL generated by CGI scripts and other dynamic page systems. Many dynamic page systems create such URLs, but you should at least try to have a normal-looking

URL for the homepage. Some sophisticated systems, such as Documentum's RightSite, can generate pages dynamically (such as the results of database searches or personalized pages for individual visitors) with normal-looking URLs, so it's a standard that sites should push software developers to uphold.

Take the example of the Minolta Printers site, which is based on software from Smart Technologies. Frankly, it could be smarter. Although a user can reach the site by typing **www.minoltaprinters.com**, when the homepage loads, the browser's URL field displays **http:// www.minoltaprinters.com/dna4/smartbroker.dll?sid=0&tp =pub_root_index.htm&np=pub_root_index.htm**.

There are a few problems with this. First, this URL is not exactly aesthetically pleasing as a component of the page design. Second, many surfers use the browser's URL field as a navigation aid, tracking what section of the site they are in through the traditional hierarchy of site sub-sections divided by levels of / marks.

Third, as noted, the homepage URL is a key component of the site's brand, and **http://www.minoltaprinters.com/dna4/smartbroker. dll?sid=0&tp=pub_root_index.htm&np=pub_root_index.htm** isn't a very strong brand.

Finally, imagine an unsophisticated newbie surfing to this homepage through a link from another page. He's impressed with the site and calls up a friend to share it with her.

She says, "It sounds like a cool site. I'd like to check it out. What's the URL?"

"What do you mean by URL?", he replies.

"The thing at the top of your browser that begins **http://www**…. Just read it to me," she says.

"Okay, it's… Sheesh, it's really long. Maybe I should just email it to you."

If he can figure out how to cut-and-paste it into an email, that is …

Figure 4.7

What's that URL again?

Cover Your Assets

Having settled on a strategic domain name that is available at the Inter-NIC, many companies register the domain and leave it at that. Another potentially big mistake.

Consider the browser's URL field (labeled "location" by Netscape and "address" by Microsoft) to be the ultimate Web search engine. If you were looking for the McDonald's homepage, would you go to AltaVista and search for "mcdonalds," or would you simply type **www.mcdonalds.com** into your browser? Probably the latter, right?

Way back in 1994, when not a lot of people had heard of the Internet yet, a journalist for *New York Newsday* and *Wired* magazine named Joshua Quittner typed **www.mcdonalds.com** into his browser. It came up blank. With a search of the InterNIC, he realized that McDonald's wasn't yet hip to the Web. So after a few weeks of vainly hounding Mickey D's PR department for comment on the matter, he registered the domain himself as a joke. He wrote some hilarious articles based on the stunt, and a few other publications picked up the story too. Finally, after convincing McDonald's to pay a paltry sum to buy Internet equipment for a grade school, Quittner gave the domain back to the fast-food giant.

McDonald's learned that lesson, but they still don't fully get it. What if you're a bad speller, and you type **www.macdonalds.com** into your browser? As of this writing, you get a page hosted by a *domain broker*, one of the crafty devils who register and hoard promising domain names, selling them to the highest bidder. Same thing happens if you type **www.mcdonalds.net**.

Figure 4.8

The hamburger giant might want to buy **macdonalds. com** from the broker Quick Domains to accommodate bad spellers who look for its site.

The Domain Name Game

If you want to have some fun, play the Domain Name Game. It's easy. Just punch random phrases and well-known brand names into the URL field of your browser (or, for advanced play, the WhoIs directory of the InterNIC). The object of the game is to see who's asleep at which marketing departments.

Virtual Vineyards is an amusing start. A darling of the press, this site is a great example of a successful online retailer, doing millions of dollars in revenue annually in wine sales. According to WhoIs, the site registered the **virtualvin.com** domain in 1994, abbreviating its name to save surfers the trouble of typing a few extra letters.

However, a surfer who assumes that the domain is **virtualvineyards.com** gets no page at all. That's because in 1996 another company registered it. This domain is presently in dispute, so the InterNIC has put it on "hold" status pending a settlement between the registrants. The subtle alternative domains **virtual-vineyards.com**, **virtualvineyards.net**, and **virtualvinyards.com** (an obvious misspelling, with no "e") are likewise registered to companies other than the wine reseller.

Microsoft, the company everyone loves to hate, gets an especially low score in the Domain Name Game. **Microsof.com**, **micrsoft.com**, **microsft.com**, **microsot.com**, **micros0ft.com** (with a zero instead of the second "o"), **microsuft.com**, **microsoft.net**, **microsuck.com**, and almost every other variation of the name we could think of are registered variously to domain brokers, competitors, anti-Microsoft sites, porno sites, and other businesses besides the warm, fuzzy software giant itself. **Macrohard.com** is registered to a gun-fanatic site that proudly proclaims it was designed on a Macintosh. **Micro-soft.com** was unregistered as of this writing.

Several clever companies prey on careless typists by registering domains with the names of popular Web sites, but without the period between the **www** and the rest of the URL. In the case of **wwwmicrosoft.com**, for example, the resulting page politely informs viewers they've made a typo and serves up an ad banner.

Figure 4.9

Making money off careless typists trying to find Microsoft's site.

No Dessert Till You've Registered Your Variables

The list goes on and on. **Amazon.com** took the trouble to register some 35 domains, including many variants of its name. But **amazon.net** is registered to another company that links to—surprise, surprise—a book site. The Good Guys electronics store registered **thegoodguys.com**, but competitor CompuWorld registered **goodguys.com**. General Motors uses the domain **gm.com**. Some guy in Georgia, however, registered **generalmotors.com** in June of 1997 for his personal homepage, which he uses to rail against greenhouse emissions, among other things.

Figure 4.10

GeneralMotors. com, doing wonders for GM's image.

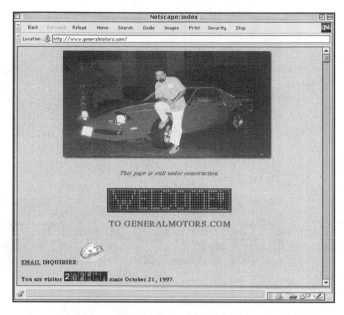

Pepsi Cola has **pepsi.com**, but not **pepsi-cola.com** (which, when typed in a browser, comes up blank) or **pepsicola.com** (which rolls over to Yahoo!). **Budwieser.com** and **budwiser.com** aren't registered to Anheuser-Busch (which spells it "Budweiser"). CNET, which has aggressively accumulated some of the choicest domain names imaginable, including **tv.com, news.com**, and **computers.com**, secured **java.com** about a year after Sun Microsystems introduced the sensational Java technology to the world. Yet CNET neglected to register **cnet.net** before someone in Canada did in October 1997. It was also beaten to **c.net** in 1993 by some academic researchers.

Sony decided that a good way to show off a variety of its properties was to launch an entertainment site called "The Station." **Thestation.com** is the domain of a Babylon 5 fan site, however. Although many people refer to Sony's site as "Sony Station," **sonystation.com** is unregistered. The actual domain is **station.sony.com**, but you have to resort to using a search engine to figure that out.

Figure 4.11

Sony's site, called "The Station," found at **station.sony. com**...

Figure 4.12

...and a Babylon 5 fan site called **thestation.com**. Who's got the better domain?

The lesson here is obvious. Register every variation of your domain you can think of. Register likely typos. Register plurals and singulars. Register both **.com** and **.net** domains. If you anticipate doing significant international business, register with specific country domains such as **.jp** (Japan), **.uk**, **.ca** (Canada), and so on. If your name could conceivably be hyphenated, register that as well. For a registration fee of $50 per year per domain, registering anything short of every variation you can possibly think of is careless.

Every company online should occasionally play the Domain Name Game as a matter of marketing strategy. Allocate a budget for leasing domains, a few thousand dollars a year if possible, to give marketers the liberty to secure all relevant variables of the company's name—a Web-marketing must—as well as to lay away promising available domains for possible future project development or resale.

Register Product Names

And don't stop there. It's amazing how many companies neglect to register their product names. Anheuser-Busch missed **bud.com**, for example, which presently is home to a cryptic page that jokes about smoking a "bud" instead of drinking it and links to a chat site. Anheuser-Busch got **budice.com** and **budlight.com** but not **buddry.com** or **budlite.com**.

The following domains are unclaimed as of this writing, despite being familiar trademarks of various companies: **hungryman.com**, **a1sauce.com** (although Heinz does have **57.com**), **wheatthins.com**, **honey-maid.com**, **liquidplumber.com**, **listerine.com**, **jiffypop.com**, and **coffeemate.com**.

Why is this so important? Is the Web really such an effective place to promote popcorn, drain cleaner, and mouthwash? Well, that depends on the creativity of a company's marketers, of course. The real point is that if those companies stopped and thought about it, they'd probably rather control their trademarked brands in cyberspace themselves than leave the names open for someone else to claim. Take a cue from the biggest conglomerate in the world, Proctor & Gamble. It controls the domain for virtually every one of its brands we could think of (**crest.com** being one exception).

On the flip side, all of the following domains are registered to "domain squatters," companies who are presumably holding the domains with the names of these familiar consumer brands for ransom: **motrin.com**, **nyquil.com**, **aspirin.com**, **501.com** and **501s.com**, **ricekrispies.com**, **frostedflakes.com**, **fruitloops.com**, **frappuccino.com**, **v8.com**, **windex.com**, **camry.com**, and **transam.com**. After much haranguing and possible litigation, the company with the most money could likely win back these domains. But negligent online marketing should not have allowed such disputes in the first place.

Figure 4.13

Looking for a Camry? If you type in **www.camry.com,** don't expect Toyota's site. You'll end up at Joseph Toyota in Cincinnati.

Same story for company slogans. Although Nike has **justdoit.com**, Pepsi-Cola has **generationnext.com**, and Burger King has **haveityourway. com**, McDonald's doesn't have **youdeserveabreaktoday.com** or **mymcdonalds.com**, Volkswagon doesn't have **driverswanted.com**, and Anheuser-Busch doesn't have **thisbudsforyou.com**.

The National Aeronautics and Space Administration now understands why defending your brand online is so important. During the spectacular Mars probe expedition in the summer of 1997, millions of visitors logged onto **www.nasa.gov** to see up-to-the-minute pictures of the surface of the Red Planet. Unfortunately, a large number, maybe even millions, logged onto **www.nasa.com** where they found pictures of the surfaces of naked bodies engaged in hardcore sex acts.

NASA succeeded in raising enough hell to have the porno site shut down. But the White House hasn't been so successful. The last time we checked, **www.whitehouse.com** still featured pictures of President Bill Clinton and First Lady Hillary Clinton superimposed on the bodies of porn models.

The Politics of Domains

As you've seen, the issue of domain names is not without controversy. In fact, it's increasingly one of the hottest topics of Internet disputes, along with privacy, security, child protection, and copyright.

The InterNIC, Network Solutions, and Friends

There are more than 100 top-level domains, although most of them designate countries, such as **.hu** (Hungary), **.de** (Germany), and **.nl** (The Netherlands). In most cases, country domains are registered with and administered by local authorities. Some countries, such as Tonga (**.to**), are eagerly selling their national TLDs to commercial entities, although the value of such a domain is questionable (when's the last time you visited a **.to** site?)

The most popular Internet TLDs—**.com**, **.net**, **.org**, and **.edu**—are registered with the InterNIC, a branch of the U.S. National Science Foundation. In 1993, the InterNIC subcontracted the behind-the-scenes administration of its huge TLD database, well more than a million **.com** domains alone, to a private company called Network Solutions, Inc. (NSI). In recent years, NSI has become a lightning rod for criticism from many quarters.

In 1995, NSI began charging fees for domain name registration: $100 up front for the first two years per domain, and $50 a year after that. Although $50 a year, roughly equivalent to a business lunch, may not seem like a lot of money to many companies, some registrants resent the fees or find them exorbitant. The fees do add up when a company covers its bases with multiple registrations, as recommended.

Moreover, NSI's would-be competitors are outraged that the government has given one company an effective monopoly over the potentially profitable business of domain management. With more than a million **.com** domains alone paying annual fees of $50, it's easy to see their point.

Figure 4.14

NSI's critics complain that, among other things, its Web site treats the **.com** domain and other TLDs like they were its private corporate assets.

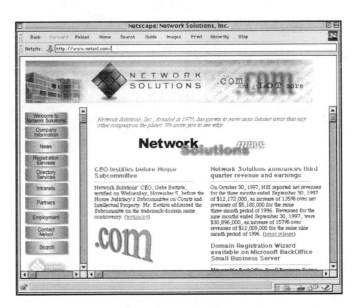

In addition, many parties are unhappy with NSI's policies regarding domain name disputes. Its original policy was to allot domains purely on a "first come, first served" basis and leave companies to settle disagreements about rightful claims to domain names among themselves or in the courts. More recently, however, NSI has caved into pressure from powerful corporate interests and has taken to freezing disputed domains, especially when the challenger has a trademark on the name.

Critics say that NSI has no legal authority to take such actions, when suspending a site's name could put a well-branded Web-only company out of business. Courts have already ruled that simply owning a trademark in a particular country or business category doesn't automatically entitle the trademark owner to a global domain name. After becoming embroiled as a defendant in several lawsuits of its own, as of this writing NSI is waffling again on its policy. (See more discussion on these issues in the "Domain Disputes" section later in this chapter.)

Pending Rush for New TLDs

NSI's critics, among both rival domain registrars and companies seeking to lease domains, would also like to see several new TLDs introduced, particularly to widen the choices for commercial Web sites beyond the predominant **.com** option.

NSI's contract with the InterNIC was originally for five years, which means it expires in March 1998. As of this writing, the future of the administration of TLDs is unclear. It does appear likely that several other firms will join, if not supplant, the NSI in the administration of domains.

Meanwhile NSI, preparing for the onslaught of competition, recently announced a new service called WorldNIC to facilitate the registration of domains more easily, particularly for smaller companies.

A group of engineers from around the world has formed the Policy Oversight Committee (originally known as the International Ad Hoc Committee) to propose new policies for the administration of TLDs. One plan of theirs, which despite its controversy seems likely to be adopted in some form, calls for the creation of seven new Internet-wide TLDs: **.web**, **.firm**, **.store**, **.arts**, **.rec**, **.info**, and **.nom**.

Although controversy over domain registration will inevitably continue and the new TLDs will likely confuse many Internet users for a while, it appears highly likely that these seven TLDs will become reality, probably by this book's publication. Other parties are pushing for even more TLDs, including **.xxx** and **.tm.int** (designating an international trademark), but the support for these is less widespread.

This means that every organization with a presence online should prepare for another land rush for domains with the new top-level extensions. Although it may not be immediately clear what **coca-cola.web** or **coca-cola.nom** or even **coca-cola.xxx** would signify as opposed to **coca-cola.com**, suffice it to say that Coca-Cola would probably like to control those domains itself rather than Pepsi-Cola or some other third party.

We all saw what happened with domain registration the first time around. Organizations that didn't register their **.com** domains before other parties did so included McDonald's, *The New York Times*, MTV, Coca-Cola, ABC TV, Dianetics, Fry's Electronics, The Gap, the Better Business Bureau, and many others. With this much advance notice in the mainstream and Internet-industry press the second time around, companies would be foolish to make the same mistake twice.

Domain Brokers

It's a popular misconception that all the good domains are gone. With a bit of perseverance and creativity, you can find plenty of unique names, combinations of words, and even some three-letter domains still unregistered at the InterNIC. And if the name you *really* have your heart set on is already taken, it may well be for sale.

So-called *domain brokers* are businesses and individuals that have amassed attractive domain names for heavily marked-up resale, like some kind of Third Wave intellectual-property commodity brokers. For an up-front $100 per name, it can be a lucrative investment for properties that may easily sell for $5,000 and up.

The Domain Name Game quickly reveals the abundance of domain brokers out there. **Donut.com**, **go.com**, **rockandroll.com**, **television.com**,

hamburgers.com, **michealjackson.com**, **audio.com**, **abc.net**, **gamer.com**, **babywear.com**, and thousands of other excellent domain names are available for sale this way.

Figure 4.15

Maybe Rupert Murdoch can afford to buy it.

Several kinds of players in the Domain Name Game collect good names for resale. There are the specialized kings of the industry, who've invested thousands of dollars in names and whose own sites are located at domains like **domains.com** or **domainnames.com**. Then there are the small-time hobbyists with credit cards. Then there are all the other Web site owners who, for a variety of reasons, have invested in surplus domains.

If there is a domain name you really want and someone else has it who isn't actively using it, you can safely assume the registrant will entertain an offer. Most starting prices, needless to say, are negotiable.

Domain Disputes

A careful domain strategy underpins the successful Web branding of many leading Web ventures. Occasionally, however, serious disputes over rightful claim to domains are bound to arise, which can pose a tremendous threat to a site's viability.

A DISPUTE RESOLVED WITHOUT RANCOR

Back when USWeb Marin was known as Cybernautics, one of our early clients was RockNet, the first online purveyor of music news and chat on CompuServe and America Online (where it was known as Rock-Line). They consulted with us regarding bringing their content to the Web.

They were interested in using their CompuServe name, RockNet, on the Web, but we discovered that a Phoenix-based car stereo company had already registered the domain **rocknet.com**. RockNet was un-daunted because they had a trademark on the name. They had launched on CompuServe in 1986, making them a true pioneer in cyberspace. With the trademark in hand, we contacted the stereo company on our client's behalf.

"At first the only person we could reach was the company Webmaster, who seemed oblivious to the issue," said Bob Heyman, USWeb senior VP of audience development. "He said, in effect, 'You don't get it, man. The law doesn't apply to the Internet.' Eventually, we reached the corporate counsel and informed her that a cease-and-desist order claiming trademark infringement was forthcoming. That got the company's attention."

Rather than leaving the dispute in acrimony, however, we were able to negotiate a settlement that made both parties happy. The stereo company agreed to give up the name, but in exchange we gave them free advertising banners on RockNet to compensate for the expenses they incurred in changing the name, such as printing new corporate stationery.

If the horse isn't already out, shut the barn doors now by researching the trademark status of your domains. If they're not trademarked yet, try to trademark them. If they're already trademarked to someone else, think twice about using them for your Web brands, especially if you're up against a larger company that could afford to bleed you dry with legal expenses.

Although trademarks, from the U.S. or other countries, may not be the final word on domain disputes in court, companies can use proof of trademark to harass domain owners, even if the two companies are in significantly different business categories. This is thanks to NSI's controversial policy of freezing domains when one party holds a trademark to another's domain name.

"The legal theories that you would use to try to get a domain name are not identical to the legal standards for getting a trademark registration out of the U.S. Trademark Office," said Carl Oppedahl, of Oppedahl & Larson, a vocal critic of NSI.

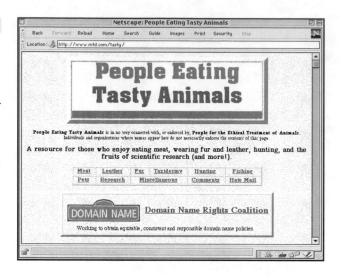

Figure 4.16

This site registered the domain **peta.org** before the well-known organization People for the Ethical Treatment of Animals thought to do so. The **peta.org** domain is suspended in dispute.

Oppedahl & Larson's Web site, an excellent Web law resource, details several case studies of domain disputes. According to those accounts, some companies with trademarks for products arriving late to the Web are clearly exploiting NSI's dispute policy to try to wrest domains away from established online brands. Several "netrepreneurs" have fought back, seeking redress in the courts to reverse NSI domain freezes, and about a dozen firms have sued NSI itself over its policy.

"The way in which the courts have been ruling on domain disputes depends on a range of factors," Mr. Oppedahl said.

"There are two extremes, depending on what type of names companies have chosen for their domains," he said. "One is the coined, unique name of some existing company, like Panovision or Intermatic. Anybody other than the Panovision or Intermatic company are going to get in big trouble if they try to register a domain name containing such a coined, unique name.

"The other extreme is words out of the dictionary that are used by dozens or hundreds of companies. That's a different legal situation. For your readers, the main point is if they're going to get a domain name, they'd better not pick a coined, unique name of some other company. And regardless of what domain name they might pick, they need to pay attention to trademarks."

Oppedahl & Larson's site describes a recent domain battle where Juno Electric, a light fixture manufacturer, invoked its trademark to pressure the NSI to suspend the domain of Juno Online, a free email service with several million subscribers. The suspension in service would have been a disaster for Juno Online, whose domain brand—found in the email addresses of millions of people—is inseparable from the company's business model.

At the last minute, NSI relented and agreed to keep Juno Online's domain running amidst court hearings. Juno Online subsequently sued Juno Electric for financial damages as a result of the threat of domain suspension, which the court rejected in favor of Juno Electric.

Figure 4.17

Juno Electric almost turned out the lights at two-year-old Juno Online by flashing its trademark to the NSI.

Oppedahl & Larson's online analysis suggests that the Juno case could give trademark holders the green light to use NSI's trademark-freeze policy to harass domain owners. The court's precedent indicates that trademark holders won't risk paying financial damages to domain owners for frivolous attacks.

But if trademark holders were to take their disputes to the courts instead of NSI, many would lose if the domain owner was in a significantly different business, according to Mr. Oppedahl.

"NSI makes no inquiry into whether the challenger actually has a bona fide legal claim, but simply cuts off the domain name if the paper formalities have been complied with," Mr. Oppedahl wrote.

In another dispute, the US Prince sports outfitter challenged the domain **prince.com**, held for several years by a British computer consultant firm. An English court found in the consultant's favor and compelled the sporting goods company to pay damages.

Stay Tuned…

Meanwhile, all speculation about NSI policy is sure to get more complicated after March 1998, when NSI's exclusive contract with the InterNIC expires. The Policy Oversight Committee's final plan is likely to effect significant changes. Their document is poetically titled the Generic Top Level Domain Memorandum of Understanding, winning the Internet's worst abbreviation contest with gTLD-MoU.

Figure 4.18

The future of Internet domain policies may be spelled out at this catchy domain.

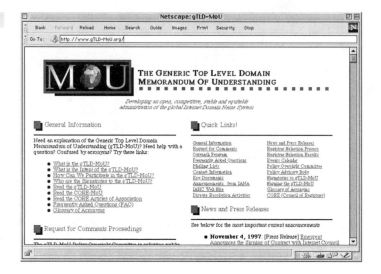

The gTLD-MoU (perhaps pronounced "Get led: moo"?) recommends the creation of a tribunal for domain name challenges where both parties can tell their stories, unlike NSI's current one-sided approach.

Given the potentially profound impact of the many looming changes to domain administration, marketers are advised to stay abreast of news on the emergence of new TLDs, changing policies for settling disputes, and other domain issues. In addition to the leading Internet industry news outlets, consult the following resources for more sites that cover these issues in depth.

Resources

InterNIC WhoIs

http://rs.internic.net/cgi-bin/whois

This is where you play the Domain Name Game. Simply type in any word or phase, followed by **.com**, **.net**, .edu, or **.org**, and see if it's registered. If it's not and you want it, it's yours for $100.

Oppedahl & Larson

http://www.patents.com

The Oppedahl & Larson law firm's Web site offers a wealth of original resources and links to further discussions of copyright, patents, trademarks, Web law, and other intellectual property issues. The extensive site contains, among other things, blistering criticism of NSI's domain name policies, domain dispute case histories, and links to other valuable resources.

John Marshall Law School Index of Cyber Legal Issues

http://www.jmls.edu/cyber/index/

Researchers at this law school have put together an excellent free resource with case studies and links to vast amounts of material on Web and intellectual property law, including trademarks and domain disputes.

Georgetown Law Center's What's in A Name?

http://www.law.georgetown.edu/lc/internic/domain1.html

This site is similar to the John Marshall site, and also an excellent resource.

Thomson & Thomson

http://www.thomson-thomson.com/

A leading trademark search service. The searches cost a fee. For other trademark search services, refer to links at the preceding sites of John Marshall, Georgetown, and Oppedahl & Larson.

The Generic Top-Level Domain Memorandum of Understanding

http://www.gtld-mou.org/

Another catchy domain, this plan by the Policy Oversight Committee, known by the hideous abbreviation gTLD-MoU, distills the contributions of hundreds of interested parties. Among its recommendations are the introduction of the seven new TLD extensions, discussed previously. Although it still has its critics, gTLD-MoU has achieved the broadest support of any domain registry proposal to date. Some or most of its recommendations seem likely to be adopted, changing the whole way the Domain Name Game is played.

http://www.iahc.org/

Internet International Ad Hoc Committee evolved into the Policy Oversight Committee, author of the gTLD-MoU proposal. The IAHC has since dissolved, but the site is full of background for the extremely curious on this issue.

Electronic Frontier Foundation on Domain Disputes

http://www.eff.org/pub/Intellectual_property/ Internet_address_disputes/

The influential EFF lobby group keeps an extensive and up-to-date list of case studies and related news.

http://www.eff.org/pub/GII_NII/DNS_control/ eff_dns_19970428.statement

Also recommended reading is the EFF Position Statement on Internet Domain Name System Policy and Evolution.

ZDNet's NetPolitics

http://www.zdnet.com/products/netpolitics.html

A Ziff-Davis site that regularly follows a number of Internet controversies, including regular looks at domain issues.

Yahoo! on Domain Controversies

http://www.yahoo.com/Computers_and_Internet/Internet/Domain_Registration/Domain_Name_Controversies/

This site has links to various accounts of domain disputes.

The American Association of Domain Names

http://www.domains.org/

This site contains links and other resources.

The Domain Name Right's Coalition

http://www.domain-name.org/

This site contains links and other resources.

Yahoo! on domain brokers

http://www.yahoo.com/Business_and_Economy/Companies/Internet_Services/Domain_Registration/Brokerages/

If you just can't find the name you're looking for, try these guys. There are lots more of these out there than listed here.

You can also figure out how to contact the owners of domains with the WhoIs database, which lists registrants' phone numbers and email addresses.

Netiva: Avoiding Information Overload

A Web site is the most important public facade many companies have. Unlike fleeting ad campaigns and remote head offices, a URL is a constant corporate representation that's instantly accessible to millions. It embodies for consumers a vision of the company, and it should reflect the same standard of quality the company associates with its products.

Netiva understood this when it came to USWeb. The company makes a Java-based system for building "intranet" applications for corporations. Its executives knew from the beginning that the site should have the same flexible, easy-to-use feel as Netiva's own software. And because the company is in the Web technology business, its site has to reflect a high standard of Web savvy.

Much more than just communicating a mood, however, the site is at the heart of Netiva's business strategy. It's where the company aims to establish its brand, attract sales leads, and let prospects demo the product for themselves.

Netiva's site is the linchpin of its corporate plan.

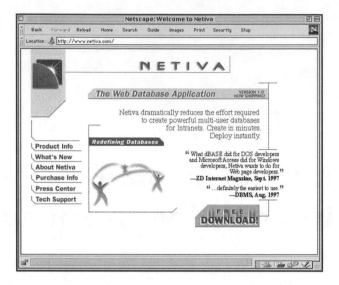

In addition to the usual features of a corporate site—executive biographies, press releases, employment opportunities, FAQs—Netiva's site is equipped for software downloads, complete product documentation, extensive customer support, discussion threads, and more.

Clear Objective, Clean Design

Netiva's executives had already planned much of their site's architecture and decided on a clean design style before visiting USWeb. They needed our help in presenting the mass of content as clearly as possible.

"The information design was the most important part of the project," said Rebecca Gilson, the USWeb producer in charge of the Netiva account. "There was so much information and functionality they wanted to put across, the biggest challenge was how to parse it out in the most efficient way for the user."

Steve Pollock, VP of marketing and Netiva cofounder, explains how he and fellow company executives approached the homepage's design. "We specced out what we were looking for. We wanted it to be graphically clean and easy to navigate. We didn't want too many choices to overwhelm the visitors," he said.

"You have to ask how important is a splash screen for the site, or should you immediately launch into in-depth information, or should the homepage be something clean. It depends on what kind of message you want to communicate," he said.

"If you go to Microsoft's site, it launches deep into information right at the homepage. It's the same with Netscape's site, where users are immediately greeted with 20-plus headlines. We wanted a simpler first impression," Mr. Pollock said.

Figure X1.2

A late 1997 incarnation of Netscape's homepage, showcasing features of Communicator 4.0, was absurdly complicated, with links everywhere. After criticism from users, the browser giant later simplified with another design.

Making Every Pixel Count

What USWeb and Netiva came up with is a quick-loading page, compact enough to fit comfortably on a 14" monitor. The page contains just a few words and a handful of simple icons and images.

At the center of the page is a series of images shown in succession, each icon corresponding to one of the main subsections of the site. Listed at the left margin of the page, the subsections are Product Info, What's New, About Netiva, Purchasing Info, Press Center, and Tech Support.

Figure X1.3

Microsoft's homepage takes nearly two minutes to load on a 28.8Kbps modem and requires a user of a 17" monitor to scroll through three screens of text.

The homepage, however, leads almost subliminally toward a seventh section of the site not listed with the others, Free Download, which details how to test a demo version of the software. In the bottom-right corner of the homepage, a button shouts "Free Download!" Originally the button was static, but we learned that we could get more visitors to click on it by animating it. Several text blocks on the page, which are all hyperlinked graphics files, also point to the download page.

Figure X1.4

Neat, eh? Who could resist clicking it?

If the user doesn't go to the download page from here, subsequent pages of the site add the "Free Download" icon to the navigation bar at the left side of the page frame.

Consistent Navigation Cues

Wherever the user goes from the homepage to another part of the site, the Netiva name and logo remain fixed on top, as do the section titles at the left, through the use of HTML frames.

Figure X1.5

There's more behind the homepage than first meets the eye.

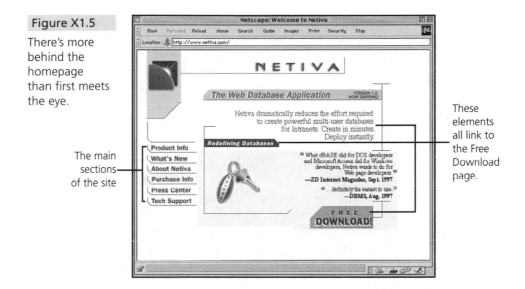

The main sections of the site

These elements all link to the Free Download page.

"It would have been really difficult to present the site the way we did without the use of frames or JavaScript," said Ms. Gilson. "But considering the target users for the product, which is written in Java, we optimized the site for users with a higher-than-average technical baseline."

We also used a subtle color-coding scheme for each section to help users understand where they are in the site layout.

Figure X1.6

Consistent design elements from page to page make the site easier to navigate.

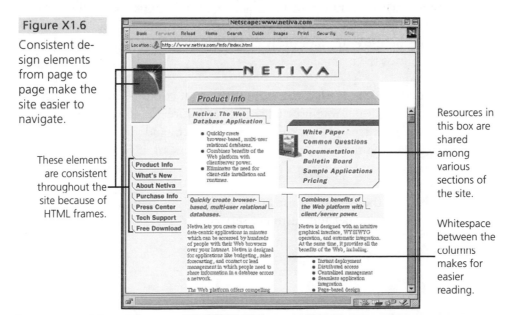

These elements are consistent throughout the site because of HTML frames.

Resources in this box are shared among various sections of the site.

Whitespace between the columns makes for easier reading.

"One of our biggest design breakthroughs was deciding to present the text on the inside pages in a two-column format," said Ms. Gilson. "The whitespace helps break up the information for the eye so it isn't overwhelming."

Built-In Flexibility

Netiva's structured site design avoids being rigid or restrictive, however. The white paper, for example, is formatted in several different ways so that users can choose how they want to view it. It's first presented within the site's standard HTML frames. A visitor who'd rather print it than read it online can choose to download a 17-page PDF (portable data file) version, viewable with the common Adobe Acrobat utility, or print it directly from an alternate Web page specially formatted in a non-frames window.

Because Netiva took the unusual step of placing its entire user manual online, we felt it better to give the documentation its own look and feel in a separate browser window. Using JavaScript, we configured the browser window more like an application interface than a typical Web page.

The manual's window is smaller than a typical Web page, and it opens without the usual browser toolbars and URL location fields. Custom buttons on the bottom of the window call up different sections and functions of the manual.

"We designed the site's basic architecture so it could be rapidly expansible as new features might be added in the future," said Ms. Gilson. "Lots of sites expand after their original launch, and you can see where they tacked on the subsequent sections. In general, if you think your design is hip and with it, it's probably already out of date."

For Netiva, the Web isn't just another advertising medium, it's a key distribution channel and customer service bureau.

Figure X1.7

The Netiva manual pops up as an independent application, so it remains accessible while the visitor surfs the rest of the site or elsewhere on the Web.

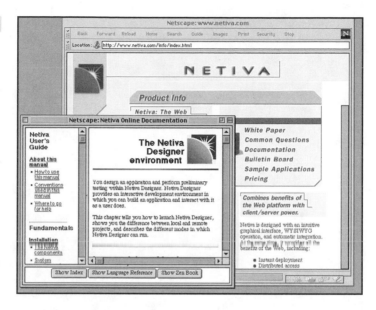

"In the world of shrink-wrap software, you end up competing seriously for shelf space," said Mr. Pollock. "You can live or die by whether there's room for you at Egghead. On the Web, it's a totally different world. Anyone can be on the shelf. The shelf, however, is infinitely wide, which changes the economics again."

In the new online economy, a company's Web site is its storefront, and the company and the site are synonymous in the minds of most consumers.

"Netiva is a very straightforward, easy-to-use product. We needed the site to have the same characteristics," said Mr. Pollock.

PART II

Audience Development

CHAPTER 5

Find and Be Found: Search Engines and Directories

A couple of years ago, registering yourself with a few search engines and Web directories was 90% of the work of online promotion. Soon your site would appear in a category next to three or four other similar sites, and you'd sit back while the traffic flowed in.

With the vast expansion of the Web since then, your site is now likely to show up alongside dozens or even hundreds of listings in a directory, and among thousands or even millions of results on a search engine query. A Web surfer has better odds of winning the lottery than of finding the ideal reference he's looking for on some Web search engines.

Nonetheless, many if not most surfers still begin their forays into cyberspace at search engines and directories. As a result, search engines generally rank among the top-trafficked sites and biggest ad revenue earners on the Web. They're growing ever more powerful and show no sign of going away anytime soon. So as a site promoter, you have little choice but to learn to love them. Or at least understand them.

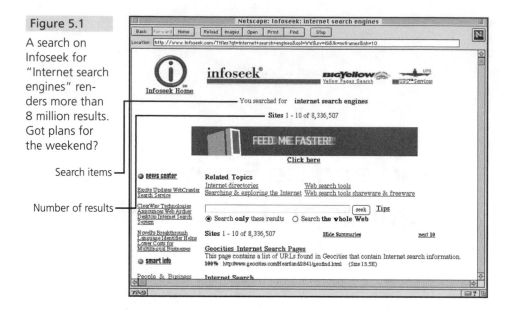

Figure 5.1

A search on Infoseek for "Internet search engines" renders more than 8 million results. Got plans for the weekend?

Search items —

Number of results —

Search Engines

First, let's distinguish between *search engines* and *directories*. To be precise, a search engine refers to an automated system, such as Digital Equipment Corp.'s Alta Vista. Such services rely on special software agents, called variously *spiders*, *robots*, *bots*, or *crawlers*, that explore and catalogue every nook and cranny of the Web (and, in many cases, other aspects of the Net, such as newsgroups). The spiders extract relevant text from the pages they discover and create digests of them in the search engine's database. When a Web surfer does a search, the system can then look at its database of pages the spider has imported, rather than performing a live search across the Web.

Directories

Directories, the largest of which by far is Yahoo!, do not depend principally on automated spiders. Rather, they index the Web the old-fashioned way, employing legions of recent college graduates for whom surfing the Web all day seems a lot more fun than a career in fast food. To a limited extent, these "surf teams" discover uncharted territory on their own and use spiders to tip them off to new sites, but to a much greater degree they depend on Webmasters who register their own sites with the directory. The directory's staff then visits the sites, qualifies them for inclusion, and edits the appropriate descriptions and keywords before putting up links to the sites.

Coherent vs. Comprehensive

The different approaches between search engines and directories produce different kinds of results, for both surfers and site promoters. For surfers, a human-edited directory is likely to organize pages in a more coherent manner than an automated program can. Yahoo! doesn't group 50,000 Web pages together into a single category, but Alta Vista will regularly return at least that many pages for a typical request.

It's no surprise, therefore, that Yahoo! is the most popular navigational guide among users. According to November 1997 data from Media Metrix, Yahoo! was visited by more than 40% of households on the Web, as opposed to less than 20% using its nearest search engine competitor, Excite.

Degrees of Site Owner Control

For site promoters, the automated approach of search engines provides a bit more control over how a listing may be displayed. Through the use of techniques such as meta tags

TIP: HOW TO SEARCH MOST EFFECTIVELY

When you're searching for a known organization or Web resource by name, you'll generally have the best results starting with Yahoo!. Due to its organized structure, a search of "search engine watch," for example, will first call up the Web resource titled "Search Engine Watch." The various search engines, however, will call up thousands of pages that contain the three words "search," "engine," and "watch," but the Web resource by that name isn't guaranteed to top the list.

Alternatively, when you're searching for a specific phrase or relatively obscure concept likely to be buried in the text of an unknown site, such as "number of emu ranches in America," a search engine such as Excite, HotBot, or Alta Vista is generally a better place to start. Search engines are more comprehensive than directories, although as the Web continues to grow exponentially, they, too, have backed away from their claim to list everything and are now aiming to reflect quality over quantity.

and the careful construction of other page elements (see the section "Maximizing Your Ranking" later in this chapter), a site designer can influence the search terms and page descriptions that many search engines will use when displaying results. Directories, on the other hand, are edited by subjective human beings who are apt to write their own description of a site and categorize it as they feel most appropriate.

Register Your Site

When your site is ready for prime time, you need to register it with all of the top directories and search engines. However, as with all types of online promotion, it is important not to jump the gun on this step before your site is ready for masses of visitors. Every site is perpetually "under construction," of course, but opening your doors for feedback when the site is still in beta is generally a mistake. You have approximately eight seconds to make that critical first impression on visitors while their twitching fingers yearn to click the Back button. Bad news travels faster on the Web than anywhere, and it will be months, if ever, before a surfer will return to a lousy site to see if it's improved.

Don't Wait to Get Found

In theory, the spiders from search engines will eventually track down your site whether you go out of your way to register it or not, but there's no guarantee of this. Registering directly with the search engines will give you greater control over how soon your site will show up (it still may take days or weeks, depending on the search engine). Manual registration may also give you more influence over which descriptions and keywords the engine associates with your site.

In the case of directories like Yahoo!, the chances that their surf teams will find you among the millions of pages on the Web are remote at best. You have no choice but to register manually with directories.

Registering your site with even 10 search services is time-consuming because each guide requires slightly different information, site descriptions of varying lengths, more or fewer keywords, and so on. Prepare a text document of basic information about your site, such as its name, contact persons, descriptions of it in 25 words, 50 words, and 100 words, sets of 5 keywords, 15 keywords, 30 keywords, and so on. As you go to each search service, you can then cut and paste the appropriate prepared texts into each field as necessary to save time.

Several services exist, both free and fee-based, both automated and personalized, that can administer this process for you. The best of these are listed in the "Resources" section at the end of this chapter.

Follow Your Browser to the Leaders

The search engine and directory market is changing faster than most other segments of the Web. Rather than naming today's market leaders only to find ourselves out of date shortly after this book's publication, we'll refer you instead to the navigational guides listed on Netscape's and Microsoft's search pages. Leading search services pay millions of dollars a year to be listed on these search pages, which are built into the "search" buttons on Netscape Navigator (**www.netscape.com/escapes/search**) and Microsoft's Internet Explorer (**home.microsoft.com/access/ allinone.asp**).

Figure 5.2

The biggest names in the search game pay megabucks to be listed on this page, with a link built into Netscape's browser.

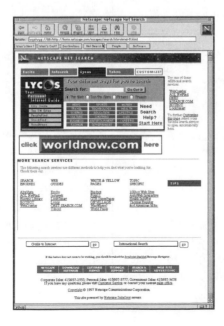

Explore all the search services listed on Netscape and Microsoft's search pages, including the smaller links to the side of and below the large graphic links. These are the industry's current search leaders with whom your site needs to be listed.

Maximize Your Ranking

Many a Web developer, after lovingly crafting a wonderful site and then registering it with various search engines, has reacted with horror to discover that the site appears as item 74,592 in a search of relevant keywords on a typical search engine.

The good news is that a responsible site designer can move his site towards the top of search results through a better understanding of how search engines rank pages. The bad news is that these guidelines aren't standard across all search engines. Most search engines even penalize sites for employing especially aggressive techniques to bolster ranking.

Unfortunately, some site designers become obsessed with a never-ending battle to keep their sites near the top of search results, at the expense of more effective methods of online promotion and even the maintenance of their site's overall quality.

Guides: Loyal to Surfers, Not Webmasters

All navigational guides, be they search engines or directories, owe their primary allegiance to surfers seeking information. Site developers who are trying to promote their pages are secondary. Of course, these search engines and directories wouldn't even be in business without sites to index, so they do recognize the promotional needs of Webmasters. They are on constant guard against attempts to abuse the system, however, and they will do their best to thwart all attempts at such manipulation.

Search engines have constructed the methods by which they rank the relevance of search results so as to provide a level playing field for all sites. They frequently change their strategies, though, to prevent Webmasters from artificially weighting search results in favor of their own sites. Meanwhile, random factors can propel completely unrelated pages to the top of search results. It's far from an exact science.

The point is that there's only so much you can do to win in the search results ranking game. After a certain point, it's okay to admit that you don't have to be number one and that it's time to move on to other things.

Keywords

When a search-engine spider finds a Web page, its main objective is to interpret various elements of the page to determine its dominant themes as they may relate to future keyword searches. Each search engine uses a slightly different formula for weighing the importance of various page elements when calculating the page's relevance to given search terms. In general, however, the following elements all play a significant role in those formulae.

Page Title

Along with the site's domain name itself, a Web page's title is possibly the single most significant factor that search engines use to determine a page's contextual relevance.

The title, indicated in HTML source code by the <title> tag, is the text that appears in the title bar at the top of the Web browser. The same text appears as the label if a user bookmarks the page.

From a search engine's point of view, the title "Sue's Cajun Flavors" would be much less effective in defining the context of a site selling hot sauce than "Sue's Cajun Flavors, for hot sauce, spicy sauce, pepper sauce, and other super-hot sauces and condiments." Although the latter title may seem clunky and doesn't fit entirely within the average browser window's title bar, a search-engine spider can read all that text and make it available for future keyword searches.

Titles should ideally focus on one theme. The "density" of the theme in the title is generally important to ranking. That is, if the title consists of only one word, and that's the word a surfer searches, it's likely to be weighted more heavily than a title that contains that word along with several other words. In our preceding example, the repetition of "sauce" and "hot" was an attempt to increase the density of that theme.

Figure 5.3

Mecklermedia's Search Engine Watch site is the definitive source for search engine advice. Notice the long-winded title pertaining to all things search engine.

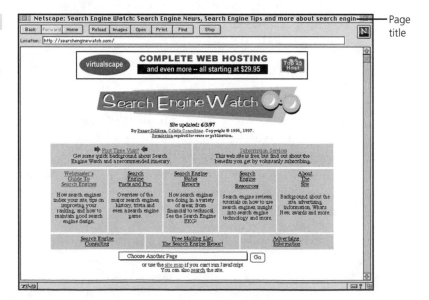

Page title

As knowledge of this technique becomes more widespread, you'll notice increasing numbers of sites with ridiculously wordy page titles that are meant less as informative labels for surfers than as rambling lists of synonyms for the sake of search engine density. Although you may still opt for short titles if you're a purist of style and design, don't neglect to give careful consideration to the few words you do choose for search-term impact. Page titles such as "index.html" and "page five" are tragically common and are usually listed 74,592nd or so in search engine results.

Likewise, a close or exact match of a domain name with the subject being searched is sure to push a site near the top of a search ranking. A site with the domain **hotsauce.com**, for example, would likely rank extremely high in a search of the keywords "hot sauce."

Headlines and Body Text

After a page's title, the headlines and first few sentences of the text are also heavily weighted by most search engines in determining the page's context. Unlike the page title, these elements are something readers will read carefully, so filling them with conspicuous lists of keywords is obviously impractical.

Nonetheless, those who live to keep their sites top-ranked in search results will counsel you to emphasize words that surfers are likely to chose as search terms when you write the text of your Web pages, and to repeat key words frequently. It's at this point—when good writing style is sacrificed for the sake of a good ranking—that the shortcomings of search-engine technology become obvious.

Joe Kraus, cofounder of Excite, advises that Webmasters stick to one theme per page. On a sports site, for example, write about golf on one page and about tennis on another. Writing about both subjects on the same page will dilute the weight a search engine will give to either category.

"It may seem like we're pigeonholing people," Mr. Kraus said. Unlike a search engine, he continued, a directory edited by humans rather than software "is a place where you can get listed in an appropriate category no matter how you present your content. But if you want a strategy for appearing at the top of a search engine's results page, it's an unfortunate fact that you're going to have to work within the bounds of how our technology tends to work."

Meta Tags

HTML *meta tags* are an important tool for prescribing how search engines should use descriptions and keywords for your pages. They are not supported by all search engines, however. Excite, for example, does not recognize meta tags as of this writing, on the grounds that site designers can too easily use them to mislead surfers.

Web browsers don't display the information in meta tags onscreen, but spiders can understand their instructions. There are several types of meta tags, but the two most common ones for the purposes of search engines are *description* and *keyword* tags.

Each meta tag, which is imbedded in the <head> section of the HTML code, is composed of two parts: a *name* field and a *content* field. The most popular use of meta tags in this context is to define the site description and keywords that a search engine should adopt. For example:

```
<HEAD>
<TITLE>Sue's Cajun Flavors</TITLE>
<META name="description" content="A one-stop, online shop
for the best hot sauces and
➥other condiments from Louisiana's Cajun country.">
<META name="keywords" content="hot sauce, Hot Sauce, hot
sauces, Hot Sauces, pepper
➥sauce, Pepper Sauce, pepper sauces, Pepper Sauces, spicy,
Spicy, red hot, Red
➥Hot, fiery, Fiery, Cajun, cajun, chili sauce, Chili Sauce,
chilli, chile">
</HEAD>
```

Most engines that do recognize meta tags will use the description verbatim in their search results and take the suggested keywords into consideration. When determining page relevance, however, they may still place greater emphasis on the page title and other factors than on the keywords suggested in meta tags.

Notice the variations of individual keywords in our example, written in both singular and plural, both uppercase and lowercase. The more variations of a word you use, including different verb forms (-ing, -es, -ed, and so on), the better. Some search engines may make these extensions naturally on their own, but others may not. Also consider common misspellings, alternate spellings, and possible typos.

More on Keywords

When you're submitting keywords into a search engine's registration and you're limited to a certain number of them, opt for plurals or longer versions (for example, "skiing" instead of "ski"). The system is more likely to match a search for the shorter version when the longer one is listed than vice versa.

When it comes to deciding which keywords are most appropriate for your site, invite friends and colleagues to look at the site and give their suggestions. You may be so close to the project that you can't see the forest for the trees, and they may have a fresher perspective on which words come to mind to describe the site. Also, plug a few keywords you're sure about into a search engine and see which sites come up, and then look at the source code of those homepages to see which other keywords your competitors are using in their meta tags. There may be some words in there you hadn't considered.

One bad idea that some sites employ is including popular search terms such as "sex" in their list of meta tags, even though the site has nothing to do with that topic. The faulty reasoning behind this is that by picking such popular, although unrelated, search terms, they may misdirect some extra Web surfers to their site. They may gain slightly inflated page view numbers with this strategy, but a wise Web marketer should focus on results, not on numbers. You're unlikely to satisfy the prurient urges of someone looking for pictures of naked ladies with a $5 bottle of hot sauce.

Popularity

Several search engines will also adjust a site's ranking in their search results based on what the engines determine to be the site's "popularity." Generally, they base popularity on the number of inbound links from other sites. Excite even attempts to take into account how many stars the site has received from certain reviewers. Of course, this isn't something a designer can influence when he's building his pages, but comes through gaining lots of inbound links to his site via all the audience development methods discussed in the remainder of this book.

Spamdexing

As if the preceding strategies weren't enough to keep Webmasters busy, those who've become deeply obsessed by their ranking in search results often partake of a range of *keyword stacking* or *spamdexing* techniques. These include various ways to repeat phrases and keywords in such a manner that they're invisible to surfers but get noticed by spiders. Popular variations of this include the use of HTML comment tags or white text against a white background.

Search engines universally despise these techniques as a kind of cheating, and most attempt to punish sites they catch employing them by deliberately lowering their ranking in search results or excluding them from the search engine altogether.

Our advice is to avoid such techniques. If you can't resist, you can keep up with the cutting-edge spamdexing methods by viewing the source code of porno sites, which can always be relied upon to pioneer the unethical innovations of Web promotion. (There, we just justified the cover price of this book in one sentence. It's the perfect excuse if your boss catches you surfing the seamy underbelly of the Web: "I'm doing stealth market research!")

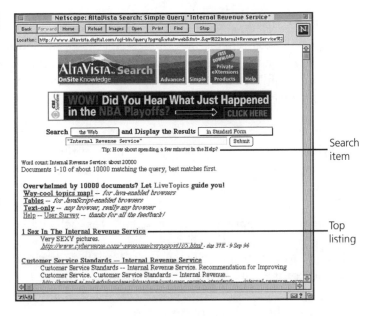

Figure 5.4

AwesomeAdult.com figured that people might like to take a break at tax time to surf for some smut. By repeating the hidden phrase "internal revenue service" more than 1,000 times in the source code of their homepage, they managed to appear as the top listing in an Alta Vista search for the IRS.

Follow the Leader

If you're really stumped about why your site still isn't appearing higher in search results, take a look at the source code of the sites that top the lists of your preferred keywords. What are they doing that you're not doing?

Be careful, though. This is where good marketing strategies can turn into obsessive-compulsive behavior. First of all, if these competitors are topping the charts due to spamdexing techniques, bear in mind that copying such strategies may help you on one search engine but bar you entirely from others. Also, while you may achieve the position of top dog for a day, your competitors are likely to copy your code and unseat you with their own modifications, leading to a never-ending struggle to remain top-ranked when your efforts would be much better spent on other site-promotion strategies.

In any event, don't cut-and-paste copyrighted material from another site's source code.

Pointer Pages

If achieving top-ranking in search results is indeed a burning priority for your site, consider contracting this task out to a service such as USWeb. Like a handful of other consultants in the industry, we've mastered rank-boosting techniques, including the complicated use of *pointer pages*.

Because the way engines weigh their rankings varies from one search service to the next, the best way to remain at the top of all of them is to customize different homepages for each search engine. To the user, the content of such pointer homepages would appear identical, but the HTML code would vary according to what meta tags and other page elements best improve the search results for each engine.

Each pointer is assigned a unique URL, such as **www.hotsauces.com/a/index** for Excite, **www.hotsauces.com/b/index** for Lycos, and so on. The different pointer pages all link the same internal site content, except the homepages are customized.

Staying abreast of the minutely different and ever-changing strategies employed by each search engine is far more complicated and time-consuming than we'd recommend any site to bother with. Hence, outsourcing the whole headache of search ranking makes sense for many sites concerned with the issue.

Avoid Dead-End Links

Search-engine spiders navigate their way around the Web by following the hyperlinks that join pages. They depend on clear text links in order to do this. Bear this in mind when you create your site navigation.

Image Maps

If all the links on a given page are contained in image maps, a spider won't be able to follow them to the next level of your site. On pages with little or no text, be sure to use descriptive meta tags so search engines that support them can still index the content of your site. More importantly, however, include text links in addition to graphic links so that spiders and visitors surfing with graphics turned off can continue to navigate your site.

Frames

Many search-engine spiders, like older versions of browsers, aren't frames-compliant and may not be able to get past your site's first page if you haven't allowed for a non-frames navigation route. Again, meta tags are useful on frames pages to allow spiders to index content topics, but you should also provide an alternative navigation structure using the <noframes> tag. (See the "Resources" section in Chapter 3, "Design Optimization," and the Appendix, "Internet Resources," for recommended HTML guides that further explain these issues.)

Password Protection

If your content is available only behind a password-protected page, be sure to make good use of meta tags on that page so that search engines will have some idea what lurks "behind closed doors." Some search engines may be able to index password-protected sites if you make special arrangements for them to have password access. That way, at least surfers will have an idea of what valuable content awaits within.

Dynamic Pages

If your site uses CGI scripts, database requests, or other methods to generate pages dynamically, you should consider creating some static pointer pages that you can register with search engines to provide some context about your site. The search-engine companies are slowly moving towards establishing a standard method of indexing dynamic pages, but no strong initiatives stand out as of this writing.

Robot Exclusion

There may be some circumstances where you want to prevent a spider from indexing your site or parts of it, such as during a beta-testing period.

You can accomplish this in more than one way. A crude way is by placing the *robots noindex* meta tag into the code of a given page, like this:

```
<meta name="robots" content="noindex">
```

There are a few shortcomings to this technique. First, as we've mentioned, not every search engine supports meta tags. Even among those that do, this particular tag is not universally recognized. Also, the tag needs to be included in the code of every page that you don't want to be indexed. This can be cumbersome if the site consists of many pages, all of which will have to be updated if you later want them to be indexed.

Better for this purpose is something called the Robots Exclusion Protocol, which allows site administrators to set up a robot.txt page with special instructions universally supported by search engine spiders (aka *robots*). A robot.txt page can tell spiders to exclude an entire site or just specified sections of it.

This page must be created by the site's host administrator. If you use an ISP or other service to host your pages, you'll need to coordinate with that administrator because you probably won't be able to upload a robot.txt page without special access.

The Robots Exclusion Protocol is a bit too technical to cover in this book, but you can find detailed instructions at the following URL:

http://info.webcrawler.com/mak/projects/robots/robots.html

If that URL is no longer valid, search **www.webcrawler.com** for "Web Robots" and you should find the current pages.

General Submission Guidelines

As we said before, wait until your site is fully ready to go before submitting it to search engines and directories. Likewise, be sure to resubmit your URL after a major redesign, with new descriptions and keywords as appropriate. Although the search-engine spiders should eventually track you down regardless, some of them take months to revisit sites.

If you have several sections to your Web site that treat significantly different topics, submit each section URL to the same search engines and directories with unique descriptions and keywords so that surfers can enter your site from various vantage points.

Whatever you do, however, don't resubmit the same page repeatedly to a search service in the space of a few weeks. Be patient. Most of these services are receiving thousands of submissions a day. Allow six weeks or so before deciding that the original submission didn't register. Most search services will penalize sites that bombard them with duplicate submissions.

Yahoo!

All of the preceding advice about optimizing keywords in your title, meta tags, and so on, for the sake of search-engine spiders has no bearing at all on Yahoo! and other search directories. Yahoo!'s surf team doesn't look at meta tags and the like. They look at each site just as any other human visitor would. They take into account the suggestions for descriptions and keywords that you enter into their registration forms, but they may rewrite any or all of it in their database and stick you into whatever category they see fit.

The most important thing is to get listed at all. Yahoo! claims to have a liberal admissions policy, but it does reject many sites. In addition to making it easier for surfers to find good content, Yahoo! sees part of its job as keeping surfers from being distracted by bad content.

Unfortunately, many sites complain that trying to get listed in Yahoo! can be tremendously frustrating. Search Engine Watch, a top resource for this aspect of Web marketing, conducted a survey of its visitors in the summer of 1997 to find out their experiences in trying to get listed in Yahoo! The results were grim. Admittedly, the survey was small and un-scientific in its methodology (perhaps those with bad experiences were more likely to complete the survey), but nearly three-quarters of the 162 respondents were unable to get listed with Yahoo! after months of trying. Those who were successful had widely varying experiences, some getting listed just a few days after they registered, some waiting nearly six months before seeing results.

The problem is one of scale. As the Web continues to grow at a phenomenal rate, Yahoo! is having trouble keeping up with the huge volume of submissions it receives. Search engines can generally throw more computers with faster processing speeds at the problem, but Yahoo!'s human staff has had much more difficulty scaling up to meet demand. As a result, it appears to have opted to become more restrictive as to which sites it will list at all.

Got the Site Right?

If your site has made the first cut, the head of Yahoo!'s surf team, Srinija Srinivasan, offers this advice on improving your positioning against competing sites: "The number one thing is to have a great site. Nothing else is going to really matter till you get that part right."

Although most of the sites in Yahoo!'s directories appear in alphabetical order in their respective categories, the surf team will raise individual sites up above the masses if they believe the sites deserve special attention. They'll also add sunglasses to sites deemed "cool" and put a "Review" icon next to those that have been written about in *Yahoo! Internet Life* magazine.

Know Your Category

You can win some points at Yahoo! by making your submission to the right subcategory, saving the editors as much time in processing your submission as possible. Yahoo strives to keep its categories small and subdivides them when they grow too large. Topics such as flower delivery don't lend themselves to simple subcategorization, however, and do contain dozens if not hundreds of listings.

On the bright side, Yahoo! doesn't break up its listings of sites into 10 items per screen in an effort to sell more banner ads, unlike many of the search engines. It lists all the sites in a category on a single page, so even if your site appears low in the list, it's more likely that a surfer will take the time to scroll the whole list.

Forget About the ABCs

Once your site is in a Yahoo! category, it will be listed in alphabetical order. So if your service begins with a "W," you can be pretty sure where it'll show up in the ranking.

A quick perusal of Yahoo! indicates that a lot of sites think "A1" is a really clever name.

We agree with Yahoo!'s Ms. Srinivasan on this one: "Personally, I think that's a very short-sighted strategy. Take ourselves, for example. Somehow we've managed to stay afloat despite the fact that our name starts with a 'Y.' If that's the only thing keeping you in business, then I think you've got bigger concerns."

Save A1 for hamburgers. Stick by a brand you can defend.

Specialty Directories

In addition to Yahoo! and the big search engines, there are hundreds of specialty directories out there, covering everything from real estate to travel to gay services to science fiction. Whatever your topic is, there's probably a specialty directory or five where you should be listed.

Where do you find such directories? Through directories of directories, of course. Yahoo! has a "Web directories" category. WebTaxi is also an interesting amalgamation of hundreds of search services. (See the "Resources" section at the end of this chapter for details.)

Finally, although there are several automated services out there to help facilitate the search-engine registration process, the best one is Submit-It. It offers a limited number of search-related services for free, but for a relatively low fee it integrates access directly into the submission pages of more than 300 search engines and directories, including many specialized ones.

We believe it's most effective to submit to the top directories individually so that you can optimize your submission for each. But if you're planning to register your site with dozens of search guides or more, Submit-It stands out among the automated submission services. For higher fees, they can also offer consulting and customized submissions.

Figure 5.6

Submit-It makes registering with dozens of search engines and directories at a time considerably easier.

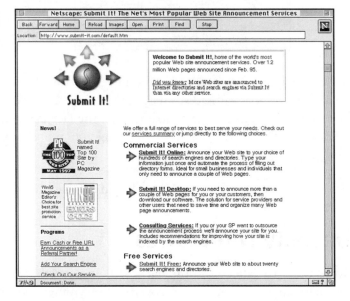

Quality Prevails

Registering your site with search engines and directories is a critical first step in promoting your site. It is by no means the lion's share of the promotion process, however. Keep it in perspective, and don't go over-board competing for top billing in search results. You'll only cost yourself ranking on other engines and waste energies better devoted elsewhere.

Along those lines, we give the final word to Jerry Yang, co-founder of Yahoo!:

"The good sites always turn up in the end. People somehow find them, not only through Yahoo! but by word of mouth. Those people who worry about superficial things, like whether their name starts with a triple-A, or who try to spoof search engines are generally running the sites without a lot of substance. Those who really devote themselves to good content or service always end up getting recognized in the end because the system is set up that way. People's patience level is very low for bad content, whereas they reward the best ones by telling other people. At that point, it's not anything that Yahoo! or Alta Vista can do. Once you're good, you're good."

Resources

Search Engine Watch

http://www.searchengine.com

Danny Sullivan of Calafia Consulting has created the definitive site about getting the most out of search engines, for both surfers and Web developers. Mecklermedia bought this resource in late 1997, although Mr. Sullivan still administers it and keeps it up-to-date. The site offers a wealth of free advice, plus more detailed information for a modest annual subscription fee. Mr. Sullivan, based in England, also maintains a mailing list about the latest developments in the search engine field, to which you can subscribe from the site.

Submit-It

http://www.submit-it.com

Founded in 1995 by Scott Bannister as a free service, Submit-It has grown into a significant online promotion company, specializing in search engines and directories. Much information is still available for free, but the more useful services are now fee-based. It's typically under $100 for a submission to dozens of search engines or more.

Netscape and Microsoft's Collection of Top Search Services

http://www.netscape.com/escapes/search

http://home.microsoft.com/access/allinone.asp

Netscape and Microsoft link these pages to the "search" buttons built into each of their Web browsers. The pages offer reliable indications of what are currently the most serious search engines.

Yahoo!'s Specialized Search Services Page

http://www.yahoo.com/Computers_and_Internet/Internet/ World_Wide_Web/Searching_the_Web/

Find links here to hundreds of specialized search engines and directories.

WebTaxi

http://www.webtaxi.com

A funky conglomeration of hundreds of specialized and regional search services. Its frames-based implementation is a bit awkward, and the site is designed more for seekers of information than site promoters, but it's a valuable resource nonetheless.

Bruce Clay

http://www.bruceclay.com

Mr. Clay's site leans towards the ranking-obsessed, spamdexing school of thought, but the private consultant does provide some interesting advice, services, and links on the topic of search engines.

Position Agent

http://www.positionagent.com

This site had room for growth the last time we checked, but the idea was interesting. The free service allows you to check several search engines at once to see how your site ranks on each, according to certain keywords. They still needed to work out the bugs as of late 1997, but it may be worth a look.

Robot Exclusion

http://info.webcrawler.com/mak/projects/robots/robots.html

This page by Webcrawler explains how to prevent search-engine robots from searching pages you want to keep private with the Robot Exclusion Protocol, or robot.txt document.

Word of Web: Online Communities

Among Web marketers who recognize that they must actively promote their sites to stand out against the masses, few think much beyond online banner advertising. That's not terribly surprising, given that advertising is the mainstay of traditional media marketing. On the Internet, however, there are many additional routes to reach audiences, in some cases far more effectively.

At USWeb, we use the term "audience development" to refer broadly to a range of online marketing strategies for building and maintaining Website traffic. Audience development includes paid media (advertisements), as well as what we call "audience creation," which encompasses techniques such as search engine optimization, contests, public relations, and other grassroots promotions.

Relatively little audience development can be automated. At least 50% of it is research. Pursuing these strategies requires hundreds of hours of Web surfing and interacting with netizens at large on Usenet newsgroups, mailing lists, and commercial online services. It means writing to thousands of Webmasters to secure inbound links to your site, applying for awards, making deals with cyber-cafes, organizing online events, and more.

Numerous sites already employ some of these techniques. Many more recognize their strategic importance but don't have the available staff or expertise to implement them effectively. For a small site, a single individual may have no choice but to handle most of these activities alone. Larger sites sometimes hire teams of surfers who are responsible in part for audience development, and more and more companies are turning to outside specialists like USWeb to manage the process.

This chapter deals with the delicate art of marketing to online communities without ruining your reputation in the process.

Usenet

In 1979, long before the advent of the World Wide Web, graduate students at Duke University and the University of North Carolina invented a way to replicate threaded discussion across networked computers. They sought to use it to share tips about UNIX programming. Thus *Usenet* was born.

Within a few years, the system spread across the country and soon around the world. Quickly its topics of discussion broadened beyond just UNIX questions to those of pop culture, hobbies, sex (of course), and much more.

Figure 6.1

Usenet has something for everyone. Seeking a magic hair tonic? Check out alt.baldspot.

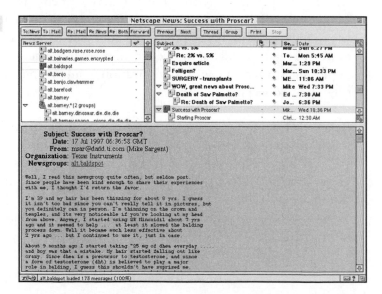

With the advent of threaded discussions on Web pages in the last year or so, the heyday of Usenet may be waning. Nonetheless, there are still more than 20,000 Usenet forums, known as *newsgroups*, many of which remain quite active today.

Certain product types, such as computer software, may lend themselves better to promotion on Usenet than products such as fast food. But with so many diverse and narrowly focused newsgroups, most marketers will be able to find a significant audience in some newsgroups.

Usenet participants come from all walks of life, but most share some common characteristics: the majority are experienced Internet users, eager for new online experiences, and most are hardcore devotees of the topic of their particular newsgroup. For every message posted on a newsgroup, hundreds or even thousands of readers may be lurking in the background, quietly following the discussions.

As loyal followers of their particular topics, newsgroup members will frequently belong to other online forums related to the subject. As a result, they're likely to pass on interesting news from the newsgroup to others via email, fan Web sites, and word of mouth.

Figure 6.2

Lots of folks find kindred spirits on Usenet, sharing their feelings about Barney the dinosaur and other important subjects.

Thou Shalt Not Spam

The Internet purists reading this may already be outraged to see us advocating commercial promotions in newsgroups at all. Blatant advertising, especially across multiple newsgroups, is called *spamming*. It's among the most reviled breaches of online conduct and can be met with serious consequences.

There are several important do's and don'ts concerning promotion on Usenet, mainly, "Don't Spam," "Don't Spam," and "Don't Spam."

Definitions of "spam" vary somewhat, and, as with direct-mail advertising, one person's spam is another's useful information. In Usenet terms, however, a spam is a blatantly commercial advertising message, especially when posted to several newsgroups (be it dozens or thousands) with little consideration for the dedicated topics of those newsgroups.

At first blush, this may seem like a good marketing tactic. With little or no programming knowledge, you can easily copy your message to thousands of newsgroups at seemingly no cost. Don't fool yourself, though. There *is* a cost. You'll get hate mail in such volumes that it can crash your servers and get you kicked off your network connection by your Internet service provider.

If you're hawking a get-rich-quick pyramid scheme through a P.O. box and a fortified anonymous remailer, and you don't mind sorting through death threats, dead fish, and possibly the occasional pipe bomb, you may find spamming to be reasonably effective marketing. If you're trying to establish a legitimate online brand presence, however, don't even think about it. The damage it will do to your reputation will destroy you, not to mention the fact that you're a sitting duck for the 100MB mailbomb files some creative hacker will arrange to send you 50 times in a row.

Figure 6.3

No matter how much this spammer claims to have earned from of his initial $6.00 investment, we doubt he has peace of mind after outraged netizens have called him at home late at night for weeks on end (a popular revenge, if they can track you down).

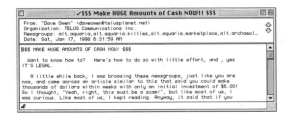

ONLINE ORIGINS OF "SPAM"

There are a few theories about how the Hormel Foods Company's product Spam (a contraction of "spiced ham") came to mean "junk advertising on the Internet."

The most amusing idea is that it comes from a prank that some MIT students allegedly played. They froze a block of the luncheon meat with dry ice and then threw it into another student's dorm room. It supposedly exploded upon impact, coating the unfortunate student's living quarters with thousands of tiny Spam fragments. This story sounds too good to be true and is likely a cyber-legend.

Others suggest that it's an acronym for something along the lines of "Stupidly Posted Advertising Messages."

However, we subscribe to the most popular theory, that it derives from the classic Monty Python routine where a chorus of Vikings at a diner burst into song in praise of the stuff, repeating "Spam, Spam, Spam, Spam…" Online spammers, then, are likewise just repeating themselves ad nauseam. (A little pun there: "ad nauseam." Har, har.)

Meanwhile, some in the marketing community prefer the term "UCE," for "unsolicited commercial email," in deference to Hormel's trademark.

The Internet's obsession with Spam doesn't end with junk mail and Usenet abuse, however. In addition to dozens of fan sites devoted to the glory of the reconstituted meat product, a distinctly '90s pop art form has swept the Internet: Spam haiku. Search for those two words on any search engine and you'll find hundreds of these delectable ditties:

Pink tender morsel,
Glistening with salty gel.
What the hell Is It?

In the cool morning
I fry up a slab of Spam
A dog barks next door

Slicing your sweet self
Salivating in suspense
Sizzle, sizzle… Spam

Pink beefy temptress
I can no longer remain
Vegetarian

Figure 6.4

One of the dozens of sites that shows up on a search of "anti-spam," instructing users how to fight back against junk email and Usenet advertising.

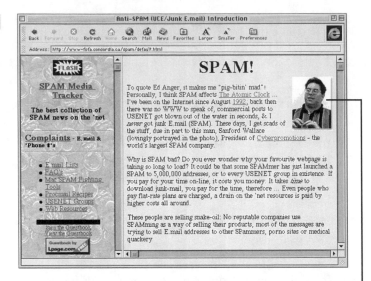

Pictured is the Web's most notorious spammer, Sanford Wallace, president of Cyber Promotions, a spam specialty service. He's so comfortable with his net.baddy reputation that he's registered a domain for his nickname: **spamford.com**.

Find the Right Audience

So how do you use Usenet for marketing without getting flamed to a cinder? First of all, find the newsgroups whose participants are most likely to care about your subject. The whole point of newsgroups is their extreme specificity. In alt.barney.dinosaur.die.die.die, participants want to discuss death fantasies about the purple-costumed children's television character, and not much else. Try to start a thread there about making money fast, kombucha mushrooms, or a new pornography site, and the members are likely to get very annoyed with you.

If you're trying to promote a site featuring your health food product, members of alt.food.lutefisk probably don't want to hear it. Members of alt.food.fat-free, on the other hand, may welcome your announcement gratefully.

There are several ways to find out which newsgroups are appropriate for you. First of all, your newsreader software should have some built-in search functions. NewsWatcher, the most popular newsreader for the

Macintosh, lets you search for words in newsgroup names or even individual message titles. Free Agent, the leading newsreader for Windows, has similar functions.

Figure 6.5

NewsWatcher for Macintosh offers a variety of built-in search options to help you find out which newsgroups are appropriate for your interests.

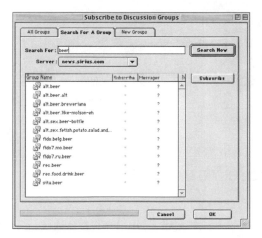

Netscape's browser provides a built-in newsreader, and the one that comes with Communicator 4.0 isn't bad (unlike previous versions). Navigator 3.0's newsreader is quite primitive, however, and should be avoided.

Figure 6.6

Netscape Communicator 4.0's newsreader offers a quick search function, much improved over earlier versions.

Deja News

The Deja News Web site is a powerful Usenet search engine. Going beyond newsreaders' built-in search capacity for newsgroup names and message titles, Deja News lets you search for words appearing in the text of individual messages across Usenet. Search for your own brand name and see if anyone is saying kind or negative things about you. Or search for terms related to your product to see which newsgroups may be interested in your site.

The service also lets you track down messages posted from a certain email address. Creepy, yes, but perhaps useful, such as in tracking down what a competitor is saying and in which groups.

In fact, you can actually dispense with a dedicated newsreader application altogether and just use the Deja News site to read and post to newsgroups, if you prefer.

Figure 6.7

By far the best Usenet search utility, Deja News is a one-stop shop for all newsgroup activities.

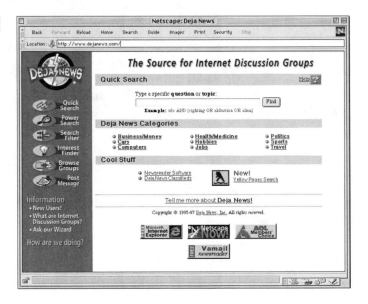

Lurk Before You Leap

Once you've identified a few newsgroups whose members you think would be interested in hearing about your product, do *not* jump straight in with a posting before getting a sense of the discussions taking place.

HOW NOT TO DO IT

An incident from the early days of USWeb's Audience Development Group illustrates how the name of a newsgroup may not indicate its true character.

Coinciding with Microsoft's launch of Windows 95, we had a client, BPR Publications, that established an area of its site to track every press release issued about Windows 95, from both Microsoft and third parties.

We identified more than 60 newsgroups that were apparently devoted to the Windows family of operating systems. We put together a short announcement calling attention to BPR's new service and posted it to those newsgroups.

The announcement was met with enthusiasm by all but one newsgroup. One of its members wrote us a civil note informing us that the newsgroup had nothing to do with the computer industry at all, but rather was dedicated to professional window washing!

Many newsgroups are close-knit communities where an outsider with the best of intentions can unwittingly breach established codes of conduct and get flamed in response.

The best way to avoid alienating your intended audience and to gauge the proper decorum for any newsgroup is to spend some time *lurking*—reading posts without participating. In theory, most newsgroups make available a FAQ (frequently asked questions) document that outlines general group policies. FAQs are produced and maintained on a voluntary basis by newsgroup regulars who are supposed to repost them regularly. In reality, you often won't find one in the newsgroup where you're lurking. Try looking for copies in the newsgroup news.answers.

Contribute, Don't Advertise

Few newsgroups, except those that contain .biz or .marketplace in their names, will welcome blatant advertisements or press releases. Most .biz and .marketplace newsgroups are little more than spam ghettos, less forums for active discussion than for free classified postings.

The key to using Usenet effectively for promotion is to serve newsgroup participants' interest in a specific topic. Craft your announcement to read more like a service to them than a service to your business. Instead of screaming "advertisement," murmur "helpful recommendation."

Figure 6.8

Everything you ever wanted to know about online Simpsons etiquette but were afraid to ask.

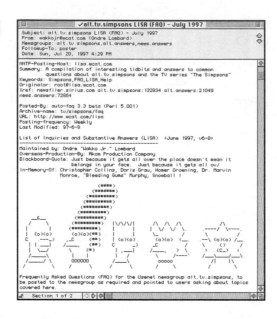

Keep posts short (one or two paragraphs), write in a casual voice, and, as with all kinds of online messages, use a descriptive and compelling subject line.

Figure 6.9

This message, one of a series that USWeb posted to promote the shareware site Dave Central, is clearly targeted to this graphics-oriented newsgroup. It's got a straight-forward subject line, it's short, and it gets to the point without exaggerated hype.

<table>
<tr><td>

WARNING: CONSIDER A DEDICATED USENET EMAIL ADDRESS

Although we sincerely hope that you'll avoid the despicable technique of spamming, sadly Usenet remains rife with it. So much so that not only do spammers broadcast their advertisements indiscriminately across Usenet, but they also troll Usenet for email addresses with software robots so they can send unsolicited commercial email messages directly to hapless newsgroup contributors.

For this reason, you may want to consider using a special email address dedicated to your newsgroup posts. If you use your primary email address in the email reply header of your newsgroup posts, you're almost certain to get on spammers' lists as a result.

Of course, it's important to be attentive to legitimate inquiries from well-meaning newsgroup members in response to your posts. The email address you use for your posts should certainly be a legitimate one whose mail you at least scan.

An alternative to a wholly separate email address is to use a *spam buffer* in your address, such as rick@SPAMBUFFER.bruner.net or rick@DONTSPAM.bruner.net. Such a buffer will normally thwart email-trolling spambots. However, you should include a note in your signature explaining that people need to delete the buffer from the address before sending you mail.

</td></tr>
</table>

Seeding Discussions

Some newsgroups remain uncompromisingly hostile to any contribution that smacks of commercial promotion in the slightest. This is true of many computer games newsgroups, for example. In such cases, there are still a couple of options available to the creative promoter.

First, you can browse the discussions taking place and look for opportunities to answer questions that lend themselves towards a mention of your site. If you're replying as an individual to a legitimate question, few could fault you for slipping in a subtle plug. In providing straight answers to real questions, your company signature may be all you need to refer to your site. (See "Tips on Signatures" later in this chapter.)

A sneakier strategy is to initiate a discussion incognito, much like a magician using a shill in the audience who pretends to be an ordinary spectator but who's actually in on the trick. Using an identity that masks your affiliation with the company you're promoting, ask a leading question such as whether anyone knows where to find such-and-such information. Then, using a second online identity, post an answer to your own question, recommending that your first personality visit your site.

Needless to say, this strategy doesn't come without risks. Make sure to use entirely separate domains in your return addresses. If you're discovered, you may well be met with outrage by newsgroup members who deem it cheating.

We don't endorse this as a regular practice, but in some cases it may be the most appropriate way to share information. Do so only when you believe your contributions would truly benefit members of a group that is otherwise unreceptive to more straightforward promotional posts.

Mailing Lists

Mailing lists (frequently referred to as *listservs* after the generic name for the software that administers them, spelled without the final "e" due to the eight-character limit on older IBM mainframe and UNIX systems) are much like newsgroups in their sense of community and devotion to a single topic. You need to be even more cautious when promoting on mailing lists, however, to avoid upsetting list members.

As their name implies, these discussions are email-based. Subscribers sign up to receive every message posted to the list directly in their email boxes. Because of this high level of commitment by users, mailing lists tend to have a strong "signal-to-noise" ratio—that is, they prefer quality information over pointless banter. The tolerance for shameless self-promotion, therefore, is especially low.

That doesn't mean members may not appreciate announcements of highly relevant information. But keep the hype to a minimum and be darn sure that your submissions are keenly targeted to the list topic.

Figure 6.10

The Net-Lawyers mailing list is one of several serving the legal profession. This one generates about 30 messages a day.

Listen and Learn

Mailing lists tend to attract those most seriously committed to a certain topic, even more so than newsgroups and other bulletin board-style forums. Many lists have thousands of subscribers, but even those with smaller distributions can provide powerful audiences for promoters because many of the readers are at the top of the influence chain within their given communities.

The need to lurk before you post is particularly important on mailing lists. At any one time, a newsgroup may have dozens or hundreds of messages available for you to peruse in order to grasp the tone of the community. A busy mailing list, on the other hand, may generate only a dozen or so messages a day. For this reason, we strongly recommend that you lurk for several days to fully appreciate a list's tone before posting. Frequently, lists archive discussions on a Web site, which can speed up a newcomer's introduction to the group.

Many lists allow, even encourage, well-targeted one-off announcements about new online services. Where possible, however, you can do much more for your brand identity by fully joining the list community and establishing credibility through ongoing contributions in answer to other members' questions.

We encourage you to subscribe to the most important few mailing lists related to the topic of your Web site. Think of mailing lists as perpetual industry seminars. Some of the participants on your industry's lists are likely to be the panelists at conferences you'll attend in the real world. Mailing lists give you instant peer access to these and other leaders in your field. It's networking, in many senses of the word.

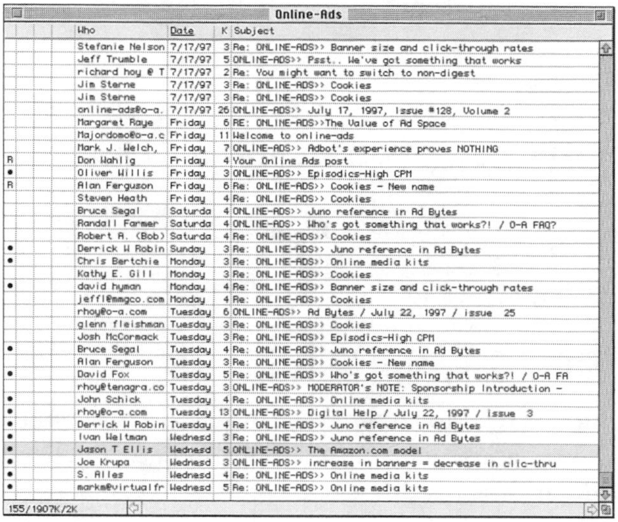

Figure 6.11

The Online Advertising mailing list is a must-read for anyone involved with online ad sales. Many companies use the list to call attention to their own products and sites, but always within the context of an example that could benefit other readers.

Tips on Signatures

An online *signature* (or *.sig file*) is more like a business card than its handwritten namesake. As anyone who's been online for a week has noticed, many netizens append their email and newsgroup messages with professional contact information, goofy mottoes, ASCII-art dragons, and the like.

Any good email software program lets users generate a canned signature automatically or on demand. The better email software programs enable the use of multiple signatures.

Brevity

As a general rule, professional signatures are best kept short and to the point—name, title, company name, corporate slogan, telephone, fax, email, and URL. You rarely need to include a snail-mail address because anyone who really needs it can just call for it.

Anything longer than four or five lines threatens the norms of good taste. Posting a message shorter than your signature is a classic faux pas.

One way to use fewer lines is to create two columns of information, using the space bar to simulate tabs, although it may not line up perfectly for readers not using the conventional mono-width fonts, such as Courier or Monaco. Or you can just string your fax and telephone numbers together with commas on the same line, do the same for your URL and email, and so on.

Figure 6.12

The author's standard signature. Just the facts, ma'am.

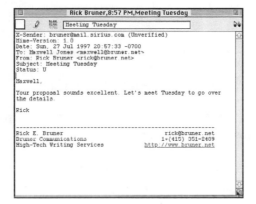

Humor

ASCII-art renditions of cartoon characters, or even your corporate logo, generally do not convey the most professional image. They are best limited to use in one's personal online life, not in the company's name.

Likewise, although many of the digerati use pithy quotes from the likes of Oscar Wilde, Winston Churchill, and Frank Zappa, often to good effect, you should indulge in this bit of flair advisedly. Witticisms need to be darn witty to impress cynical cybernauts. Once-clever tags get dull quickly for regular list members, who may see such .sigs as a waste of screen space.

Figure 6.13

Dave Del Torto is known in some circles for his masterly use of 200+ .sig files, each in perfect context.

Moderated vs. Unmoderated

Most mailing lists come in one of three flavors: unmoderated forums, moderated forums, and newsletters.

Getting mentioned in non-interactive email newsletters is a matter of public relations (see Chapter 8, "Media Savoir-Faire: Public Relations for a Digital Age").

Most good interactive lists have a moderator who reviews every submission before allowing it to be posted. In addition to leading discussions on occasion, the moderator controls the quality of the list, filtering out spam, offensive language, name-calling, and the like.

Befriend Moderators

If you want to post an announcement to a list that you don't regularly read, a useful tactic is to send your announcement directly to the moderator. Explain that you don't know the list's policy on announcements, but that you believe your post would be of interest to the readers. Include the post and invite the moderator to decide whether or not it's appropriate, with thanks either way.

This tactic has two advantages. First, you win points with the moderator for being respectful, rather than just spamming the mailing list. Second, if the moderator does submit your brief announcement, it will bear her mark of endorsement to the rest of the readership.

Finding Lists

Discovering which mailing lists serve a given topic isn't as simple as it is with newsgroups, which are listed together on every Usenet server. Mailing lists are maintained by thousands of separate servers across the Internet.

The best directory of mailing lists is Liszt. At last check it claimed to index more than 70,000 lists.

New lists are springing up all the time, and just because you don't see it in Liszt doesn't mean it's not out there. Ask colleagues and fellow netizens for referrals to the most important online forums for whatever audience you're trying to reach.

Figure 6.14

The huge Liszt directory is the place to start researching mailing lists.

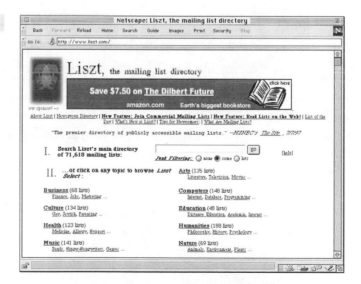

Commercial Online Services

Also part of the online community are the subscribers to the big commercial online services, namely America Online, CompuServe, Microsoft

Network, and Prodigy. These services have more than 15 million combined users, who are included in most estimates of the 30–70 million Internet users worldwide.

Reinventing Themselves

All of the commercial online services have been struggling to re-engineer their businesses in the face of the surging popularity of the Internet in the last few years. The big services, dating back to the '70s in CompuServe's case, were happy to be a near-monopoly in online access for the masses. Their mix of services principally featured email (consistently the Net's most popular application), news and feature content from large print publishers, live chat, and message boards.

The sudden explosion of the Web's popularity in '94–'95 caught the online giants off their guard. Now, as they labor to provide full-service Internet access to their millions of members through proprietary network gateways, they must also justify their added value to customers who can get on the Net directly through thousands of local ISPs nationwide.

While former market leader CompuServe peaked in the early '90s, AOL grew rapidly through aggressive marketing (the inescapable gazillions of free log-on disks it sent everywhere), surpassing 10 million members in 1997. By that time, however, the service had infuriated many subscribers with busy access lines, email outages, and perceived abuses of members' privacy. As a result, AOL experiences a constant user "churn rate" of more than 50% of their membership per year, according to the Yankee Group industry analysts.

Figure 6.15

Welcome to McCyberspace. Millions and millions served.

Meanwhile, Microsoft Network, which ranked a close third behind CompuServe with just under 3 million subscribers in mid-1997, has gone through several metamorphoses since its 1995 launch. Back then, Mr. Gates still insisted the Internet wouldn't amount to a hill of beans, and MSN started as a closed-protocol network like AOL, CompuServe, and Prodigy. Soon after, Microsoft turned 180 degrees and gave the Internet a bear hug. MSN transformed into a private Web entertainment network and access provider. Lately, analysts say it's looking more like an educational network. Speculation persists that Microsoft eventually wants to get out of the Internet access business altogether and turn MSN into a pure subscription content service.

Figure 6.16

Microsoft's second strategy turned MSN into a content-rich Web environment for subscribers.

Prodigy, sorry to say, is the least relevant of the commercial services for marketers these days. A pioneer of commercial cyberspace, the service launched in the late '80s and never quite found its way. In the summer of 1997, CNET wrote, "Before joining the company, its own former chief executive, Edward Bennett, had described Prodigy as 'slow, lame, and ugly' in an interview with *The New York Times* a year ago." The company's latest gambit is to pioneer commercial cyberspace again, this time in China. Good luck to them.

JoeConsumer@AOL.Com

For sheer numbers, AOL is the most important commercial service for most marketers. Although it's the subject of much derision on the Net, AOL is a handy Internet-on-training-wheels for the newbie masses. And as such, it's a great place to find ordinary consumers and establish online brand loyalties when they start.

Of the various basic services AOL offers, the most effective for the online marketer is their message boards. These are basic discussion bulletin boards, much like Usenet. AOL's captive audience, however, often generates considerably more dialogue on their message boards than most Usenet newsgroups ever see.

Figure 6.17

Women in business for themselves. Not a bad demographic. AOL's got them, as well as many more juicy slices of middle America.

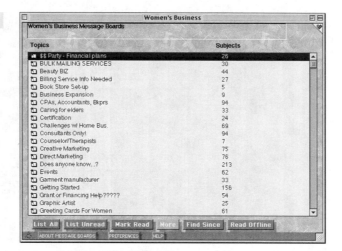

All the same rules of online marketing netiquette discussed earlier in the chapter apply equally to the commercial services.

If you're using AOL's discussion forums to promote a Web site, bear in mind that some of AOL's users are likely to be new to computers, much less the Internet. Make sure your site is friendly to AOL's primitive browser, and don't assume much technical sophistication on the part of your audience.

CompuServe, et al.

Unless you're already a member of one of the other big services and are familiar with its benefits, it may be more trouble than it's worth to get accounts with all of them for online marketing.

A possible exception could be if your service were targeted towards a specific professional group, like lawyers, accountants, or realtors. If so, you may want to investigate CompuServe. CompuServe has long had a reputation as the preferred service for professionals, and the quality of discussion in their forums often reflects that. Following AOL's purchase of CompuServe in late 1997, AOL officials announced plans to continue emphasizing CompuServe's professional character as a point of differentiation between the two services. If there's another $20 a month available in your budget, you might consider it.

CompuServe also has the largest presence in Europe, if you have a significant stake in those markets.

Figure 6.18

Like most CompuServe forums, the Architecture Forum includes numerous message sections where members pursue lively discussions.

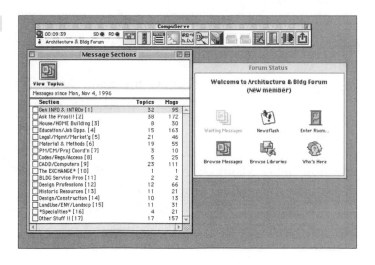

Web Discussion Boards

In addition to newsgroups, mailing lists, and commercial services, you should look into the bulletin-board-style discussion forums that many Web sites present. Marketers can leverage these to spread the gospel about their products and sites. Like mailing lists, these forums are generally closely monitored by moderators, in the form of Webmasters, so blatant self-promotion is unwelcome and may be removed as fast as it's posted.

Again, the same rules of netiquette apply to Web forums as the others we've discussed. Posts should be in the spirit of sharing experience rather than bald-faced hawking.

Certainly, bulletin boards maintained by a competitive site probably won't tolerate plugs for your rival site. Such contributions are better suited to neutral sites with a tangential, rather than direct, thematic similarity to your own.

Many sites archive their discussion threads indefinitely, increasing the chances that a pointer to your site would be seen weeks or months after you originally posted a message to the discussion, particularly if a surfer turned up the message in a keyword search. More effective still is securing permanent pointers to your site on an affinity site's resources page, as discussed in the following section.

Affinity Sites

What makes the Web a web, of course, are the hyperlinks connecting sites together. By its very definition, the Web encourages sites about related interests to point to each other, and indeed most sites maintain a collection of recommended destinations.

Securing inbound links from so-called *affinity sites* to your homepage is an important part of online promotion. In most cases, Web publishers with an interest in providing good links charge nothing to maintain long-term pointers to other quality sites.

"With banner ads, once the banner is gone from a site, the link is gone," notes Leland Harden, USWeb Marin cofounder and senior VP of sales and marketing.

"Not only are most links free, the credibility of a link is higher than an ad for most surfers. A link bears the esteem of an editorial endorsement rather than the stigma of a paid ad," Mr. Harden said.

In fact, many of the bigger sites *do* charge to link to other sites, and strategic cross-promotions and content-sharing arrangements can be hard-bargained business deals (see Chapter 9 for more on this subject). Most smaller and medium-sized sites, however, are still happy to link for free. Some may ask for a reciprocal link, which may or may not be in your best interest, but frequently they will link to you regardless if your site is good enough.

Figure 6.19

Doug tries to pitch LegalZone on a link for Tumbleweed Software.

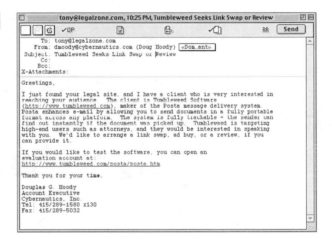

Complements, Not Competitors

Obviously, some direct competitors may see a conflict in linking to each other. That only leaves hundreds of thousands of other sites to choose from. Affinity sites complement, they don't compete. A romance fiction site and a personal dating service might both benefit from reciprocal links, for example.

In other cases, similar sites have found it to their advantage to band together. For example, hot sauce retailers online seem happy to link to others in their field, so much so that some of them have founded the Ring of Fire mutual appreciation network. Such cross-promoting *Web rings* are relatively common within certain fields.

Figure 6.20

Mark Stevens, perhaps a man with too much time on his hands, belongs to the Ring of Fire hot sauce network.

Real Value of Links

The incoming traffic generated by links can vary tremendously depending on the affinity site's quality and the character of its audience. In USWeb's experience, a rule-of-thumb average is about 20 visitors a week for each inbound link to your site.

Comparing that rule of thumb to the cost of banner advertisements, it's easy to appreciate the real value of affinity site links. Let's assume you have a banner that is receiving the Internet industry average clickthrough rate of 2% (that is, one in 50 Web surfers who sees it clicks on it), and that you're paying only $10 per thousand impressions shown of the ad. That means you'd have to show the banner 1,000 times, at a cost of $10, to get 20 visitors a week.

However, given that most links stay up on their pages indefinitely, you may be able to secure 1,000 inbound links after two or three months of a diligent affinity link campaign. Then, according to our 20-visitors-per-week rule of thumb, you'd have 20,000 visitors a week from those free links, for an equivalent banner ad value of $10,000 a week.

Figure 6.21

At least some of the carefully chosen links at Moms Online are the subject of serious negotiation.

Über-links

Not all links are created equal, of course. Some might produce only one or two visitors a week. Others may pass along 20 visitors a day or more. These are the prized *über-links*.

Über-links (a term coined by USWeb's account executive Doug Moody) are sites that have become leading resources within their audience groups, whether that's lawyers or computer gamers or Star Trek fans. They're the sites that everyone else in the field invariably links to, and where every Web surfer searching the topic quickly ends up.

USWeb tapped into an über-link in the summer of 1997 for our client Cosmo, Silicon Graphics' virtual reality server and player products division. Right at the beginning of the media sensation sparked by NASA's exploration of Mars with its Sojourner robot buggy, we secured a link from NASA's Jet Propulsion Laboratory's site to Cosmo's site. SGI's engineers had used real images from Sojourner to map out a 360-degree picture of the landing site, which Web surfers could explore in 3D with the Cosmo browser plug-in. Traffic to Cosmo's site went through the roof, its Web servers barely able to keep pace with the unprecedented volume of visitors.

If you get yourself listed on an über-link site, other related sites may discover you and decide to add a link to you as well. Thus, linking gains its own momentum.

Identifying which are the über-links and which are the also-rans requires hours of online research and experimenting.

Figure 6.22

Mark Holtz's Star Trek site may be nothing special to look at, but a link here can transport legions of Trekkies to your site.

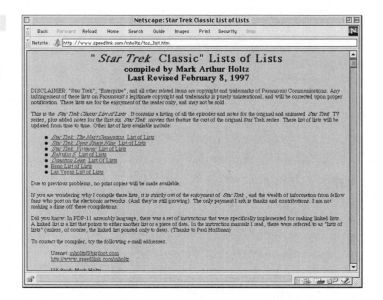

Although emailing Webmasters is the most direct way to solicit inbound links to your site, a large part of that process is also organic. Essentially, all audience development marketing—search engine registration, seeding online forums, contests, public relations, online advertising, and so on—has the residual effect of interested Webmasters discovering your site and volunteering links to you without further prompting.

Paying for Links

Of course, an easy way to convince sites to link to you is to reward them for doing so. A fast-emerging trend on the Web is paying for traffic on a per-clickthrough basis.

Cashing in on the trend is Submit-It, a service that has gained prominence by automating the process of registering with search engines (see details in Chapter 5, "Find and Be Found: Search Engines and Directories"). In late 1997, Submit-It launched a new service called ClickTrade, which brokers payments on a per-clickthrough basis between sites that are willing to pay other sites for hosting links to them.

ClickTrade automates the process of linking sites to each other, tracks the clickthrough visits, and administers the accounting, taking a 30% transaction fee for the service. Submit-It founder and VP of technology, Scott Banister, told us that advertisers are willing to pay in the neighborhood of 10 cents per clickthrough.

Tracking Inbound Links

Tracking which sites have linked to you is a bit complicated. Many Webmasters you write to requesting free links may never reply but will still go ahead and put up a link. Others may add you to their pages unsolicited.

Most of the main search engines will let you search for a URL to determine which pages are linking to you. They generally don't make it straightforward to do so, though. Alta Vista, for example, allows you to omit all references of your own site's internal links from the search results, but you have to know the arcane search commands to use:

```
link:usweb.com/ -host:usweb.com
```

On HotBot, you need to change a pop-up menu on the homepage from the default that tells the engine to search for "all the words" to "links to this URL." On Infoseek, choose the "Ultraseek" option and follow the link to "Search URL" or "Search Link."

Figure 6.23

HotBot makes it relatively easy to search for sites linking to your homepage, if you explore the pop-up menus.

For a thorough review of how to search for inbound links on the big search engines, the excellent site Search Engine Watch features a detailed description (see the "Resources" section at the end of the chapter for the URL).

For a whopping fee of $500 a month, Lycos offers Link Alert, a great improvement on the free URL searches (although it still seems over-priced for an automated service). Link Alert lets you analyze data in various ways, including downloading the raw spreadsheet data for your own report format without banner ads breaking up the results every 10 listings.

Announcement Sites

When a site is first readied for public consumption, a good way to generate initial traffic is to register with various *announcement sites*. The most famous of these is Net-Happenings, run by the computer department of the University of Wisconsin. Dozens of other similar services also exist.

Figure 6.24

Lycos's Link Alert, an over-priced but handy tracking service for in-bound links.

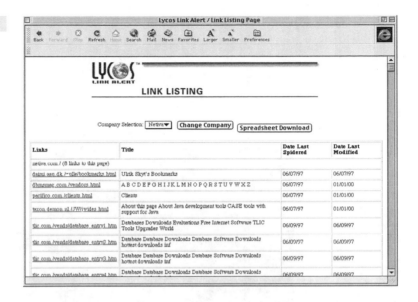

Announcement sites are subscribed to by many Webmasters, Internet journalists, surf-junkies, and various other chroniclers of cyberspace who are likely to give exponentially wider distribution to interesting announcements that issue from these central hubs. They're great for generating volunteered links via interested Webmasters who monitor them.

In addition to using announcement sites for your site's initial launch, many can be revisited for special cyber-events, although administrators won't appreciate you abusing the service with abundant and frivolous postings. (See the "Resources" section for references to the leading announcement services.)

Awards, Reviews, and "Cool Sites"

"Webocracy" gives every netizen an equal chance to be heard online, so nearly everyone is a critic. Many Web connoisseurs have gone so far as to issue their own awards of excellence. The "Cool Site of the Day/Week" award is a favorite of countless sites.

Being cited for excellence or coolness by a well-recognized award site may indeed benefit your online venture. Many reviewers and Webmasters who follow such lists may check out your site and create links to you themselves. Certainly, you'll experience a spike in traffic for the day or week the award is featured, and of course you can forever display the award icon with pride (preferably somewhere tactful, not as the first image that loads on the homepage).

Figure 6.25

ProjectCool.com is the latest and greatest from Glen Davis, who originated the cool-site-of-the-day genre.

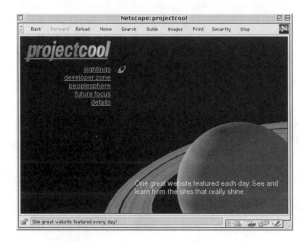

As far as making an effort to seek out awards, it's worth a rainy afternoon's work at most. Although a virtual plaque from peers is heartwarming, the true impact of awards on developing audience is not profound. If you do your job well, building a good site and promoting it with the tactics described in the book, awards should come your way unsolicited.

For that rainy afternoon you do want to invest, however, check out Yahoo!'s Best of the Web sub-category (see the "Resources" section for the URL).

Resources

Tips on Netiquette

Netscape on Netiquette

http://home.netscape.com/menu/netet/

Netscape maintains a reasonably good set of Net user guidelines, so-called "netiquette" and "forum decorum."

Tenagra's Links

http://marketing.tenagra.com/net-acceptable.html

Tenagra has a collection of links on this page to rules of the road. The resources focus especially on how to advertise appropriately on Usenet.

news.newusers.questions, news.announce.newusers, and news.answers

These three newsgroups are good starting points for those new to Usenet, with lots of FAQs and advice for online promoters.

Anti-Spam

Junkbusters

http://www.junkbusters.com/

One of many sites preaching the gospel against Usenet and email spam, this one has a particularly good set of resources.

Yahoo! on Spam

http://www.yahoo.com/Computers_and_Internet/Internet/Policies/Abuse/

Yahoo! has links to oodles of sites raging against net abuse. This URL has lots of cross-references and links to various such pages.

Announcement Sites

Net-Happenings

http://scout.cs.wisc.edu/scout/net-hap/index.html

Thousands of Internet hardcores subscribe to the Net-Happenings mailing list to find out what's going on online. A posting here can provide a critical jumpstart for a new site and for special online events.

WebStep Top 100

http://www.mmgco.com/top100.html

This is a good list of some of the best announcement and other online promotional services.

Yahoo on Announcement Services

http://www.yahoo.com/Computers_and_Internet/Internet/ World_Wide_Web/Announcement_Services/

Pointers to a variety of announcement and promotional services.

Other Resources

Deja News

http://www.dejanews.com

This is a key resource for marketing on Usenet and by far the most powerful way to search topics being discussed in newsgroups. Engage in competitive analysis by searching for what your competition is saying, and see what users are already saying about your product.

Liszt

http://www.liszt.com

This is the most comprehensive directory of mailing lists, and lets you search in a variety of ways.

Search Engine Watch on Inbound Links

http://www.searchenginewatch.com/popularity.htm

This page of Search Engine Watch, the excellent resource discussed in Chapter 5, describes in detail how to use each of the leading search engines to discover which sites have links to yours.

Visibility Index

http://www.visibilityindex.com

This site, run by Word of Net, has a neat utility that sees which of two sites has a higher online visibility by counting in-bound links to each, as well as counting mentions in newsgroups and online news stories, among other measures. For a fee, the service provides much more detailed data.

ClickTrade

http://www.clicktrade.com

A service of the popular Submit-It promotion company (see a discussion of them in Chapter 5, ClickTrade brokers fees between sites willing to pay others for links.

Yahoo! on Award Sites

www.yahoo.com/Computers_and_Internet/Internet/
World_Wide_Web/Best_of_the_Web/

This page lists dozens of the top award and cool-site-of-the-day sites.

Women's Wire: Sisterhood of Demographic Excellence

I n recent years, women have rapidly closed the geek gap on the Web. Recent studies, such as a spring 1997 joint survey by CommerceNet and Nielsen, indicate that women now account for more than 40% of all Web users. Furthermore, in 74% of households, women are the principal shoppers for most goods, according to Mediamark Research, Inc. Statistics like those leave Women's Wire sitting pretty with one of the highest concentration of women surfers on the Net.

Women's Wire, one of USWeb's most successful clients, illustrates well the power of audience development techniques for driving traffic online and targeting users. After careful analysis, executives at the Women's Wire site have found that our grassroots techniques can be more cost-effective at driving traffic than banner ads, and are highly efficient in identifying specific groups of users with a strong affinity for a site's content.

Roots in Grassroots

The brainchild of Ellen Pack, Women's Wire has grown from a modest dial-up bulletin-board service in the San Francisco Bay Area with a few thousand subscribers in 1992 to the largest women's interest site on the Web today, with more than 5 million page views monthly from an audience that's 90% female. Thanks to its choice demographic audience—mostly upscale, tech-savvy female professionals—Women's Wire commands among the highest advertising rates on the Web.

The site's parent company, Women.com, with a staff of around 60, has leveraged its experience with Women's Wire to create two other successful sites as well. Beatrice's Web Guide is a joint venture with Yahoo! with shortcuts to the Web's best content, and Healthy Ideas is a health-oriented joint venture with *Prevention* magazine.

"Women, who make up 51% of the general population, are destined to become the majority online," said Marleen McDaniel, CEO of Women.com. "We see Women's Wire's role as being a central point for women online to gather to explore ideas important to them and to network with other people with similar interests. As a business, Women.com is also seeking opportunities to match our audiences with marketers who have something valuable to offer them."

On the subject of female empowerment, Ms. McDaniel knows of what she speaks, having played executive roles in six successful startups, including 3Com and Sun Microsystems, before joining Women.com.

Figure X2.1

Serving the women who are shaping the Internet and society today. And not a bad marketing segment, either.

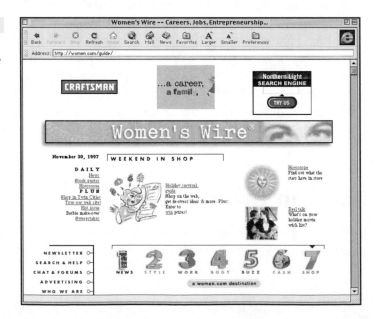

Given Women's Wire's own background as an online discussion group, it's not surprising that the company's executives had faith in the kind of online marketing techniques in which USWeb's Audience Development group specializes.

"From my perspective as a marketer, I view the Web as still somewhat anarchic," said Ramona Ambrozic, VP at Women.com. "If you could find those thousands of people who belong to newsgroups and other special-interest communities online and tell them about content they are likely to be interested in, it seemed to me you could build traffic relatively inexpensively and with a good likelihood of converting them to loyal visitors."

Building Audience for Cash, Buzz, and Style

With those clear objectives for building traffic within niche communities, Women's Wire retained USWeb in a rewarding 14-month partnership. Women's Wire has experienced strong, steady growth since its inception, and in 1997 averaged a 10–15% rise in traffic per month. USWeb's audience development techniques—which in this case have concentrated on topical promotions within newsgroups and other online communities and affinity link building—have complemented a wide range of other traffic-building activities at Women's Wire, including banner advertising, aggressive public relations, print and television coverage, and more.

The role that audience development techniques played in that growth was important. In some cases, Women's Wire concluded, the results were half again as cost-effective as banner ads.

For the purposes of this case study, Ms. Ambrozic pored over Women's Wire's traffic logs for a two-week period in May of 1997, when USWeb was charged with three traffic-building promotions. One was Stock Quotes, a brand-new feature within the Cash section of the site that was devoted to financial issues. The second was a celebrity profile with actress Elizabeth Hurley within the Buzz entertainment section. The third was Fashion Wire, a recently introduced fashion industry news column within the site's Style section.

Figure X2.2

For women who take their investments seriously, Stock Quotes was a welcome addition to Women's Wire's existing financial content. The trick was figuring out where money-minded women hang out online.

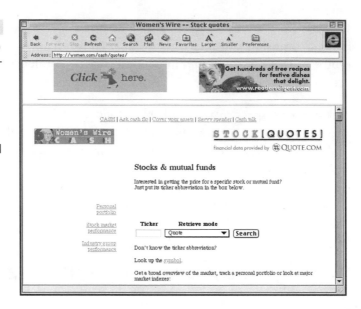

"These features were sub-components of the major sections of the site, so we're drilling pretty deep into the content. We gave USWeb very specific URLs to promote," said Ms. Ambrozic.

She also noted that none of the features in question had been promoted via advertising, PR, or other means, so the grassroots audience creation techniques could pretty well be isolated as responsible for the increase in traffic beyond average overall traffic growth.

"The results were good," Ms. Ambrozic cheerfully reported.

Because each of the promotions lasted two weeks, Ms. Ambrozic chose the two-week period prior to the promotion as a base to measure the change in traffic. In addition, she also examined the two weeks following the end of the promotions to see if the audience creation resulted in a sustained growth in traffic, indicating that a portion of visitors may have become repeat visitors as a result of the promotions.

In each case, traffic at the specific features rose substantially above the 15% growth that the overall site experienced during the same period.

And two weeks after the promotion ended, both Stock Quotes and Fashion Wire continued to see a rise in traffic significantly greater than the whole site experienced in that time.

Taking the Message to the Masses

"Promoting Stock Quotes was a fun challenge," said Heidi Paul, USWeb's account executive in charge of the Women's Wire account. "There are lots of sites and discussion groups out there that focus on finance, but not many that cater especially to women. We decided to approach finance-specific groups and target the women within them, as well as turning to a range of women's groups online that we thought would be interested in stocks and finances."

During the two-week promotion, traffic to the new Stock Quotes feature jumped 250% and has continued to grow substantially ever since.

"Elizabeth Hurley was a bit more difficult to promote," Ms. Paul said. "We didn't find too many fan clubs for her on the Internet at the time, but we were able to promote it in a variety of online entertainment circles, including newsgroups such as alt.fan.britishactors and rec.arts.movies.people."

During the promotion period, traffic rose 72% from the page views on the previous celebrity profile. After the promotion ended, however, traffic for the celebrity profile section fell back to the same level as before the promotion.

"There are not as many fashion sites and discussion areas on the Net as you might think," Ms. Paul said. "But when we dug around, we found several places to promote the new Fashion Wire feature, including some newsgroups, Webzines, and Generation X-oriented online communities."

Fashion Wire saw a 54% rise in traffic during the promotion period, of which it maintained a modest 16% growth in visitors for two weeks after the promotion.

Figure X2.3

Elizabeth Hurley didn't have the same number of devoted fan sites as, say, Madonna or Pamela Lee. But with some work, we found a number of netizens interested in this feature.

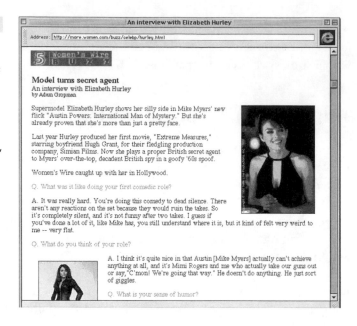

The table shows the rise in traffic to select Women's Wire features during two weeks of USWeb's grassroots audience creation promotions.

Table X2.1

For much less than the cost of an ad banner campaign, traffic to the promoted features was up markedly above the overall site growth during the same period.		
Site Feature	Rise in Traffic During Two-Week Promotion *	Rise in Traffic Two Weeks After Promotion *
Stock Quotes	250%	240%
Celebrity Profile	72%	0%
Fashion Wire	54%	16%
Overall site, including promoted features	15%	7%
Overall site, not including promoted features	13%	6%

* Relative to two-week period prior to promotion

Figure X2.4

Denizens of high fashion appear still to be warming up to the Net, but we were able to tip off some couturiers that Fashion Wire is an important new outlet for the industry.

Audience Creation Versus Advertising

"As these three features were not promoted any other way during that period, I would have to attribute the success of their growth in traffic to USWeb's activities," said Ms. Ambrozic.

"Next, I estimated what the traffic cost me. And it was very efficient," she said. "Probably the best way to characterize it is versus online advertising. And I would say it was 50% more efficient than advertising during that period. I'm reluctant to attach a real CPM [cost per thousand impressions] to it, because I would have to make a lot of assumptions to do so. But based on this kind of rough analysis, I would say these audience-creation tactics are very competitive with advertising in terms of driving traffic."

As we will discuss further in Chapter 9, "Paid Media: The Many Faces of Web Advertising," there is no conflict between online advertising and grassroots audience-creation techniques. At USWeb, we consider non-paid promotions and online advertising to be the two foundations of audience development. Women's Wire is a premier example of how combining these strategies can produce tremendous marketing success.

7

The Era of Innovation: Contests, Sweepstakes, and Other Creative Promotions

A nything written about the Internet in the 20th century, including this book, is going to fail to appreciate its full potential. Imagine writing in 1955 about the future of television. Who could have envisioned the political power of CNN, the "MTV generation," or the multibillion-dollar video rental market?

The incredible pace of the Web's development (1994 already seems like ancient history) may occasionally fool us into thinking that the medium has already arrived. In reality, it's barely poked its nose in the door. These are the salad days of the Internet, when conventions are being broken as fast as they're written. Anyone who says, "It can't be done," simply hasn't thought to try it yet. So you may as well be the first.

This is true of Internet marketing as well. When HotWired first introduced advertising banners in 1994, many observers disparaged the idea, predicting that users would reject banners and that few advertisers would pay for them. Today, banners underwrite a huge portion of the Net's content and are as ordinary as highway billboards.

The creative marketer should accept no boundaries. Clearly, this chapter cannot describe what hasn't yet been tried. Rather, it aims to provide you marketing mavericks with food for thought by highlighting some online innovations that we and other companies have found successful. Consider modifying them for your own use or as inspiration for ideas of your own.

Free Stuff

With more than a million sites competing for users' attention, providing good content is often not good enough. Web ventures need to build traffic quickly to reach marketing objectives. A favorite strategy is to appeal to netizens' base human greed by offering a chance to win free stuff.

Figure 7.1

Sweepstakes Online is one of dozens of sites specializing in the newest Web contests. Until the rest of the world comes online, the odds are better than the state lottery.

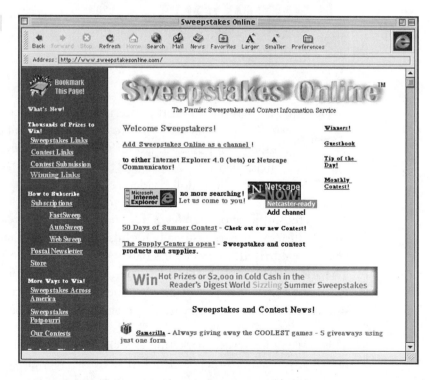

Sweepstakes, treasure quests, scavenger hunts, trivia quizzes, interactive mysteries, and writing, recipe, and photo contests have all become staples of Web promotion. T-shirts, CD-ROMs, vacation packages, computers, bumper stickers, and good old-fashioned cash have all brought in registered users to grateful site operators.

Of course, contests, like the sites that host them, must themselves be promoted. In addition to alerting visitors of contests through ad banners (such as the familiar "Click here to win $10,000!"), there are dozens of Web sites, mailing lists, and newsgroups that specialize in announcing new contests (see the "Resources" section at the end of the chapter).

However, with the right prizes, partners, and/or creative spin, the best contests have a way of promoting themselves, attracting tens or even hundreds of thousands of entries.

ichat: Tune In to Win

ichat, maker of popular Web-chat software, came to USWeb to build an audience base quickly for Open 24, a new chat service they were launching. The new chat service is a showcase for Rooms, the company's server software.

ichat's previous chat service, Chat Now, had taken six months to attract 450,000 registered users, and ichat wanted Open 24 to be an even bigger sensation in the world of online chatter.

In addition to USWeb's typical audience development services, such as directory and search engine registration, announcement services, newsgroup alerts, and affinity site linking campaigns, we came up with the idea of a series of live chat sweepstakes. Much like a radio contest where listeners have to be tuned to the station to win, participants of the ichat sweepstakes had to be logged into the Open 24 chat rooms at appointed times to respond to their names being announced in group chats.

ichat allotted USWeb a number of banner impressions that we traded with manufacturers for prizes. We found companies that were eager to give away modems, graphics accelerator cards, computer video cameras, Nintendo 64s, and a grand prize "chat dream machine" tricked out with all of the above plus a top Pentium processor, large monitor, speakers, and so on.

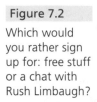

Figure 7.2

Which would you rather sign up for: free stuff or a chat with Rush Limbaugh?

At the time, the spring of 1997, these live chat contests were the first of their kind. Several prominent directory services featured the contests as big attractions, including Yahoo!'s Pick of the Day.

ichat topped out Open 24's server capacity for simultaneous chats quickly at each of the six weekly prize drawings. In large part due to publicity from the live sweepstakes, Open 24 registered 450,000 users in only two months, three times faster than Chat Now.

Yahoo!: "360 Degrees Every Time"

"The Internet is all about change. It thrives on change," said Bill Miltenberger, sales promotion manager for Yahoo! "You have to come up with ideas that take the advertising model and turn it 360 degrees every time to come up with something new. You have to stay ahead of the competition and continue to give your advertisers a compelling and interesting concept."

He speaks from experience. Miltenberger and his fellow Yahoos have dreamed up some terrific promotions, including Halloween and Valentine's Day treasure hunts and live online chats with NBC TV stars (cross-promoted during NBC's prime-time programming—how's that for driving traffic?). In the autumn of 1997, Yahoo! staged a virtual road rally sponsored by Volvo.

One of Yahoo!'s most memorable promotions, however, was its 1996 "Find the Y" sweepstakes, featuring tech-industry cartoon hero Dilbert. For the event, the Web guide teamed up with cartoonist Scott Adams, his syndicate United Media, and NYNEX's Big Yellow business directory.

Figure 7.3

Who could resist helping poor Dilbert in his hour of need, especially when the prize was two vacations, one for you and one for your boss ... in separate places.

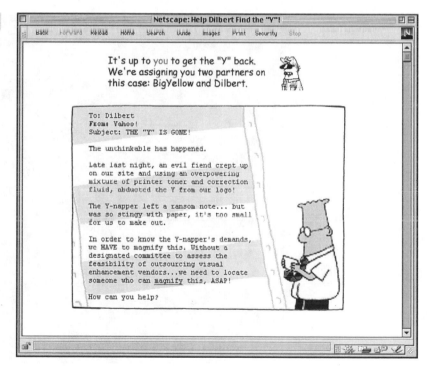

During the week-long contest, visitors who hit Yahoo!'s homepage—the site averages more than 30 million page views a *day*—immediately noticed that the capital "Y" of the site's famous brand name was missing! "Drat, what scoundrels could be responsible for this evil deed?", millions of netizens asked themselves.

It was then that they noticed the trustworthy visage of Dilbert smiling at them from an ad banner, asking for help in locating the missing "Y," with a chance to win fabulous prizes to boot. When they clicked the banner, they learned that to help Dilbert find the "Y" and be eligible to win, they needed to use Big Yellow to search for clues. For Big Yellow, it was clearly a great way to familiarize new users with its product.

While enjoying Adams' wry wit, entrants uncovered a trail of amusing clues, searching for a detective in Big Yellow, decoding a random note, and consulting a swami in the guise of Dilbert's contemptuous dog/management consultant, Dogbert.

Figure 7.4

If only all consultants were as wise and efficient as Dogbert.

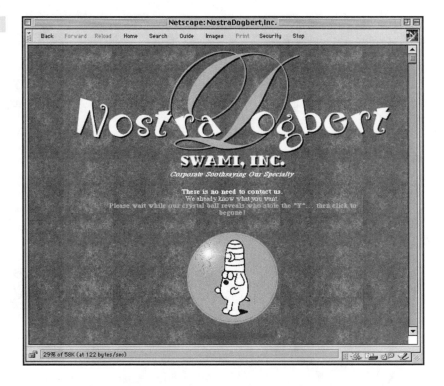

Upon solving the mystery, participants still had to register themselves with Yahoo!'s then-new personalized Web guide, My Yahoo!, to be eligible to win the sweepstakes. In all, nearly 200,000 visitors followed the contest links to Big Yellow's site, and 41,000 registered with My Yahoo!

Oh, in case you're wondering, it was Dilbert's pointy-haired boss who stole the "Y" for no particular reason.

Yoyodyne: Instant Internet Millionaire

Online game company Yoyodyne Entertainment came up with a good way to attract attention for their client, the WebCrawler search engine: give away a million dollars. Best of all, it didn't cost Yoyodyne or Web-Crawler a dime.

"We looked at the way sweepstakes work in the conventional world," said Jerry Shereshewsky, VP of marketing and business development at Yoyodyne. "There are many consumers who believe they will increase their odds of winning by entering the maximum number of times allow-able. If the rules say you can enter 150 times, there are people out there who will enter 150 times. So we figured, if people will make multiple entries, why don't we make that part of sweepstakes? But instead of let-ting them make multiple entries willy-nilly, let's make them go visit a sponsor's site."

Figure 7.5

If only life were so easy for the rest of us.

The result was the "Million Dollar Webcrawl," the first time Internet sponsors were able to pay a fixed price just for the visitors who clicked through to their sites. (Pay-per-clickthrough ad pricing models are now relatively common, as we'll discuss in detail in Chapter 9, "Paid Media: The Many Faces of Web Advertising.")

Contestants who visited the promotion's page on WebCrawler found a list of links to participating sponsors' sites. To enter, contestants had to visit those sponsors' sites and find the contest logo at each one. By clicking the logo, the contestant arrived at a page where she could enter her email address, thereby entering herself in the sweepstakes. Every additional site she visited increased her odds of winning. With more than 20 sponsors, some of whom had multiple logos on their sites, a contestant had the chance to submit her name nearly 100 times, and many did.

Sponsors paid 50 cents or less for each visitor who clicked through to their sites. Most contestants didn't just arrive at the sponsors' sites and click immediately on the contest logo, though. According to Mr. Shereshewsky, the average contestant visited 3.5 pages of each sponsor's site, making it a cost-effective way for sponsors to introduce their sites to the sweepstake's players.

More than 500,000 people entered the contest, submitting approximately 2.5 million entries. The 50 cents per visit thus covered the $1 million prize money.

WebCrawler and Yoyodyne gained huge publicity for the contest, the results of which were covered by TV news stations, newspapers, and magazines across the country. And Ray Burns, a 30-year army veteran from Lancaster, PA, is now $1 million richer.

Yoyodyne has since continued the format of the contest as a regular feature on its site, called "Get Rich Click."

"It's not the U.S. mint yet, but it's getting there," said Mr. Shereshewsky of the ongoing contest's earning potential for Yoyodyne. The company now awards only $100,000 to winners, but it still receives the same number of entrants. "We discovered that while $1 million sounds great to people, a hundred grand isn't so bad either," Shereshewsky said.

Figure 7.6

$100,000 might not make you exactly rich, but it would probably settle the Visa bill. Not bad for a few clicks' work.

Amazon: The Greatest PR Coup Ever Held

One of the best online promotions to date has been Amazon.com's "Greatest Story Ever Told" contest. Locked in a high-stakes battle with Barnes and Noble for online bookseller supremacy, Amazon.com scored big points with this interactive writing contest.

In a major coup, Amazon.com enlisted the help of Pulitzer Prize-winning author John Updike in the contest. For a $5,000 honorarium, Amazon.com commissioned Updike to write the first paragraph of a story, which he titled "Murder Makes The Magazine," about a mild-mannered Miss Tasso Polk who notices an unusual man in the elevator as she arrives at work one morning at a magazine called simply *The Magazine*. For 44 days in August and September of 1997, Amazon.com invited Updike-wannabes to put their talent to the test and advance the story one paragraph at a time.

Each day's author, chosen from the submissions by a panel of Amazon.com editorial staffers, was awarded $1,000 and the honor of sharing a byline with one of the greats of contemporary literature. At the end of the contest, Updike stepped back in to provide a masterly wrap-up of the outlandish murder mystery that had unfolded over the course of the event.

"Mr. Updike was phenomenal to work with," said Kay Dangaard, director of media relations, who played a large role in organizing the contest. "He hadn't kept up with the story at all during the contest. On the last day, I sent him the entire story. Within 2-1/2 hours, he sent back his conclusion. He's some writer."

Figure 7.7

Sometimes it takes more than luck to win online. Amazon.com asked contestants to write like Pulitzer Prize-winner John Updike.

One lucky winner, drawn at random on the last day of the contest from among the 380,000 who submitted paragraphs for the story, was awarded a cool $100,000.

On average, 8,500 people entered the writing competition each day. On the most active single day, more than 18,800 writers submitted entries. Bleary-eyed Amazon staffers worked around the clock to review submissions for the six weeks of the contest, giving each entry an average 30-second read.

The objective of the contest was brand recognition for Amazon.com, who spent nearly $150,000 in prize money alone on the contest. As *The Washington Post* noted in an editorial about the contest, it was a publicity bonanza for the bookseller. According to Ms. Dangaard, the contest received write-ups in nearly 300 prestigious outlets, including *The New York Times, The Washington Post, Newsweek, People, The New Yorker* (written by Mr. Updike himself), the front page of *USA Today*, television's *Today Show*, and other leading news media around the world.

"You can't buy publicity like that," Ms. Dangaard said.

AT&T: Putting the Brand in Consumers' Hands

AT&T launched a promotion in the spring of 1997 that aimed not only to boost its online presence but to help it gain market share in collect calls, a key area of the telecom market that rival MCI dominates with a 60% share. With the help of Modem Media Advertising, the interactive arm of True North Communications, AT&T developed a contest named "Win Thing" (obviously the result of some late-night brainstorming).

Players first encountered Win Thing in the form of an AT&T banner with the curious call to action, "Don't Click Here." Thanks to a Java trick, curious surfers needed only to pass their cursors over the banner for a small browser window to pop up and automatically download a Shockwave game in the form of a telephone keypad. Players were then instructed to take their best shot at typing AT&T's collect calling number, 1-800-CALL-ATT, five times as fast as they could.

Figure 7.8

A little reverse psychology just might do the trick, with the help of Java.

The game, which users could play with even while disconnected from the Internet, selected the player's best time and uploaded it to AT&T's game site to be entered in a daily competition. For the four weeks of the competition, each day's fastest dialer won a pair of Ray-Ban sunglasses.

Figure 7.9

Gen-Xers who competed for Ray-Bans in this AT&T contest won't likely forget what number to call when phoning Dad for emergency rent (or beer) money.

AT&T wanted to aim the promotion at 16-to-24-year-olds, the mainstay of the collect-calling market, so Modem Media placed the banners on sports, gaming, and music sites, as well as search engines. In all, more than 240,000 people downloaded the game. Of those, more than 10,000 entered the competition, and many more probably experimented with the application, achieving AT&T's actual goal of having them practice dialing the 1-800 number.

Silicon Graphics WebFORCE MediaBase: Screaming Streaming

The goal of holding a contest isn't always to get the most entries possible. Silicon Graphics, a company known for high-performance Internet serving, asked USWeb to come up with a promotion to drum up sales leads for WebFORCE MediaBase 2.0, a server software package that helps manage rich content, such as video or audio, on the Web. USWeb recommended a sweepstakes dubbed "Screaming Streaming," in which the lucky winner would be awarded the server software and a Silicon Graphics computer to run it on.

The price of the software and hardware package was around $15,000, so Silicon Graphics wasn't eager to give the prize away to any kid who submitted his email address. In this case, getting several thousand entries in the contest would have been a failure.

The account team set out to monitor professional discussions on news-groups and mailing lists pertaining to streaming video and audio, corporate intranets, and particular industries that might benefit from the product, such as long-distance education, library information services, and hospital administration. After lurking on the discussions for a couple of days, we then sent private emails to selected forum participants with consumer surveys in exchange for T-shirts, further assuring ourselves that typical forum members closely matched the demographics of prospective WebFORCE MediaBase customers. Only after thoroughly vetting each forum this way did we post announcements about the contest to the discussion groups.

On the contest pages, we asked entrants a series of questions to further qualify themselves as potential sales leads: What positions did they hold within their organizations? Were they currently working on a rich-media Web project within a near time frame? What size budget did they control? We also asked them whether they'd like to be contacted by a Silicon Graphics salesperson in the future.

At the heart of the contest was an essay question. The contest page showed a photo of a woman seated in front of a computer with her hair blowing back as if by the intensity of the content on her screen. We asked entrants to describe in 50 words or less how they would use WebFORCE MediaBase to create such a powerful Web experience. By picking the winner subjectively, we could consider not only the quality of the writing, but also which entrant might provide the best publicity value.

In the end, 458 people entered the competition, of whom approximately 15% met all of Silicon Graphics's qualifications for good sales leads. The winner we chose was a computer administrator at Notre Dame University's library who would otherwise not have had the budget to buy the system.

Silicon Graphics and WebFORCE are registered trademarks of Silicon Graphics.

Online Events

After free stuff, the most popular motivation for your average American to visit a Web site is probably the chance to chat with celebrities. Live online chats with heroes of TV, film, and pop music are more common today than appearances on Letterman and Leno. And easier to manage, too.

In the early days of celebrity chat, much effort was made to sit the stars down in front of a computer terminal as chatters around the world suffered through their hunt-and-peck replies. Today, the typical celebrity chat barely interrupts brunch at the latest Beverly Hills hotspot, with the stars doing their part by cell phone while speed-typists transcribe their replies, hangovers barely an issue.

Jefferson Cybership: Everything Old Is New Online

How is an aging hippie band without Paul McCartney's artistry or the Rolling Stones' enduring sex appeal supposed to stay relevant in the '90s? Why, jump on the Internet, of course.

That's what brought Jefferson Starship to USWeb Marin's door in 1995. For a band that wags had begun calling Jefferson Wheelchair, a modern makeover was required to prevent them from fading into the obscurity of garage-sale record bins.

The band's existing sci-fi image, since its earlier transformation from Jefferson Airplane to Jefferson Starship, lent it some affinity to a portion of the Net's early adopters. To leverage that foothold, USWeb worked with the band to create the most spectacular live concert the Net had seen up until that time.

The band staged a concert at San Francisco's Maritime Hall, calling itself Jefferson Cybership for the one-time event. Although bands before them had already used Internet technology to broadcast live, none had tried to tie together so many different kinds of technologies.

For the Cybership performance, USWeb coordinated live video and sound streaming using Xerox PARC's IP Multicast Backbone (MBone), a high-speed Internet channel that allowed real-time transmission of high-bandwidth applications like video streaming. We also used Cornell University's CU-SeeMe video conferencing technology and Xing MPEG audio and video, which were accessible to a wider audience than the higher-quality MBone. Beyond that, chatters could talk with band members and follow a live onstage commentary on the Web's RockNet site, as well as on CompuServe and America Online.

Figure 7.10

Wouldn't you love somebody to still vaguely remember? A few on the Net still do.

The event was a big hit. The respective servers for all the various technologies quickly reached their user capacity and several of them crashed, which was the definitive standard of success for an online event in the early days on the Web.

In a terrific example of creative online promotion, a little-known but technically savvy band called Severe Tire Damage reserved access to the MBone channel for the two hours immediately preceding the Jefferson Cybership concert. Although they never shared a physical stage with the legendary '60s band, Severe Tire Damage still claimed the honor of being the opening act for Jefferson Starship.

Today, typing "Jefferson Starship" into a search engine turns up legions of fan sites across the Web, so perhaps the band found the younger audience they were looking for. Unfortunately, they did little to follow through on that momentum. The site that USWeb built for the band,

www.jstarship.com, is now defunct. On the other hand, Severe Tire Damage is still pushing the envelope of the online music experience, even if few people have noticed.

Star Trek: The Online Frontier

If ever there was a topic that netizens could feel passionate about, *Star Trek* is it. Although scientific research on the topic is lacking, it seems likely that 70–80% of early Internet adopters were weaned on the sci-fi TV classic. Incredibly, a whole generation of Trekkies—anyone age 29 or under—is younger than the series itself.

When Paramount asked USWeb to help promote the online activities for the *Star Trek* 30-year anniversary celebrations, we figured it would be a piece of cake. In November 1996, Paramount was staging the two-day *Star Trek* convention to beat all *Star Trek* conventions in Huntsville, Alabama, dubbed "One Weekend On Earth." Stars from all four *Star Trek* TV series would attend: the original show, *The Next Generation*, *Deep Space Nine*, and *Voyager*.

Figure 7.11

Just what the world needs, another spaced-out lawyer.

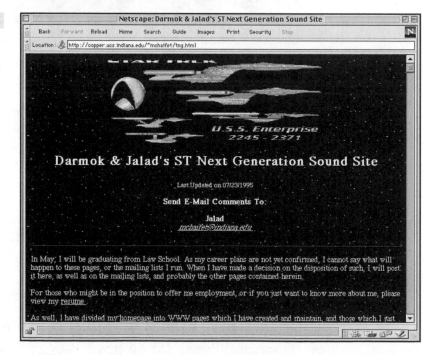

To coincide with the event, Paramount was preparing an online extravaganza featuring constantly updated convention news, streaming audio and video feeds, and interactive chats with cast members.

The studio complicated things for us, however, with some special conditions. First, in a cross-promotion deal that Paramount worked out with Microsoft, the online activities would be available only to subscribers of the Microsoft Network. The event was to be a special promotion to gain new subscribers to the network.

And then Paramount's lawyers weighed in, saying that we couldn't contact any of the hundreds, if not thousands of unofficial *Star Trek* fan sites to help promote the event. Paramount considered all of the unofficial sites to be in violation of its copyright. Asking them to alert their readers of the MSN event would have meant legitimizing them and compromising Paramount's position in any potential future legal actions against them.

Our first tactic was to turn to our old friends, the newsgroups and mailing lists. Luckily, there are *lots* of newsgroups and mailing lists devoted to *Star Trek*, and many of the Webmasters for the *Star Trek* Web sites participate in them. As a result, we ended up getting a fair amount of voluntary publicity from the affinity Web sites anyway.

Being the fanatic breed they are, Trekkies' discussion groups can be extremely specific and passionately devoted. So much so that we found a willing volunteer in alt.startrek.klingon to translate our announcement into the Klingon language for posting in that newsgroup. (Yes, believe it or not, there is a well-developed Klingon language, composed by linguist Marc Okrand for scenes in the third *Star Trek* movie. Mr. Okrand later published *The Klingon Dictionary* with Pocket Books, which in turn spawned the Klingon Language Institute (**www.kli.org**), now with more than 1,000 members.)

In addition to promoting the event in online communities, USWeb also contacted dozens of cyber-cafes around the country and asked them to help publicize the event to their customers. Almost all were happy to oblige. We sent them specially designed posters announcing the online anniversary, which they hung on the walls by their computers.

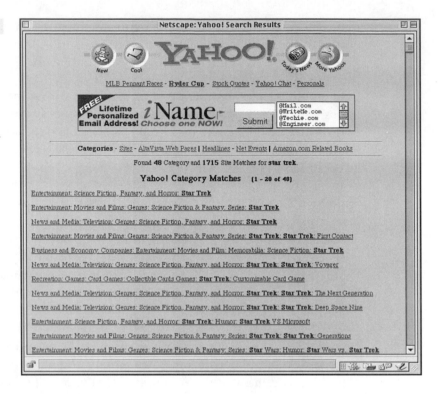

Figure 7.12

Despite the abundance of Star Trek sites online, we had to work around them in our Web promotion.

Both Paramount and the Microsoft Network were delighted with the response they got. The online event received thousands of visitors, and Microsoft signed up hundreds of new users who joined the network specifically to participate in the event.

Mailing Lists

Some marketers have realized that instead of trying to drive surfers to their Web sites, it is sometimes easier to drive their Web sites to the surfers. Hence, the whole concept of *push technology*.

Email is the original and most enduring push technology. For all the hype in late 1996 and early 1997 surrounding push technology—the ability for publishers to "push" content directly to end users instead of waiting for them to "pull" it from Web sites—the trend has so far failed to gain much popular momentum with consumers beyond the category's pioneer, PointCast.

Part of the problem has been the lack of a standard application for consumers. To receive push content from various publishers, end users have been required to download incompatible client applications from a variety of different companies, including BackWeb, First Floor, inCommon, Individual, InterMind, Marimba, NetDelivery, Wayfarer, and others.

Push may experience a second wind with the recent introduction of standardized push platforms bundled as part of Netscape Communicator (NetCaster) and Microsoft Internet Explorer 4.0 (Active Desktop). However, the early versions of both of those push platforms, as well as PointCast, more or less require users to have constant Internet access through high-speed connections. Although the technology may hold promise for business-to-business applications, it still seems seriously handicapped for general consumer marketing in the near future.

The one exception to this may be HTML-compliant email. Recent versions of most of the popular email applications enable email to be formatted in HTML so that messages can be displayed as Web pages, complete with graphics.

Which brings us back to the point that email is the original push technology. Although few marketers have used push applications successfully for consumer marketing much beyond simple sports or stock tickers, thousands of companies have found that maintaining an email mailing list is an excellent way to keep users engaged with the brand without waiting for them to visit the company's Web site.

Global Exposure: Money for Nothing and Clicks for Free

Adam Boettiger operates Global Exposure Internet Marketing out of his home, consulting companies about their online marketing and advertising strategies. He has more prospective work than he can handle, despite the fact that he doesn't pay to advertise his services anywhere. In fact, the only marketing he does conduct for Global Exposure actually earns money for him.

In early 1997, Mr. Boettiger began the Internet Advertising Discussion List, or I-Advertising, a daily interactive discussion forum for Internet marketers delivered via email. Despite the existence of at least three similar advertising discussion lists, I-Advertising secured more than 5,000 subscribers in a matter of a few months. (See the "Resources" sections of Chapter 9 and the Appendix for subscription information for this and other advertising mailing lists.)

The archives for the list, which Mr. Boettiger hosts on his company Web site, get 40–60,000 page views a month. The list generates around 15–20 submissions a day. Mr. Boettiger, acting as moderator, filters out advertising spam and other inappropriate submissions, reducing the count to 10–12 messages that he forwards to subscribers.

"As far as marketing tools go, mailing lists are one of the best branding mechanisms I've seen on the Internet," said Mr. Boettiger. "After you set up your business on the Net, you establish a related discussion list, distributed free by email, that would be well-received by same target market you're trying to reach with your business. The idea is, you visit my Web site once, and from there afterwards my Web site visits you."

Global Exposure's name and Web site URL appears in several places at the top and bottom of each list message, in the context of a brought-to-you-by notice, instructions for subscribing and unsubscribing from the list, the location of the archives, and so on. Mr. Boettiger also frequently participates in the discussions. As a result he has gained tremendous name recognition among the readers, who are typically vice presidents of sales and marketing at companies worldwide.

Not only does the list bring him money indirectly by generating business leads, but it pays him cash on the barrelhead via advertising. Given the list's high-quality readership, he's able to charge $35 per thousand impressions for a few lines of text advertising in daily submissions of the list. This works out to more than $500 per week. After the $100 a month he pays the RevNet service to operate the software that distributes the messages, that's not bad money for the hour a day it takes him to act as moderator of the list.

"I'm profiting from a branding mechanism that's generating business for me," he said.

Figure 7.13

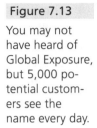

You may not have heard of Global Exposure, but 5,000 potential customers see the name every day.

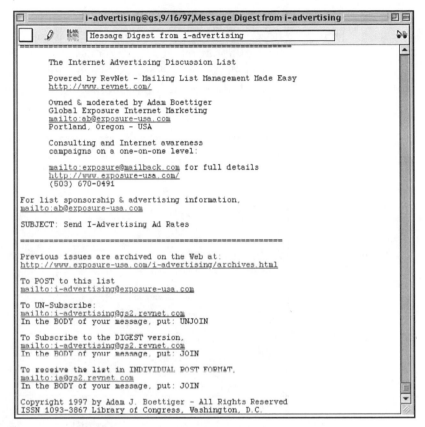

```
┌─────────────────────────────────────────────────────────────────────┐
│ □          i-advertising@gs,9/16/97,Message Digest from i-advertising □ ⊟│
├─────────────────────────────────────────────────────────────────────┤
│ □    ⬓  ▤▤▤   │Message Digest from i-advertising                │    🔊│
│                                                                        │
│ ========================================================               │
│   The Internet Advertising Discussion List                            │
│                                                                        │
│   Powered by RevNet - Mailing List Management Made Easy                │
│   http://www.revnet.com/                                               │
│                                                                        │
│   Owned & moderated by Adam Boettiger                                  │
│   Global Exposure Internet Marketing                                   │
│   mailto:ab@exposure-usa.com                                          │
│   Portland, Oregon - USA                                               │
│                                                                        │
│   Consulting and Internet awareness                                    │
│   campaigns on a one-on-one level:                                    │
│                                                                        │
│   mailto:exposure@mailback.com for full details                       │
│   http://www.exposure-usa.com/                                        │
│   (503) 670-0491                                                      │
│                                                                        │
│ For list sponsorship & advertising information,                       │
│ mailto:ab@exposure-usa.com                                           │
│                                                                        │
│ SUBJECT: Send I-Advertising Ad Rates                                  │
│                                                                        │
│ ========================================================               │
│                                                                        │
│ Previous issues are archived on the Web at:                           │
│ http://www.exposure-usa.com/i-advertising/archives.html              │
│                                                                        │
│ To POST to this list                                                  │
│ mailto:i-advertising@exposure-usa.com                                │
│                                                                        │
│ To UN-Subscribe:                                                      │
│ mailto:i-advertising@gs2.revnet.com                                  │
│ In the BODY of your message, put: UNJOIN                              │
│                                                                        │
│ To Subscribe to the DIGEST version,                                   │
│ mailto:i-advertising@gs2.revnet.com                                  │
│ In the BODY of your message, put: JOIN                                │
│                                                                        │
│ To receive the list in INDIVIDUAL POST FORMAT,                        │
│ mailto:ia@gs2.revnet.com                                             │
│ In the BODY of your message, put: JOIN                                │
│                                                                        │
│ Copyright 1997 by Adam J. Boettiger - All Rights Reserved            │
│ ISSN 1093-3867 Library of Congress, Washington, D.C.                 │
└─────────────────────────────────────────────────────────────────────┘
```

Yoyodyne: A Personal Voice with a Corporate Agenda

Yoyodyne Entertainment takes a different tack with its mailing list. Instead of a discussion forum, it simply publishes a weekly newsletter for readers.

As far as company newsletters go, Yoyodyne Entertainment News has a pretty informal feel. Its editor, Wendy Hall, writes about whatever the heck she's thinking about each week: her cat got sick; she's been having trouble sleeping; she's secretly been taking stand-up comedy classes.

"It's not very corporate," she says, which is an understatement. "It's just me babbling most of the time. Other people here [at Yoyodyne] or from elsewhere send me stuff. Anything I like, I'll put it in."

Basically, it reads like a Gen-X angst report. The mishmash of items also includes a horoscope and a surprisingly sincere advice column answering readers' questions about relationship troubles and the like. Oh yeah, and it also contains updates on new games, which happens to be Yoyodyne's business, although the prosaic job of promoting the company definitely takes a back seat.

Figure 7.14

Find out the latest news about Wendy's cats and other breaking developments at Yoyodyne.

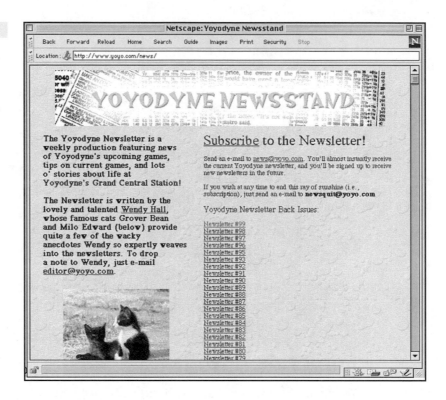

But it seems to have struck a chord. With virtually no promotion, the newsletter presently has more than 30,000 subscribers.

"The first week we had 10 subscribers," Ms. Hall said. "I think all 10 of them wrote me afterwards. It's funny, it was very intimate. It continued like that first six months, when there were probably a few hundred readers. It's grown solely through word of mouth, people forwarding it to their friends."

A newsletter that takes her three to four hours a week to prepare has been a great source of brand awareness for the company. Many first-time visitors to Yoyodyne's site say that they discovered the game company through the newsletter, forwarded by a friend.

URL-biquity

The cheapest way to promote your site is to print your URL on *everything* associated with the company. For the fraction of a cent it costs for a line of ink, your URL should be on corporate business cards, letterhead, and brochures. Put it on the sides of product packaging and in all advertisements, be they print, TV, radio, direct mail, whatever.

And where would new media marketing be without the age-old marketing tool of tchotchkes (Yiddish for knickknacks)? Print your URL on the pens, bottle openers, and stress balls you already hand out at conventions. From there, see how creative you can get.

Web Fuel: The URL-iously Strong Mint

New York-based World Packaging Corporation, a specialty food supplier, may be the only food producer to sell online advertising space on its products.

Cofounder Amy Katz explained that she and partner Donna Slavitt saw the popularity of Altoids, "the curiously strong mint" from England, especially among workers in the high-tech industry. They decided they could get a piece of that digerati market by styling their mints specifically to it.

"In the Internet arena, there aren't many tangible products," Ms. Katz said.

Capitalizing on this, in the summer of 1997 World Packaging introduced Web Fuel, a tin of triangular mints specially formulated by a Swiss confectioner. Besides the mint's appealing taste, the product immediately stands out due to its tin, which is shaped like a computer mouse.

Figure 7.15

Powerful branding and fresh minty taste!

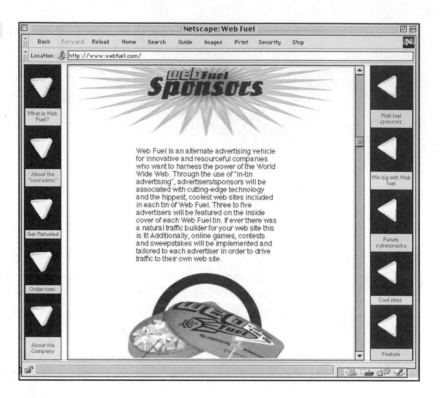

For a fee comparable to a magazine's ad rates, companies can print their URLs on the inside of the candy's lid. World Packaging charges $5,000 for an ad in 50,000 tins, with spots for three ads per tin. Among the first companies to try the unusual ad medium were Talk City, Amazon.com, and AudioNet.

Ms. Katz said the candies were selling swiftly in specialty food stores, cyber-cafes, computer stores, and other outlets.

ZapWorks: Drink, Think, and Link

ZapWorks is a San Francisco-based company that's figured out a clever, non-electronic way to get advertisers' URLs in front of netizens while they're surfing. The firm sells advertisements to companies like Yahoo!, Lycos, and Apple, displaying them on mouse pads that it sends to cyber-cafes around the world for free. The company resupplies the cyber-cafes with new advertiser mouse pads each month.

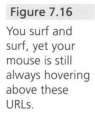

Figure 7.16

You surf and surf, yet your mouse is still always hovering above these URLs.

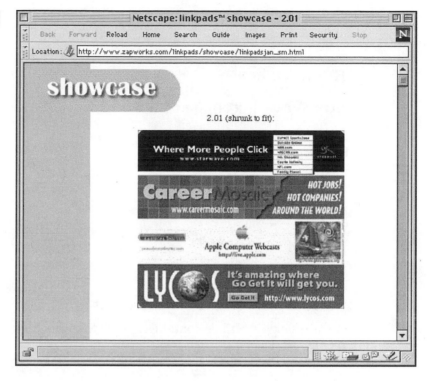

"The cafes love it," said Mark Dolly, president of ZapWorks. "From their point of view, the mouse pads encourage users to stay on their computers longer by giving them new ideas of where to surf. At the end of each month, they can give the old mouse pads away to customers, which makes everyone happy."

ZapWorks fits four ads on each mouse pad, and charges advertisers $7,500 for around 7,000 pads per month.

Resources

Contest Indices

Yahoo! on Contest Indices

http://www.yahoo.com/Entertainment/
Contests__Surveys__Polls/

This section of Yahoo! shows dozens of sites that specialize in the latest online contests.

Huron Online

http://www.huronline.com

High-traffic sweepstakes-listing site.

Volition

http://www.volition.com

The oldest free-stuff site on the Net. High quality and lots of traffic.

Beth's Sweepstakes

http://rapidnet.com/~tiger/sweeps.htm

An amateur site with current, high-profile contests eager for submissions from contest organizers.

Brian's Free Stuff Home Page

http://come.to/freestuff

Another amateur site with current, high-profile contests eager for submissions from contest organizers. Gets lots of visitors.

Online Events

Yahoo Net Events

http://events.yahoo.com/

The most influential events-listing online. Good luck getting listed because the competition's fierce.

Netguide

http://www.netguide.com/Happenings

CMP's events listing.

Yack

http://www.yack.com

"The ultimate guide to Internet chat."

Mailing List Tools

RevNet

http://www.revnet.com

One of the most affordable and efficient services to outsource the management of mailing lists.

Cyber-Cafes

Yahoo! on Cyber-Cafes

http://www.yahoo.com/Society_and_Culture/Cyberculture/
Internet_Cafes/

A starting point for listings of cafes as well as indices and associations of cyber-cafes.

Global Computing Cyber Cafes

http://www.globalcomputing.com/cafes.html

A list of 100 or so U.S.-based cyber-cafes.

CyberiaCafe

http://www.cyberiacafe.net

An index specializing in European and Asian cyber-cafes.

Cyber InterCaptive

http://www.clearlight.com/~kireau/cafe.shtml

A cyber-cafe search engine.

Macromedia: Realizing Visions of Success

M acromedia came to USWeb's Audience Development Group with a classic marketing challenge: to build fast awareness of a new product. Together, we came up with a sweepstakes promotion that served both to publicize the new product to its target audience and to gain valuable market research for Macromedia's development and sales teams.

Although Macromedia's award-winning development products, such as Director and Flash, were already well-known to Web designers at the end of 1997, the company was then preparing to enter into an unfamiliar product category with Dreamweaver, an HTML authoring tool. The product effectively pioneered a whole new type of product, combining the convenience of a graphical Web design program with the control of a text-based HTML code editor. Nonetheless, it had to contend with competitive "mindshare" from a dozen existing HTML editors, including the well-established likes of Microsoft FrontPage, Netscape Navigator Gold, and Adobe PageMill.

Rather than waiting for the product release and trying to gain brand recognition through user testimonials and press reviews, Macromedia sought to create a substantial buzz about Dreamweaver among developers prior to its availability. Having heard of USWeb's Audience Development Group through other satisfied clients, Don Marzetta, Macromedia's director of marketing, put the challenge to us like this:

"We really had three goals for this promotion," he said. "To build advance interest in an unannounced product; to gain user input on what qualities they were seeking in such a product and validate that we were on track with the product's key features; and to generate sales leads."

Delivering Convenience with Confidence

Dreamweaver's principal breakthrough is that it overcomes a major shortcoming of other graphic Web editors on the market. Namely, they rob the designer of control over the page code by inserting nonstandard HTML instructions generated by the program. Although other graphical editors provide conveniences such as drag-and-drop positioning of images—whereas positioning images in straight HTML code is an often tedious matter of trial and error, substituting numbers in tables until the right effect is achieved—the resulting source code is often difficult to understand.

If a designer wants to combine the program-generated instructions with his own traditional code, the outcome can be a nightmare, requiring a lot of troubleshooting for software bugs. As a result, many experienced HTML programmers sacrifice the convenience of graphical editors for the reliability of doing it the old-fashioned way.

Dreamweaver delivers the best of both worlds, producing what Macromedia calls *round-trip HTML*. This means that the code generated by the graphical interface appears as standard code, allowing programmers to switch easily back and forth between the text- and graphical-editing environments.

In order to get developers excited about the product, gain their feedback on what other features they'd like to see in such a program, and test the marketing messages, we developed with Macromedia what we called the "Dream Sequence" contest. To attract users to participate in the contest, Macromedia offered prizes such as digital cameras, MPEG (digital video) cameras from Hitachi, and certificates redeemable for $1,000 worth of Macromedia software products.

Figure X3.1

Macromedia invented a new kind of Web editor, allowing *round-trip HTML* coding, and sought a new kind of online publicity to get the word out and gather feedback.

The Dream Theme

"In designing the contest pages, we wanted to stick with the 'dream' concept, given the product's name and the idea that it is a dream come true for Web developers," said Chris Frey, the project director of the account at USWeb. "The pages featured a dreamy look with clouds and soft colors, and we highlighted quotes about dreams from famous writers, such as 'Every dream is a prophecy,' by George Bernard Shaw."

When contestants came to the site, it didn't directly extol the virtues of the product. Rather, it presented them with a series of questions about what kinds of features their dream Web design product would contain. It led them through a series of yes/no questions about whether they'd like to have certain functions that only Macromedia's upcoming product would feature.

"Instead of simply repeating 'Yes' and 'No' for the possible answers, we kept the tone lighthearted with colloquial language, such as 'Yep/Nope,' 'Way/No Way,' 'Hot/Not,' and other slang as replies to the questions," said Mr. Marzetta.

Figure X3.2

With wit and style, we asked contestants whether their dream of the perfect HTML tool would match what Macromedia was preparing to release.

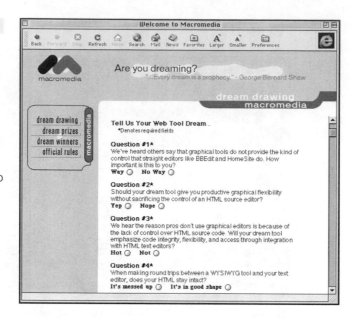

In addition to the yes/no questions, the form allowed entrants to provide additional comments of their own about what they would like to see in such a product. We qualified how many hours a week they spent developing Web pages, what HTML editors they currently used, and, of course, their names and contact information, both so we could contact the winners and for future sales leads. We did let them choose whether they'd like to be contacted when the beta version of the software was available. Over 80% checked Yes.

Separating Dreamers from Schemers

"It was important that we got highly qualified respondents for the survey," said Mr. Frey. "Sheer numbers of contestants was not the goal. Since we were genuinely interested in the survey results as well as in generating strong sales leads, we didn't go to sweepstakes announcement sites to drive traffic. We used our audience development methods to seek out Web developers who spent several hours a week actually working on sites, preferably 15 hours or more."

Accordingly, we focused on three key target audiences: HTML programmers, existing Macromedia product users, and graphic designers, many of whom have added Web design to their traditional desktop publishing skills.

We referred to the contest internally as the "Dream Sequence" because we conducted it in four waves, each a week apart, with different sets of questions and new prizes awarded each time. We invited participants from each round to come back for the following rounds, with renewed chances to win prizes.

In the first round, we simply sent emails to Macromedia's extensive base of users. In all, that was more than 140,000 potential contestants, of whom nearly 20,000 participated.

Figure X3.3

USWeb's Michael Sheehan sent letters to editors of selected sites, like this one to the MacDirectory, encouraging them to promote the contest. Most were happy to oblige.

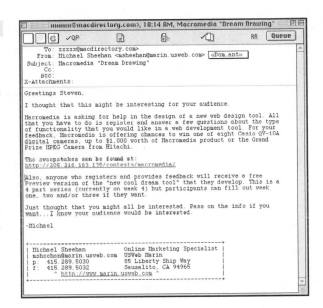

In the second wave, we concentrated on Mac users and HTML programmers. Although Mac users make up only 30–40% of Dreamweaver's overall target market of site developers, they are a passionate user group who frequently drive the adoption of leading products on the Windows platform, such as the formerly Mac-only packages Photoshop, Illustrator, and Macromedia's own Director. To reach them, we sent emails to the editors of more than a dozen leading Mac-oriented Web sites and newsletters, such as Mac Addict, TidBits, Mac Central, and others. About two-thirds of these sites announced the contest to their readers, from which word spread further to other smaller sites and forums. For HTML programmers, we again targeted leading sites and newsletters, as well as several relevant newsgroups such as alt.html.writers and comp.infosystems.www.authoring.html. About 5,000 highly qualified contestants responded to this wave of announcements.

In the third week, we broadened the target audience. We sent announcements of the contest to general Internet news sites and posted to a select few sweepstakes sites. We received more entrants for this round, but on average they were less qualified, spending less time coding per week and using mostly the low-end competitive products. Dreamweaver is targeted at professional designers, not hobbyists.

The last round focused again on HTML programmers, plus graphic designers, targeting the sites and discussion groups frequented by those audiences.

Figure X3.4.

The grand prize of an MPEG camera made digital designers' mouths water.

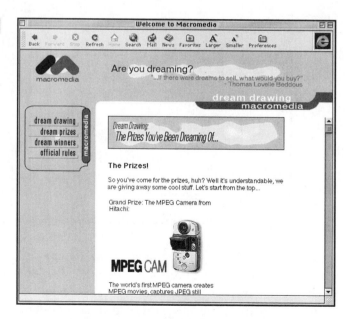

When Dreams Become Reality

"We were quite satisfied with the results of the promotion," said Macromedia's Mr. Marzetta. "It was great for developing interest and leads.

We had about 5,000 people a week participate, and they were highly qualified, so it was definitely well worth the money."

"The promotion achieved all of the set marketing goals," Mr. Marzetta said.

"For us, it was unique way to develop leads and interest for something that wasn't even introduced yet," he said. "We wanted to get a real head start on the publicity. It also verified some of our thinking. For example, when I was about to purchase advertising, it was interesting to see the number of people with certain platforms of computers so I knew how to target my ad messages."

Most importantly, the contest was valuable market research, confirming that the target users indeed were seeking the unique features that the program delivers.

"Most of the contestants were very qualified developers, about 50% of them doing more than 15 hours a week of HTML development," Mr. Marzetta said. "They pretty much endorsed every feature we asked about. About nine out of 10 of them really wanted all the features we had planned."

For example, one question in the fourth round of the contest got right to the heart of the product's competitive advantage: "We hear the reason pros don't use graphical editors is because of the lack of control over HTML source code. Will your dream tool emphasize code integrity, flexibility, and access through integration with HTML text editors?"

"Ninety-nine percent of the respondents answered 'Yes,' so we knew we had hit the nail right on the head," Mr. Marzetta said.

Taking the promotion to the next level, Macromedia hosted Dreamweaver parties in five cities with major Web-development communities—New York, Boston, Chicago, Los Angeles, and San Francisco—and invited local entrants from the contest who had said they spent more than 25 hours a week coding.

"We did a lot of integrated things to create a buzz," Mr. Marzetta continued. "Between this, the press tour, and the launch of the beta product, by the time we shipped the product at the New York Internet World trade show in December, there was so much buzz we had twice as many leads as we had expected. At our Internet World booth, there were crowds of people wanting to hear about it. Word of mouth had begun to spread, and great press articles started showing up. It was one of those situations where everyone knew what the product was very quickly. The Dream Sequence was definitely part of that."

Figure X3.5

Strong press reviews like this one, combined with the contest and other audience development strategies, created a powerful buzz about the product by the time it was available for sale.

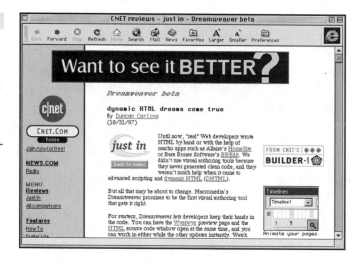

At the prestigious Internet World show, Dreamweaver won the Best of Show award for the category "Outstanding Web Development Software Product." Sales of the product have been brisk ever since.

Maybe George Bernard Shaw exaggerated when he said, "Every dream is a prophecy," but with the right strategies, some marketers' dreams can come true.

Media Savoir-Faire: Public Relations for a Digital Age

A properly executed PR campaign can be among the most valu able means of building an audience for your Web site. Positive press coverage is far more credible to potential customers than any amount of advertising, and getting your URL printed in *USA Today* will drive more traffic to your site than any banner campaign.

The Internet is not so much a mass medium as a massing of media and communities. When you want to reach people en masse, turn to PR. But only if you're going to do it right. It's what we prefer to think of as media savoir-faire.

Most of what's discussed in this chapter applies equally to journalists working in print, broadcast, and radio as it does to the new breed specializing in online publications. All journalists are driven by the same need to generate stories on deadline, and PR helps them meet that need. Journalists in all media have been quick to adopt the Internet for research and communication, which only benefits the PR specialists who are trying to reach them.

The relationship between the media and publicists is a delicate one. Some journalists have a flat-out allergic reaction to "flacks." Most reporters and editors accept that publicists play a significant role in the information food chain, however, and are willing to tolerate them and even occasionally befriend them.

PR is an inherently good idea. Journalists need information about companies. Companies want to give journalists information about themselves. So everybody's happy, right? Not always. The problem lies in the fact that most attempts at PR are so badly executed that journalists despair, setting trash cans under their fax machines and filtering their email to delete all messages from certain company addresses.

The favorite technique of clueless publicists is to send long, badly written press releases, bereft of any genuine news value, to every journalist in their database with no regard for each writer's particular focus. Then, for good measure, they top it off with a follow-up call just when the reporter is on deadline to ask if she's going to write about the announcement. You can guess the answer.

Figure 8.1

This hapless publicist has me on his bulk email list even though this release has nothing to do with what I cover for *Advertising Age,* which is ad management products. Notice that he's addressed the message to himself, while my address is hidden in the blind copy field along with probably hundreds of other journalists.

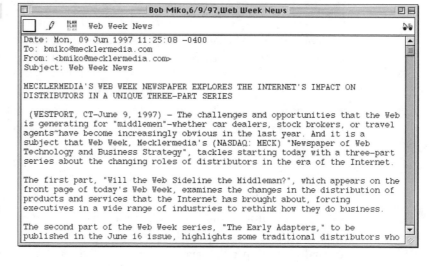

More than anything, good media relations requires time and planning. Marketing managers who decide on a Wednesday that "we have to get this release out by Friday" should just throw their press releases out the window for all the good it does them. Well-executed PR is among the most cost-effective marketing strategies available to any business. Bad PR, however, all too commonly accounts for a tremendous waste of marketing resources.

Understanding the Press

A publicist must empathize with the press. Press rooms are bustling, noisy, and chaotic places. The typical journalist has a phone receiver pinched in his neck while he types frantically into an arcane word processor as colleagues shout to each other across a crowded room above the sound of several ringing phones.

"Jump." "How High?"

That's not to say that most publicists, or for that matter almost all workers in modern America, don't also work under tremendous stress. But in the special symbiotic relationship between journalism and PR, publicists get the short end of the stick. When a journalist calls wanting something, she wants it now. If you succeed in dropping everything and turning the information around immediately, you probably won't get extra points. But you'll definitely lose points if you don't.

The publicist's role is to be a problem-solver, not a problem.

The dynamic between reporters and their sources is essentially one of mutual manipulation. The source wants publicity and is willing to massage the facts and leave out the ugly parts to get coverage. The journalist wants a compelling story and won't regret upsetting some people to get one. When these two objectives overlap, everyone wins. The journalist always has the upper hand in this game, however. Don't think that just because you two were chummy yesterday that your latest misfortune won't look great tomorrow in 36-point type.

With Friends Like These...

Becoming a journalist's trusted source can be your most powerful marketing advantage. Journalists rely far more on their Rolodexes than on press releases to generate stories. But never forget that "off the record" is entirely subjective. Absolutely never *assume* you're speaking off the record. Even if you've explicitly heard your reporter "buddy" agree to those terms, think three times before letting your words slip out if seeing them in print could cost you your job or sink your stock price.

Nor do you have a lot of recourse if you're unhappy about how you've been treated in print. Haranguing the reporter's boss, threatening lawsuits, citing advertiser privilege, or vowing allegiance to the publication's competition will certainly only make matters worse. At best, your company will be ignored forever after; at worst, it'll be subjected to vendetta journalism. As the old saying goes, don't pick a fight with someone who buys ink by the barrel. If absolutely necessary, politely seek a correction. Otherwise, you're probably better off not calling further attention to a damaging story with any follow-up.

Pitches: Personalize, Don't Commoditize

The starting point for any successful PR strategy, as in all aspects of marketing, is to know your audience.

First, identify who will be using your site, which, if you haven't done by this stage in your marketing development, means you're in big trouble. Second, determine which media those customers pay attention to. Just because you're promoting a Web site doesn't necessarily mean that technology and Internet-oriented publications, both print and online, are the place to start (unless your core customers are technologists). Although you, as a site developer and Internet devotee, may live by *Wired*, *News.com*, and *Web Week*, are those the first media your readers turn to? If you run an animal services site, it's possible you may be able to get it covered in *Web Review* if you work hard enough at it. But you'd get better results by devoting the same energy to placing a story with *Dog Fancier* magazine.

Third, and most importantly, find the right journalist at the right publication who will be interested in the story you want to tell. For example,

Walt Mossberg writes an influential technology column for the *Wall Street Journal*. But if you sent him a press release about your fantastic new site for Java developers, or your company's strategic partnership with another industry-leading firm, or your new software that's going to revolutionize corporate computing, count yourself lucky if all he does is ignore you. Mossberg's column is called "Personal Technology," and if your news announcement isn't targeted to personal computer users, he's not going to care about it.

Journalists' most common complaint about publicists, particularly since the advent of email, is being sent press releases that have nothing to do with the topics they cover. Spamming is bad enough when a company's trying to sell a product, but it's a hopeless strategy for gaining media exposure. Although recipients of sales spam have little real recourse, journalists who get annoyed by enough spam PR from the same company can always do a less-than-flattering write-up about that company.

Go to bookstores, libraries, and the Web, and find out for yourself which journalists are actually covering what your customers are reading about. Read their publications regularly, tune into their broadcasts, and bookmark their Web sites.

In most cases, all the contact information you need—phone numbers and email addresses—can be found in the publication's masthead or hot-linked to the author's byline on the Web site. Beginning an email message with, "I really enjoyed your recent story about..." will dramatically increase the chances that the writer will finish reading your message, first of all, and then decide to write about you.

Become a Source

In truth, press releases are among the least-effective ways to get a story written about your company. According to a 1996 MediaSource survey of more than 600 magazine and newspaper business editors, press releases accounted for only 14% of stories, compared to 59% that journalists generated based on their own sources.

Figure 8.2

Even Walt doesn't mind receiving email if you're telling him something he wants to hear.

His email address——

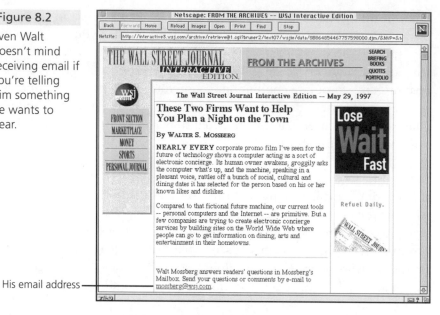

Figure 8.3

MediaSource's third annual online press survey shows that journalists still like to get their stories the old-fashioned way: through their own contacts.

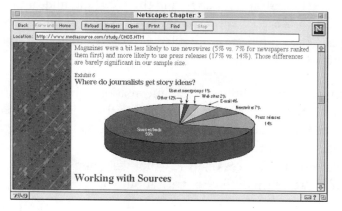

So how do you go about becoming a "source?" First of all, target a reasonable number of publications. Develop an "A" list of not more than 10 publications and a "B" list of another 10 or so. Journalists get their leads from sources they know by name. Unless you're a full-time publicist, you probably won't get to know more than 10 to 20 journalists personally. You may want to develop a "C" list as well, for those to whom you simply send announcements after they're public. But anticipate poorer results from reporters who will know your name primarily as a bulk-emailer of press releases.

The Personal Touch

The best way to find out whether a journalist would be interested in covering your company is to ask.

Plan well ahead of an announcement and simply drop a brief email to the journalist, explaining that your company is going to be making some announcements in the future. Say that you believe, based on your familiarity with the journalist's work, that she is the appropriate contact for your type of company, but you want to confirm that before sending her any unwanted press releases. Keep it to a couple of paragraphs in a friendly, professional tone. Almost without exception, the journalist will be grateful for your direct approach. If she isn't the appropriate contact, she'll likely refer you to whoever is. If she *is* the right one, chances are she'll take the opportunity to ask you a few questions about your company and pending announcements.

How to Find Contact Addresses

Finding email contacts for the press is no great challenge. The first place to look, as we've said earlier, is in the publication. In many cases, print publications will list email addresses for their principal editorial contacts. Online publications almost always do.

Figure 8.4

Computerworld, like many publications online, lists extensive editorial contact information.

You may sometimes find only one main editorial email address. Such a generic address is likely to be read only by a junior staffer. In that case, you're best off asking that your email be forwarded to the journalist you're trying to reach. If you simply email a full press release to such a generic address, your chances of it reaching the appropriate person are slim.

If you can't find a contact's email address through other means, try a name search directory on the Web, such as Four11 or WhoWhere. These services contain the email addresses only of those who have volunteered to be listed, but lots of Web-savvy journalists have done so.

Figure 8.5

Did the *New York Times'* technology reporter Peter Lewis list his email address with the Four11 directory?

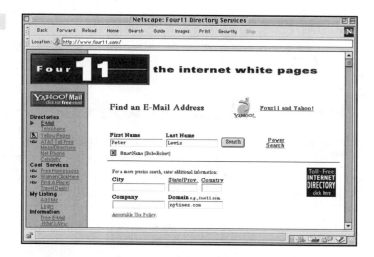

Figure 8.6

Of course he did.

If all else fails, here's a novel idea: call the journalist on the telephone. Use a phone book if necessary, and simply ask to speak with the journalist. When you get her on the line, use the same frank approach, explaining that you want to verify that she's the right reporter to follow your company. And could she please tell you her email address for future reference?

If the front switchboard can't connect you because the writer is a freelancer, or for some other reason, ask to be transferred to the managing editor. Explain briefly why you're trying to contact the writer. If the editor won't give out the writer's personal email address, ask if you can have him forward a message to the writer. The editor will almost certainly oblige.

It's not in journalists' best interest to make themselves hard to reach. They depend on information, and if you're offering information that's useful to them, they and their editors will open the channels to receive it.

Telephone Etiquette

Although email is in most cases the best way to make initial contact with journalists, especially those writing for Web publications, judicious use of the telephone is still an important tool for a publicist even in the digital age.

Here's the golden rule for calling journalists: Begin every call by saying, "Hi, [whoever], am I catching you at a bad time?"

You have immediately made clear to the journalist that you respect her time. If she answers "Yes," follow through on that respect and say, "Can I call back tomorrow?" Quickly agree on a time and hang up. Don't try to squeeze in a fast pitch, unless she explicitly invites you to do so, or you will have blown that trust. Save it for the agreed-upon time. If the journalist really is on deadline, you're too late to pitch to her for the next edition anyway.

If you get a journalist's voice mail, leave a message only once. If it's really urgent, leave that one message and then play "Dialing for Dollars."

Call and call and call until you actually catch her in, and then act casually like it's the first time you picked up the phone since leaving your message. (Pretend you're back in college, trying to get a date.)

Quality Time

Once your A-list journalists know your name, and aren't cursing it, it's important not to be a stranger if you want to be a good source. Don't wait until you have a press release to check in. Touch base once a month or so.

Whoever said "There's no such thing as a free lunch" definitely wasn't a journalist. Forget about sending trinkets along with press releases. No reporter every wrote a story because of a refrigerator magnet. If you really want to bond, get some face time.

If you're in separate cities, find out when (if ever) your A-list reporters are likely to be in town and recommend a get-together. Likewise, plan time to see them when you're in their neighborhood, and keep track of which conferences you're both attending. Although the top reporters at *Business Week* and *The New York Times* may be above the flattery of a classy meal, most hacks are not.

Another way to ingratiate yourself to your A-list press is to feed them hot industry tips. Dirt on a competitor is always a favorite. Don't cry wolf with any old grime. But when you know without a doubt that the CEO of a rival company is on the way out, for example, that's something your best reporter contact would like to have a scoop on. A scoop means an exclusive, of course, so don't mitigate your impact by shopping the same hot tip around to every reporter on your list.

Editorial Calendars

Whenever you have a chance to speak with a journalist, ask what else she's working on to see if you can fit something into a story underway for next week or next month.

Although hearing from a reporter firsthand what stories she's working on is the best way to keep abreast of her activities, many publications also maintain "editorial calendars," which they make available publicly. By perusing the feature stories the publication has committed to covering, you may find some topics that fit well with your company. Some publications post their editorial calendars on their Web pages, while others will fax them to you upon request (ask the editorial assistant to do so, not your key reporter).

Figure 8.7

Computerworld posts its editorial calendar on its Web page.

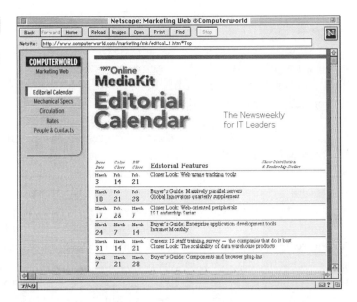

Although such calendars are often useful, they're not 100% reliable. They're usually designed months ahead of time to give advertisers notice of special editions. Often the editors are only dimly aware of the calendar commitments, and it might be challenging to figure out who's in charge of preparing a special feature. Such articles are usually prepared well in advance of the publication's normal deadlines, so concentrate on the opportunities several weeks or months in the future.

Planning News Announcements

Having sufficiently emphasized some avenues for getting recognized in the press, we can now discuss how effectively to use that old PR staple, the news announcement (aka, press release). The point is to avoid overly relying on press releases to get your company exposure in the media. Nonetheless, a well-written, properly disseminated release announcing significant industry news can certainly build awareness.

Timing

The most important factor in a successful news announcement is to allow enough time to prepare properly. Calling a journalist *after* you've issued a press release to make sure she got it is not only the number one pet peeve of most reporters, but it's also too late to have much effect. If the publication has a strong news agenda, the chances of a reporter caring about a press release after it has been publicly issued are slim at best. This is especially true of weekly publications.

Consider it from their point of view. You release your announcement on PR Newswire or Businesswire (see the section "Disseminating Your Press Release" later in the chapter for more on these services), to which thousands of news organizations across the country subscribe. Then you send it by email specifically to the publication you'd most like to see print it. Reuters, Associated Press, and various news Web sites may indeed pick up the release off the wire, if it has genuine news value, and rewrite a story that same day. That means if a daily print newspaper picks up on it, they're already a day behind Reuters, AP, and the news sites. By the time a weekly publication has a chance to print it, the news is already a week old. Don't think that a weekly magazine doesn't view a daily newspaper as competition. They certainly do. And a newspaper feels the same way about a news Web site that can turn a story around in hours instead of a day.

By definition, it's only news while it's new.

The point is, you have to let everyone know to expect the release ahead of time. For weekly publications, this means you have to *pre-brief* the journalists around a week in advance. For dailies (including Web news sites), it's a day in advance. For monthlies, you might as well forget about briefing them on news. Few monthlies even attempt to cover news because they typically finish their editorial production of an issue anywhere from two to five months in advance of publication. Unless you're extremely well-organized and can brief them that far in advance, just send them the release when it's public and concentrate on getting feature and profile coverage from them, instead.

Figure 8.8

No weekly publication wants to cover next week what **News.com** just ran online today.

NDAs and Embargoes

"But if I brief them in advance," you ask, "couldn't they go ahead and publish the news before we've put out our press release?" If what you're really interested in is publicity, that's the least of your worries. The straight answer, though, is yes they could, but they probably won't.

Every journalist is familiar with the concept of a *non-disclosure agreement (NDA)*, or *embargo*. This essentially means that the journalist promises not to release the information until an agreed-upon date, namely when your press release officially goes out on Businesswire or PR Newswire. Although we mentioned earlier that speaking off the record is subjective, most journalists are pretty clear about whether or not they'll honor an NDA. Generally, it's not necessary to have them sign an agreement to that effect, but most would be willing to sign one if you're really paranoid about it.

There are some publications and journalists that refuse to agree to NDAs as a matter of principle, but they're the minority. As long as you don't start giving them the news before you've agreed on an NDA, this shouldn't be a problem. They'll tell you up-front that they don't agree to NDAs, and you can decide at that point to pre-brief them or not accordingly.

Be prepared to share a draft copy of your press release with your A-level journalists when you pre-brief them. Even if the release hasn't completed its rounds of official approvals yet, the journalists will expect to use it as a reference. Clearly label the release as a draft that's subject to non-disclosure. The whole point of a non-disclosure agreement, however, is that it's an *agreement*. Simply writing "NDA" at the top of a draft release and sending it to a journalist who's not expecting it is not an agreement. They now have the news without having made a promise to honor your embargo deadline.

Pre-Briefing in the Online Era

Although pre-briefing the press is a time-honored tradition among publicists, the Internet has complicated that process. In the pre-Web era, there wasn't much a weekly publication could do to scoop your story even if they wanted to, as long as you timed your briefing a week before your announcement date. Now, however, most publications are putting daily news on their Web sites in addition to their weekly print editions and are eager, therefore, for daily scoops.

In most cases, the risk is manageable. Mostly it comes down to being clear with the journalist that your NDA includes the Web site. If a journalist regularly goes around burning her sources, she'll soon have no leads for news, so you can usually count on her word on NDAs. In some cases, however, the journalist may not have ultimate control over that process. A different team of editors may produce the Web site and sneak peaks at the material in the production cycle for the weekly print edition. Ask your journalist contact ahead of time if that's likely to be the case.

Figure 8.9

Advertising Age prides itself on always respecting non-disclosure agreements, relying on companies to give it a heads-up on important announcements.

For some companies the risk of an early news break is too great, so they never pre-brief reporters. This is frequently the case with companies whose stock is publicly traded because they don't want to be accused of not sharing information equally with all investors. This is a viable position for companies prominent in their industries, such as Microsoft or Netscape. Journalists have no choice but to react to these companies' announcements, regardless of whether they were pre-briefed. For most smaller companies out there, however, this isn't a luxury they can afford.

Pitch on Fridays or Mondays

If your A-list includes weekly magazines, officially release your announcements on Mondays. Most weeklies begin their reporting cycle on Fridays and continue collecting news on Mondays and Tuesdays. Wednesdays and Thursdays are the deadline crunch and are the worst days to try to call them. By Friday the cycle starts over, with each edition hitting the streets on Monday. Some magazines come out on other days, such as *Business Week,* which is on newsstands by Friday (despite an official Monday cover date), but those are the exceptions.

When you make initial contact with your A-list reporters, ask them to clarify their deadline schedule and find out the best time to brief them. Again, you'll gain points for expressing consideration for their hectic jobs.

Understand News

The biggest challenge for most PR people is understanding what reporters consider genuinely newsworthy and what they consider fluff. This is generally due to a lack of perspective. Being as close as they are to their firms' daily struggles, many marketing directors, product mangers, and CEOs think the whole world ought to care as much as they do about their company's every success. Save the self-congratulations for the weekly staff meeting. The press will see you as crying wolf if you issue fluff press releases too often.

What *Isn't* News?

All journalists are guided by what is called the "hype detector." With so many mediocre publicists trying to snow the press every day, this is a necessary defense mechanism. When you're evaluating whether or not to issue a release, give it a thorough testing with your own hype-o-meter first.

The following are some common topics that companies think the press should care about, and are then disappointed when they don't.

A New Web Site

This one is a matter of spin. Of course, the launch of a new online service should be a significant news event for most companies. The point is that the novelty of simply launching a Web site hasn't been newsworthy in and of itself since early 1995.

"I tell my clients not to even use the phrase 'Web site' anywhere in their press releases," says Marissa Verson Harrison, a principal at San Francisco-based InterActive Public Relations. "If you open a retail business, it's not news that you have a storefront. It's news that you have a business."

The customer benefit behind the HTML interface needs to be the compelling news story. Find a way to demonstrate that your venture satisfies an important market need, with the Web simply being the most efficient way to deliver it.

Redesigned Site, Upgraded Product

How compelling do you really find the words "new and improved" on a box of detergent or cereal? It's no more convincing as a news message than as an advertising pitch. Significant changes to your venture's business model might make interesting news, but cosmetic changes to your site design aren't even worth a media alert.

Similarly, if you're a software company, don't count on the general media getting excited about your upgrade from a 2.0 product to version 3.0. The computer press might take notice of this, but if your customers are in a non-technical industry segment, the publications that serve them aren't likely to care about the bells and whistles. Extolling theoretical benefits doesn't cut it. The press wants installed users who can talk about results, and not just about a few weeks of limited beta testing.

Staff Appointments

A new CEO is news, but may be a signal that there was something wrong with the old one. It might not be the best news to crow about without a well-considered spin. Unless they're major industry celebrities, your vice presidents, directors, financial officers, and the rest probably don't merit more than a brief in the local daily paper. Some publications do have a "Movers and Shakers" column that you can target, but your A-list reporters will probably value new-hire releases only as background.

Customer Wins

In a capitalist society, companies are in business to win customers. Failing to win customers and going out of business is news. Winning customers is business as usual, not news. Unless the likes of Intel, General Motors, or the White House have standardized on your product, issuing a press release about a "customer win" is unlikely to spark the press's imagination.

What *Is* News?

A good news story needs a hook. It should contain some sense of drama, importance, or righteousness. It may appeal to human interest, local pride, or fascination with celebrity. Or it could click due to humor, surprise, or irony.

The following are some possible news hooks for Web ventures.

Embrace What's Topical

Stage an online event, or introduce a feature on your Web site focusing on something that's already prominent in the news or is destined to become so. For example, you could hold a forum on an important trial, congressional controversy, or foreign event. Or target an upcoming event, such as a holiday, an election, or Black History Month.

Issue a Report

Find a topic related to your site's main theme, conduct a survey, and issue a report on the findings. Being the first to report which percentage of women executives are shopping online, for example, will certainly get you immediate press exposure. Plus your findings are likely to be cited repeatedly over time, and many other sites may link to your survey from their pages. Continue to update the research monthly, quarterly, or annually, and your report could become a perpetual source of exposure for your site. Paying an outside consulting group to actually conduct the research would be money well spent, considering its genuine publicity value.

Rent a Celebrity

It's a sad comment on our society, but almost anything to do with a well-known personality is newsworthy enough to guarantee you some press. Find some way to incorporate a big name into an event on your site, and it's worth a press release.

Form a Strategic Partnership

Unlike winning a customer, partnering with another company can be newsworthy if the union brings a new level of value to your mutual customers or puts you in a stronger competitive position against industry rivals.

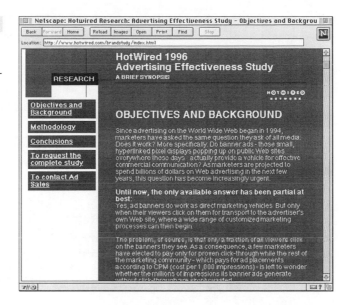

Figure 8.10

HotWired's ad survey, which came to the not-so-surprising conclusion that advertising on its network is effective, is still cited as proof of online advertising's effectiveness more than a year later.

Buck a Trend

The press loves nothing more than controversy. If everyone in the industry is jumping on the same bandwagon, be the first to charge loudly in the opposite direction. The half-life of an online fad is normally a matter of weeks, so editors will tire of the latest overhyped trend quickly and be eager to give voice to someone who disagrees. Just be sure you can stand by your convictions, and don't set a corporate strategy based on a publicity opportunity that later turns out to go against the company's best interest.

Celebrate a Milestone

Don't overdo this idea, but large round numbers are cause for attention. Celebrate your millionth customer, a million page views a month, $10 million in revenue a year, and so on.

Present an Award

Rise above being a mere player and become a judge of industry excellence.

Figure 8.11

Tenagra, an online marketing company, appointed itself the expert on who else deserves recognition.

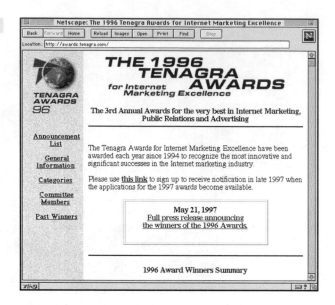

Do Public Good

Join a just cause, such as fighting a disease or raising money for a charity. Team up with organizations such as a mayor's office, a university, or, especially, other media outlets such as a newspaper or TV station, to champion a heart-warming cause. Your contribution could be no more than online promotion, but the event could provide you with substantial goodwill exposure.

Take a Political Stance

Is there a legislative debate affecting your industry? Boldly declare a position. Become a leading proponent of one side.

Co-found an Industry Association

Does your industry need to agree on common standards, or lack a body to represent its interests? Don't let someone else steal the thunder. Act first to get the ball rolling. If the association already exists, run for its top office. Show leadership.

The Model Press Release

The three most important guidelines for writing an effective press release are:

1. Keep it short.

2. Keep it short.

3. Keep it short.

As any journalist can tell you, only one in 10 press releases actually manages to obey these three important rules. "Short" means a maximum of two double-spaced pages, *including* the "About Our Company" boilerplate. For an emailed press release, it means no more than one-and-a-half screens of text. That's about six or seven paragraphs, or 400–500 words.

If you can't say it in that few words, you're not being clear about what you're trying to say. Imagine the journalist who only has room to report the announcement in a two-sentence brief. Is it possible to reduce your news to two sentences, or would you rather not have a newsbrief at all?

If the announcement involves complexities that you feel need a detailed explanation, relegate it to a *white paper* or other supplemental material. Focus on the customer benefit in the news announcement.

There's no question that writing so concisely is difficult. Henry David Thoreau said in a letter to a friend, "Not that the story need be long, but it will take a long while to make it short." All the more reason not to rush the press release process.

Consider that each journalist reading your release probably receives more than 100 email messages a day, the majority of which are other press releases. Every extra paragraph begs her to skip to the next email. If the release is short but compelling, she will call you with further questions as necessary.

Death to Buzzwords

"Robust," "scaleable," "next-generation," "industrial-strength," blah, blah, blah. These sorts of terms are the bane of the high-tech industry. Jargon just makes your announcement sound unoriginal. Decide what you really mean to say and say it.

Similarly, resist hyperbole and superlatives, such as "the first," "the leading," or "revolutionary." Even if they're true, they sound insincere and invite challenge. And don't promise emotions, such as "exciting," "wonderful," or "incredible." Let the press, and ultimately your customers, be the judge of their reactions. Just the facts, ma'am.

Figure 8.12

This company has a broad vision indeed. What the heck does the software actually do, do you suppose?

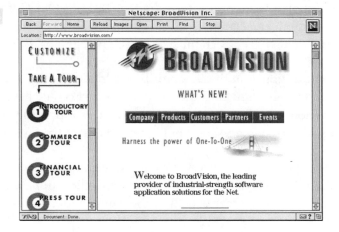

Component Parts

In general, press releases follow a predictable formula. Unlike poets, publicists don't get much creative license. It may seem stifling, but if you want to create art, you're in the wrong profession. If you get too clever with anecdotal, feature-like ledes, journalists may become confused and move on to the next release on the pile. Rules are made to be broken, of course, and we don't want to inhibit the next William Faulkner of PR, but venture forth so advised.

The goal of a release is to communicate the news clearly and directly enough that the journalist can rewrite a short item based entirely on it.

Or at least pique his interest enough to call. Leave the details to interviews, white papers, corporate backgrounders, and other follow-up material.

Headline

In the headline, state the news in as few words as possible, focusing on the customer benefit. Be straightforward, and leave the clever puns to the editors. Follow the Associated Press style rules on grammar, tense, and so on.

A sub-headline is optional. If you opt for one, use it to express a secondary message, not simply to reiterate the same point as the main headline.

Date and Dateline

Don't forget to date the release. A reporter may reference it months from now to note when a certain company event occurred. The tradition of printing "For Immediate Release" at the top of a press release, on the other hand, is fairly redundant and can be ignored. Obviously it's for immediate release once it's made public.

A dateline—that is, the location from which the news was filed—indicates where the company is headquartered, although that same information should be contained at the bottom of the release in the contact information. Often, if a release is issued in conjunction with a conference, the dateline will reflect that location.

(Issuing press releases at industry conferences, however, is rarely a good idea. Many other companies will do the same, and therefore most announcements are lost in the noise. Better to jump the gun and make announcements the week prior to a conference, so the story appears in the publications while all of your competitors are gathered at the event.)

Lede

After the headline, the lede is the most important part of the release, perhaps the only paragraph the journalist will bother to read fully. Imitate news style. Be direct, immediately stating the news while emphasizing the customer benefit. Cover the news basics: who, what, where, when, why, and how.

> **NOTE**
>
> "Lede," by the way, is a peculiar spelling of the word "lead" that's traditionally favored by journalists in this context. The origin, like other strange journalistic spellings such as "graf," "hed," and "folo" (for "follow-up), come from shorthand instructions to typesetters that were intentionally misspelled so they wouldn't accidentally get set into print.

Quotes

Quotes from the company's president, customers, or industry analysts are optional. Make quotes advance the story, not just reiterate what's already been said. Use them to express opinions. Avoid clichés and hollow claims such as, "Our service is a breakthrough that will revolutionize the industry."

Boilerplate

It's standard for a release to contain a brief description of the company and its positioning. This text remains the same for all the company's press releases. Keep it to one or two sentences.

Price and Availability

If applicable, the last section of a release before the contact information should note the price and availability of the product or service. Don't avoid the question of price; journalists will want to know this and won't appreciate having to call just to find out.

Contact Information

Be sure to include contact information at the very bottom of the release. This should include the company's full address and URL, as well as a publicity contact. Include both email address and telephone number for the publicist. You may choose to include a sales department contact as well as a publicist, given that press releases that are broadly issued are likely to end up directly on the screens of potential customers via Web news sites.

Page Numbers

Be sure to number each page on printed copies of the release, and print "- more -" at the bottom of each page. Remove these page markers when formatting the release for email, however.

Abstract

If you're positively unable to limit the release to two pages, use an abstract at the top of the release. When alerting journalists by email, send only the abstract, with a URL where they can find the complete release if they desire.

Media Alerts

When your company feels compelled to make some official announcement for the record, yet you believe it doesn't merit serious news coverage (such as a staff appointment), consider issuing a "media alert." This is a very short item of one to two paragraphs, sent out over PR Newswire or Businesswire, that you don't pitch to any individual press.

An Example of an Effective Press Release

Here's a sample of an effective press release. The subject is genuinely newsworthy. The body of the release is under 500 words. The quotes advance the story and contain the only opinions in the release. The writing style is direct, newsy, and avoids hyperbole and jargon.

> **NOTE**
>
> This press release is only a model. While it purports to announce the launch of this book, it was obviously written before the book's actual availability. If USWeb and I do, in fact, issue a press release along these lines, it may read somewhat differently.

NEW BOOK, "NET RESULTS," BLENDS STRATEGIES WITH TACTICS FOR INTERNET SALES AND PROMOTION
EXPERTS USWEB AND RICK E. BRUNER WRITE DEFINITIVE WEB MARKETING TEXT FOR HAYDEN BOOKS

Sausilito, CA, March 17, 1998—The Audience Development Group of Internet services giant USWeb Corporation (Nasdaq: USWB) and Internet strategist Rick E. Bruner announcedtheir new book today, "Net Results: Web Marketing That Works," published by Hayden Books.

The nine-chapter guide brings together high-level marketing strategies with hands-on tactical methods. It aims to help companies improve sales through intense Web exposure to key audiences. The book goes behind the scenes with leading Net marketers to discuss successes and challenges in online marketing. It includes in-depth case studies with USWeb clients Macromedia, Women's Wire, and Netiva, as well as conversations with Amazon.com, Fingerhut Industries, Lipton, The Internet Shopping Network, Yahoo!, Federal Express, Excite, Tower Records, and many others.

Part I, "Get the Site Right: Web Marketing Fundamentals," focuses on strategic corporate goals, user benefits, and bottom-line return on investment on the Web. It offers important advice on design and choosing an effective domain name. Part II, "Audience Development," delves into the practical details of online promotion. It describes secrets for optimizing search engine results and tells how to leverage newsgroups and other forums without offending Internet norms. It recounts great contests, live events, and other promotions that leading online marketers have used to build site traffic. It also details how to survive in the fast-changing worlds of media relations and advertising in the cyber-age.

"Too many companies arrive to the Web with a 'Field of Dreams' mentality: 'Build it and they will come,'" said Bob Heyman, partner in charge of audience development at USWeb. "Then they're discouraged when visitors don't magically flock to their sites, and they think the Web is over-hyped. Our clients and many others, meanwhile, are benefiting hugely from the Web because they set realistic goals and strategies for getting there. That's what we hope this book communicates to readers, because the Web has a lot to offer marketers who get it right."

Hayden Books

Hayden Books is an imprint of Macmillan Computer Publishing (MCP), a unit of Macmillan Publishing, the world's largest reference book publisher. Macmillan Publishing is a division of Simon & Schuster. Find more information about MCP and its books at its Web site: **http://www.mcp.com/**.

Rick E. Bruner

Rick E. Bruner has an extensive background in journalism, publishing, and publicity. He is president of Bruner Communications, a strategic Web marketing consultancy, and writes regularly about the Internet for *Advertising Age* magazine and other media. Find more information about Bruner Communications at its Web site: **http://www.bruner.net/**.

USWeb Corporation and its Audience Development Group

USWeb Corporation is a leading, strategic Internet services firm helping clients nationwide develop Internet strategies and improve business processes by using Internet-based technologies. The Audience Development Group specializes in audience creation, cutting-edge research, and media placement to help clients raise Web site traffic, increase brand awareness online, and maximize their return on investment online. Find more information about USWeb and the Audience Development Group at the corporate Web site: **http://www.usweb.com/**.

Product Information

Net Results: Web Marketing That Works
By USWeb and Rick E. Bruner
Price: $29.99
ISBN: 1-56830-414-5

Sales Information
Hayden Books
201 West 103rd Street
Indianapolis, IN 46290-1097
1-800-428-5331

Press Information

Priti Choksi
USWeb Audience Development Group
(415) 339-1067
pchoksi@marin.usweb.com

Disseminating Your Press Release

Now that you've created a newsworthy event, written a short and to-the-point press release about it, and rigorously checked it for spelling, grammar, and writing style, you need to get it into the hands of some journalists.

The Wire

When publicists speak of *dropping* a press release on *the wire*, they generally mean issuing it via PR Newswire and Businesswire, two subscription-based announcement services that have dominated the industry of disseminating press releases for decades. Issuing a press release on one of these two services is synonymous with making your announcement public. The average fee for a basic wire announcement is around $500, depending on the length of the release and the breadth of the distribution.

Figure 8.13

PR Newswire is one of the two leading press announcement services, with thousands of media outlets worldwide subscribing to its feed of press releases.

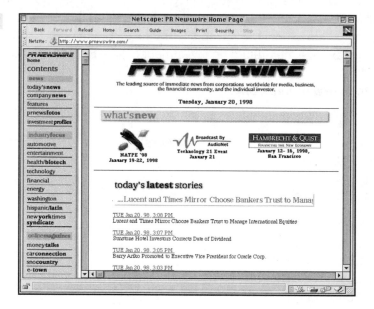

These services provide at least two important benefits. First of all, thousands of news media outlets around the country and the world subscribe to them, and many editors scan them attentively according to their various topics of interest. News services such as Reuters and the Associated

Press routinely rewrite press releases with no further research and forward them to thousands more outlets. You're unlikely to find any other way to reach as many media outlets as quickly and efficiently.

Second, in the Internet age, releases from these wires are reissued directly for public consumption by many Web sites and other online services. Whereas it used to be that only editors were likely to read press releases and decide whether or not to rewrite them for their readers, the Internet has cut out the middleman. Putting a release on the wire has effectively become a direct publishing channel between companies and potential customers. Such online services also extend the life of a press release indefinitely through searchable databases.

Figure 8.14

Free online news services such as NewsPage present "stories" straight from Businesswire and PR Newswire to Internet readers at large.

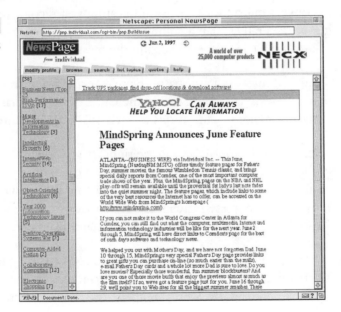

Another class of press release distribution services has emerged recently that automates the distribution of releases directly to editors' email addresses. The benefit of such a service is marginal, at best. For one thing, PR Newswire and Businesswire offer the same added service. They will customize distribution lists for individual clients, or use their in-house lists that are specially tailored for narrow industry topics, for the same prices as the new breed of specialized Internet news wires. The new services don't offer the traditional wires' breadth of distribution, however.

More to the point, mass distribution of press releases to individual editors is far less effective than sending personalized messages yourself.

Individual Distribution

As discussed earlier, you should alert your key press contacts from your A- and B-lists before the actual release date of your announcement. You can send C-level contacts the release the same day it goes out over the wire.

In all cases, it's highly preferable to send the release to each journalist individually rather than placing all their names in the blind copy field. This conveys much more respect, indicating you recognize them as individual writers rather than a commodity. Write a sentence or two of introduction to the release, personalizing the message.

Of course, you can cut and paste the release and the introduction into individual messages, typing in just the name of the journalist separately and making minor modifications to each introductory note as required.

Be sure to get the journalist's name right. It's an axiom of journalism that if you can't get the names right, no one can trust the rest of the facts in the story. Don't assume a familiar name for the writer (such as "Kathy" for "Katherine") unless it's clear that's how she's known publicly. By default, use the same name the journalist does in her byline.

Any standard email program will allow you to keep an address book of contact addresses so that you don't need to retype the email addresses every time you send out a press release. The process of cutting and pasting and customizing each message will obviously take longer than copying a mass of addresses at once, but the extra half hour or so is time well spent. A good email program, such as Qualcomm's Eudora, makes creating form letters even easier with a "stationary" function (consult your software's Help or manual to see if it provides a similar feature).

If you insist on copying multiple journalists with the same message, never add a mass of names to the To: or CC: fields. The result is a long, extremely tacky list of names dominating the first screen or more of the message. Instead, place all the addresses in the BCC: field (short for "blind carbon copy," from the days of typewriters and carbon paper). Address the message to yourself or, in the case of Eudora, leave the To: field blank so the resulting message will automatically display "Recipient List Repressed" in the To: field.

Formatting for Email

Most journalists these days prefer to receive press releases via email, but you should try to determine individual preferences ahead of time. Some traditionalists would still rather receive them by fax or snail mail and may react unkindly to email submissions.

When sending a release by email, *never* send it as a binary attachment. Always cut and paste the text of the release into the body of the email message. Unsolicited email attachments are an online no-no. Attached files can contain viruses (Microsoft Word files are notorious for them), they frequently get garbled or deleted by corporate email gateways, they take a long time to download (the writer may be checking email on her laptop via a long-distance phone connection), and so on.

60–65 Characters Per Line

When copying text from a press release into an email message, make sure the message is neatly formatted. The most important consideration is to put a hard return at the end of each line, creating relatively wide margins. Between 60 and 65 characters per line (including spaces) is ideal. More than that and your recipients' email software may cut off the ends of each line and leave just a few words dangling at the beginning of the next line. Use fewer characters than 60 and the release starts to look like a column of newsprint.

Macintosh users have a rare occasion to gloat that a terrific application exists for their platform that makes text formatting a breeze, with no equivalent for Windows. Namely, it's Bare Bones Software's superb program, BBEdit.

In addition to line-wrapping, be sure to put a blank line between each paragraph to make the ASCII text much easier to read.

Figure 8.15

Ouch! What an eyesore. Most messages formatted like this get quickly deleted.

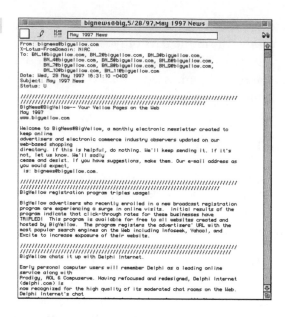

Death to Dumb Quotes

It's also important to eliminate all non-ASCII-standard characters, such as bullets, trademark symbols (replace with just "tm" in parentheses), em dashes (use two hyphens), and especially so-called "smart quotes," which are in reality dumb quotes. These insidious characters, which curl to the right at the beginning of a quote and to the left at the end, are supposed to be a clever enhancement to text. In the ASCII-based world of the Internet, however, smart quotes and all other non-ASCII-standard characters turn into accented "i"s, square blocks, or strings of gobbledygook.

Figuring out how to turn off smart quotes on your word processor can be a challenge. Consult your program's manual or online Help. On Microsoft Word 6.0, smart quotes can be found under the Tools menu, Option/AutoFormat.

Press Kit Basics

With every announcement you send out, you want to have an up-to-date press kit available for those journalists who request it. Don't send press kits unsolicited because reporters who didn't ask for them are liable to throw them away. A professionally packaged press kit isn't cheap to assemble, so save yourself the expense and send them only when requested.

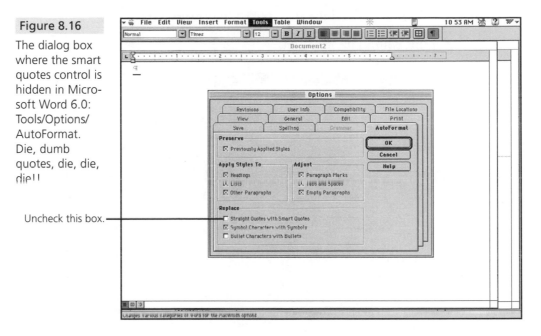

Figure 8.16

The dialog box where the smart quotes control is hidden in Microsoft Word 6.0: Tools/Options/ AutoFormat. Die, dumb quotes, die, die, die!!

Uncheck this box.

In addition to a *physical* press kit, every Web site should have a *virtual* press kit as well. This includes more than just recent press releases, which is all most sites seem to bother with, but also most of the items noted below. This is a cost-effective alternative for smaller businesses for whom the production of professional physical press kits might be a prohibitive expense.

Corporate Fact Sheet

The corporate fact sheet is the chance to expand upon the standard boilerplate at the end of most press releases. It's a one-page summary of key company information for quick reference:

- Founding date

- Key executives' names and titles

- Product names and short descriptions

- Short mission statement and company history

- Corporate headquarters contact information

- PR contact information

Figure 8.17

Marimba, Inc.'s Web site provides a good example of what should be contained in an online press kit.

Some companies also include in their press kits a several-page "corporate background" document, with more narrative extolling the company's vision and positioning. This is generally less useful to journalists. If you choose to include one, include a simple fact sheet as well.

Executive Biographies

Executive biographies should be limited to the top members of the executive team, the only people the press are likely to interview. Keep them as short as possible, one paragraph for each person if you can. More than one biography on a page is fine. Include hobbies as well to round out the character of the individuals.

Press Releases Digest

Press kits typically include one or two recent press releases in addition to the current one being pitched. If the company has produced several press releases in recent months, it's useful to include a digest of one or two pages with a paragraph abstract for each press release. Refer to a URL where full copies of the releases are located.

Graphics

Graphic images are extremely important in increasing the attractiveness of any story and can easily make the difference between a story being printed or not. They can include screenshots of your site or products, as well as portraits of executives. Try to avoid overly corporate headshots of executives. Opt instead for more relaxed images.

Be sure to make the images available on the press area of your Web site in several digital image formats, including GIF and TIFF. In addition, be prepared to accommodate technophobic reporters by mailing the images on a disk, as well as making them available on an FTP server for the technophiles. Some editors prefer printed copies or slides of images.

Product Descriptions/White Paper

As necessary, you may want to go into further detail about products and services in separate documents.

Customer/Analyst References

You may want to provide customer and analyst quotes and contact information (with their permission, of course). Most journalists will prefer the contact information to the canned quotes. Be prepared to surrender control of these interviews because a journalist will not be comfortable interviewing a third party with a company publicist monitoring the call.

Frequently Asked Questions

A Q&A or FAQ document for journalists is only useful if you truly antic-ipate the hard questions the press might ask or that past reporters have asked. Don't use this document as an opportunity to spoon-feed them marketing fluff. Keep in mind the BS-o-meter. Rather, use it as a chance to prepare the best spin for the difficult questions.

Reprinted News Stories

A reprinted news story as part of a press kit can be a double-edged sword. On one hand, a journalist might find a third-party report to be a more objective explanation of a company's positioning than the compa-ny's own marketing and PR material. On the other hand, the reporter may be turned off to see that the company has already been well-covered by her competition. Use no more than two or three of the best stories, if any.

Other Publicity Opportunities

Beyond print and the Web, there are still other ways to get the word out about your business and your site. Consider some of the following ideas.

Speaking Opportunities

Get your CEO or other top executives on the speaking circuit. Although maybe only a few hundred people will hear them speak on a given day, the caliber of audience you reach through public speaking is valuable in influencing the rest of your industry. The "trickle-down effect" may be dubious in economics, but it's certainly real in the world of publicity.

Christie Dames, director of the Speakers Bureau at Niehaus Ryan Group Public Relations, offers this advice to would-be speakers:

"Whatever you do, don't sell your company from the platform. The most important thing is to educate the audience. You might never even mention your company in your speech, but the next time anyone there thinks about the subject you spoke on, you and your company will come immediately to mind. If you try to sell yourself from the stage, they'll never ask you back again."

Keeping track of upcoming speaking opportunities can be difficult in this fast-paced industry. One of the better online resources is the Association for Interactive Media's Web site (see the "Resources" section at the end of this chapter for details). Speaking opportunities normally get booked months in advance, so look ahead.

Figure 8.18

The Association for Interactive Media has a comprehensive directory of high-tech conferences year-round.

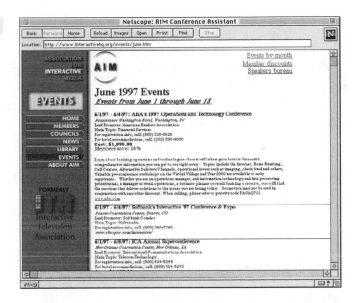

Ms. Dames urges clients to stick to the requirements of the conference applications. "If it says to provide a 50-word description of your speech, stick to 50 words. Write 51, and that might make the difference of not getting it."

In your application, target industry trends for discussion. Downplay any mention of your own company in the abstract.

Opinion Pieces

Newspapers, magazines, and Web publications are often eager to receive opinion pieces for their editorial pages. Have your CEO write such a piece (or commission a freelancer to ghostwrite it for you), again discussing an industry trend without putting your company in the middle of the discussion. Having your company name and URL printed at the bottom of the piece is effective enough. Many of those who are inspired by your opinions will check out your site on their own.

Similarly, writing letters to the editor is another option for publications that are more competitive in their opinion pages, such as the *New York Times*.

Web 'Zines and Email Newsletters

From a PR perspective, the larger Web publications are generally not much different from traditional media, other than their immediate turnaround time is closer to radio, TV, news wires (like Reuters), or even newspapers, which require a day to turn news around.

Smaller Web publications, sometimes called *'zines*, as well as email newsletters, are often more malleable, however. Although many offer reasonably high quality information, particularly in narrow niches, they are almost all run on shoestring budgets. As a result, they may welcome your CEO becoming a regular columnist (pro bono, of course).

If a regular column is too much work, consider tailoring your news releases to read like actual stories. Doug Moody, an account executive in USWeb's Audience Development Group, explains:

"We've found that if we take the time to rewrite press releases to make them read more like news stories, and we send them to the editors of smaller sites or newsletters, they will frequently reprint them verbatim. Even though they know we are working as publicists, if the news is good and the writing sounds reasonably objectives, it's too convenient for them to pass up," Mr. Moody said.

Call-In Radio Shows

If you call in to a talk radio program, the host will generally let you tell the audience your URL if your comments are on-topic.

VNRs and B-Roll

If you have the budget for it, video news releases (VNRs) and *B-rolls* are a great way to get coverage on television. A video production company will charge in the neighborhood of $10,000 to prepare a mock TV news story about your company's latest announcement, which you can submit to TV stations. Some smaller stations are likely to broadcast the VNR in its entirety if it has been professionally produced.

Either as a separate undertaking or as part of the process of making the VNR, you can produce B-roll. This is background footage of your company, showing employees at work, your executives answering general interview-style questions, a computer screen with someone navigating your site, and so forth. You can continue to submit B-roll material to TV stations long after any specific announcement, which the station's news team may edit together to make their own story. Most of the images could be used as background for the news reporter's original voice-over.

Small TV stations with limited resources for sending out their own crews are especially receptive to this technique, and are quite likely to follow through on a story once you've made it this easy for them.

Resources

Sites and Services

PR Newswire

http://www.prnewswire.com

One of the two leading services for disseminating press releases world-wide. The Web site explains the company's services in detail and contains links to several valuable PR resources.

Businesswire

ttp://www.businesswire.com

Ditto.

Ragan's Interactive Public Relations

http://www.ragan.com

An excellent newsletter produced by Ragan Communications. The corporate Web site has subscription information (including a free trial offer), as well as many good links and resources for publicists.

Info Scavenger

http://www.infoscavenger.com

Another very good newsletter. Published on a small scale by Info Scavenger Communications, it meets a high standard of general online marketing advice. The Web site has a wealth of information for online marketing.

Association for Interactive Media

http://www.interactivehq.org/

Formerly the Interactive Television Association, this organization offers a wide range of marketing and promotional services to members from all sectors of the Internet community. Their Web site's events listings, available for free, is one of the best calendar of industry conferences and events we've seen.

Books

The Associated Press Stylebook and Libel Manual

Available at any good bookstore, this is the bible of journalistic style and should be used for press releases as well.

Elements of Style

By William Strunk, Jr. and E. B. White

Every writer should own a copy and reread it annually. Also available in part on the Web at **http://www.columbia.edu/acis/bartleby/ strunk/**.

On Writing Well

By William Zinsser

A better-than-average guide to good writing.

Paid Media: The Many Faces of Web Advertising

Many companies take their first stab at Web marketing by simply building a basic Web site. Once they've dipped their toes in the water, they eventually realize that they need to promote the site. So in the next wave of budgeting, they design some ad banners, buy several thousand impressions on some leading sites, and sit back to wait for the 2% or so of those who see the ads to click on them and come to the site.

And for a great many online ventures, that remains the extent of "Web marketing."

Now that you, dear reader, have read through to this last chapter, we hope you appreciate that online marketing is more complex and rewarding than simply putting up one Web site and a shower of ad banners. As described in Part I, your site needs to be not ordinary, but extraordinary, representing real strategic goals for the company and true benefits for visitors. And as covered in the preceding four chapters of Part II, there are many other, more cost-effective ways to promote a site and develop a loyal audience than online ads, including newsgroups, mailing lists, affinity site links, contests, media relations, and more.

Why Advertise Online?

This is not to say that online advertising plays *no* part, of course. It can be very important for many sites. USWeb's definition of *audience development* is made up of two key components: the audience creation techniques described in the previous four chapters of Part II, and paid media, also known as advertising. This two-pronged strategy of paid and non-paid promotion is directly akin to how public relations and advertising are counterparts in most traditional marketing campaigns.

Internet advertising is definitely coming into its own, experiencing a surge in 1997 that even surprised many in the online industry. At a June 1997 meeting of the Internet Advertising Bureau, whose members include many of the biggest sites and online advertisers, a membership poll said that online ad spending for the year would be in the range of $500–700 million, up from around $300 million in 1996. By the end of 1997, however, it appeared more likely that advertisers had spent close to $1 billion. And this in only the third year that any ad dollars had been spent on the Web at all!

However, it is strategically important to understand where the real benefits of online advertising lie and how to use ads in harmony with the free media placement techniques we've been describing.

CPM Versus CTR: Conflicting Measures

Most sites use banners to drive inbound traffic. Although there are clearly cases where this makes sense, the kinds of audience creation techniques discussed in previous chapters are often more cost-effective for generating traffic. Furthermore, the strategic importance of banners for brand building is often overlooked by many Web marketers, as discussed later in this chapter.

One reason more sites don't question the cost-effectiveness of using banners to drive traffic is a confusing incongruity between the two key measurements popularly used in Web advertising. For whatever reason, online advertisers have accepted the CPM (cost per thousand) measure as the standard for banner pricing. CPM comes primarily out of the broadcast and print worlds, where branding is the prevailing advertising objective. Yet at the same time these advertisers have deemed click-throughs to be the most common measure of advertising success, which is a clear extension of direct marketing principles.

Figure 9.1

Does IBM communicate much more about its brand message in its similar TV commercials? Seems like this animated Web banner ad more or less says it all.

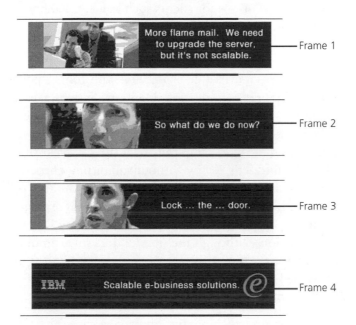

If you're paying for branding but you're measuring for direct results, it's hard to know if you're getting what you're paying for. To the extent that you're interested in paying for branding, it makes sense to quantify the costs in terms of sheer numbers of impressions registered with desired audience segments, as in other media. Measuring the success of branding is complicated, as we'll discuss later in the chapter. Clickthroughs are a poor measure of branding success, and this measurement shouldn't be forced to fit this objective. If driving traffic is indeed the goal, on the other hand, it is useful to translate the CPM rate into a cost-per-click measure to make sure you're getting a fair price.

For example, say an advertiser pays a typical $20 CPM and receives an approximate industry average 2% clickthrough rate (CTR). It makes for easy math: $1 per clickthrough (see "The Math" sidebars later in this chapter). At this fairly typical ad cost, a company would pay $10,000 to generate 10,000 visits to its homepage.

However, $10,000 spent on the type of nonpaid audience creation techniques described earlier in Part II should render a lot more than 10,000 page views. In the Women's Wire case study, you read that Ramona Ambrozic said that such audience creation techniques were 50% more cost-effective than the company's typical banner advertising campaigns. USWeb's promotions for clients such as ichat, Paramount, Macromedia, Jefferson Starship, and others generated tens to hundreds of thousands of page views for substantially less than $1 per click.

Amazon.com's remarkable promotion with John Updike, discussed in Chapter 7, "Era of Innovation: Contests, Sweepstakes, and Other Special Promotions," cost the company a bit over $140,000 in prize money. Yet the site received nearly 400,000 story submissions, to say nothing of the multitudes more who came daily over the six weeks of the contest to follow the interactive story without submitting entries. A fair percentage of those visitors likely bought books while at the site, offsetting marketing costs, to say nothing of the resulting press coverage in almost 300 prestigious outlets worldwide. According to Kay Dangaard, director of media relations, although the site did do a small amount of banner advertising for the promotion, it worked out to pennies per visitor because the real volume of traffic came in response to word of mouth, grassroots, and PR promotions.

Scalable and Complementary to Audience Creation

One way in which banner ads are clearly more effective than nonpaid audience creation techniques for driving traffic is their ability to scale their results proportionally to a company's spending. Marketers can try to target audience segments in only so many newsgroups without resorting to spamming. Companies such as Microsoft, Intel, and Procter & Gamble are committing multimillion-dollar budgets to online advertising. It would be hard to spend such amounts effectively just on search engine registration, sweepstakes, or even public relations, along with the other nonpaid techniques discussed in earlier chapters. However, successful banner campaigns delivering better-than-average CTRs can easily be expanded to the purchase of more impressions across more sites, and, theoretically, can continue to generate the same proportion of click-through traffic indefinitely.

Figure 9.2

Microsoft and Visa can afford to spend what-ever it takes to drive traffic. Presumably their crack marketing teams have taken the time to thoroughly analyze the cost of acquiring new customers and have found banners an effective means.

Web advertising is also an excellent strategic complement to the unpaid promotional strategies of audience creation. Advertising with a publisher opens the door for additional levels of cooperation, including exclusive sponsorships of select content, joint promotions, affinity links with top sites, and so on.

Furthermore, the $1-per-clickthrough cost depicted previously is an oversimplification of the deeply nuanced strategies and rewards available in Web advertising today. That's what we'll cover in the rest of this chapter.

REI: Playing Ads Against Free Placement

Since 1938, REI has been selling quality outdoor gear and clothing in retail outlets around the country and through its mail-order catalogue. The company ventured into online retail in 1997, and by the end of the year, Web sales were booming.

A few months after launching its site, the company retained USWeb to help build traffic. Through our usual tactics of promoting REI's site and doing online sales promotions in recreational newsgroups, mailing lists, and the like, we were able to effect a significant rise in traffic immediately. REI expanded its promotional budget five months later, and USWeb launched a banner advertising campaign, after which traffic and sales surged dramatically again.

Figure 9.3

The sporting set has reacted well to REI's online store. After the company opened up an online advertising budget, outdoor-oriented sites were more accommodating than ever to link to REI and recommend the store to readers.

The jump was not entirely due to the success of the banners alone, which experienced average CTRs and ran mostly on medium-sized sites focused on biking, hiking, climbing, camping, environmentalism, and the like. Rather, the paid media gave us new bargaining power with the publishing sites to expand our free media-placement tactics.

Although publishers might be loath to admit it, the policies at many sites are much looser than the traditional church-and-state division between editorial and advertising departments at established print publications. As the medium matures, a little advertising grease can generally loosen editorial favoritism.

"I worked closely with Guy Hill, our media planner, to add value to the REI media plan," said Molly Parsley, the online marketing specialist who led REI's audience creation campaign.

Ms. Parsley wrote emails to the Webmasters of all the sites where Mr. Hill bought advertisements, explaining to them, "Part of my job as Online Marketing Specialist is to get links established for REI, and I would like to know if you could offer any added value to our client by providing a link to REI."

To make the point clear that future advertising may hinge on their cooperation in giving REI some free exposure, she added, "We will be reporting back to REI with a list of links from our current media buy, so please let me know if I can add your site to this list."

The results were powerful. Nearly every site contacted added links to REI, and several added a few lines about REI's services to their member newsletters and other editorial services.

Online Ad Objectives

As in other media, there are two principal objectives in advertising online: branding and direct response. Both can be had online in a wide array of flavors and give you much greater control than other media over market segmentation, performance review, speed to execution, and other advantages. Most online marketers can benefit from a combination of the branding and direct-response characteristics of Web advertising, but it pays to appreciate the distinctions between the two.

Branding

By and large, marketers have been slow to embrace the brand-building potential of Web ads. It's not hard to see where some of that reluctance comes from. For one thing, page banners, the most common form of online advertising, are small. The most popular size, 468×60 pixels, fills about 10% of a Web browser window on a 14-inch or 15-inch monitor, and proportionally less on a larger monitor. For advertisers used to full-page newspaper ads, 17-foot-tall billboards, and 30-second TV commercials to achieve their branding objectives, a one-by-six-inch rectangle doesn't seem like much to work with.

Figure 9.4

Two of the most popular banner sizes, standardized by the Internet Advertising Bureau (IAB) and the Coalition for Advertising Supported Information and Entertainment (CASIE), don't take up much real estate on a 14-inch monitor.

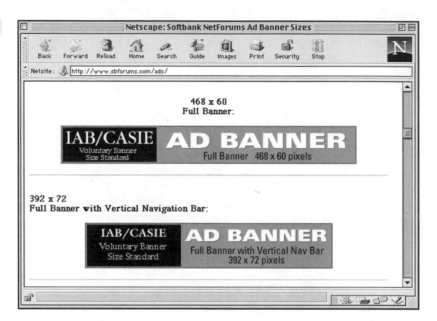

Add to this the easy-to-measure clickthrough ability inherent in the ads, and the appeal of a direct-response model has generally overshadowed branding as the key online advertising objective for many sites.

"Measuring the success of Web advertising can be complex, taking into account many different factors," said Guy Hill, media planner at USWeb. "We try to communicate some of that in our reports to our clients, but often the top bosses don't have the time for such subtleties. They want to be able to glance at one number and make a decision about whether a campaign is working or not. So, by the time our contacts present our reports to their bosses, everything gets reduced to a clickthrough rate."

This is regrettable. Not to take anything away from the power of direct response online, but there's also real potential to achieve strong branding on the Web. Without a doubt, the best evidence of this comes from the Internet Advertising Bureau (IAB) and Millward Brown Interactive's 1997 Advertising Effectiveness Study.

IAB & Millward Brown Interactive's Advertising Effectiveness Study

Millward Brown, a 20-year-old international advertising research group, meticulously designed a study to demonstrate how giving users a single exposure to a Web banner could have a significant positive impact on their recollection of the ad, affinity with the brand message, and even their intent to purchase the product. After surveying nearly 17,000 Web surfers' reactions to 12 real ad banners on 12 leading Web sites, the report concluded that after only one viewing of a banner ad, Web surfers were on average 5% more aware of the brand and 4% more likely to purchase the product over a competitor's product.

The concept of measuring branding may seem a bit like herding cats—abstract at best. Yet Millward Brown has established itself as an expert of brand measurement, with a third of the Fortune 100 companies on its client list. The methodology of the study is too complex to explain in detail here, but we'll sketch it out briefly. (Copies of the report are available free on Millward Brown's site. See the "Resources" section at the end of the chapter for the URL.)

Collaborating with the IAB's prestigious roster of members, Millward Brown's online division, MBinteractive, was able to experiment with visitors to sites including CNN, CompuServe, ESPN SportsZone, Excite, Geocities, HotWired, and Pathfinder's *People* magazine, running real advertisements for companies such as Schick, Toyota, Toshiba, Deja News, Kenwood, Delta Business Class, Volvo, and MasterCard.

MBinteractive picked one link at each site, such as the Celebrity News link on *People*'s homepage, and randomly intercepted a certain percentage of folks who clicked it. Instead of taking them to the intended page, the system invited them to partake in a survey. Nearly half agreed to do so. At this stage, the survey just requested basic demographic information "to help the site better understand those who use its service." After submitting the completed survey, the participants were thanked and sent to the page they wanted.

Unbeknownst to the participants, when they submitted the demographic information they were randomly split into two equal groups—equal both in terms of absolute numbers and demographic balance. On the following page, one group was served a test ad and the other was served a control ad, with all other conditions exactly the same.

Then, between a day and a week later, the participants were emailed and invited to come back and answer further questions. This time the survey focused on their recollection of the test banner, its brand message, their opinion of the product, and so on. Again, roughly half participated in the second phase of the survey, a total of 16,758 respondents.

Some of the results were remarkable. Bear in mind that all of the test banners used were in normal circulation throughout the test sites and elsewhere on the Web, so both the test and control participants may have already seen the test banners before or after the tested exposure. With all other things equal between the test and control groups, the survey precisely measured the impact of at least one additional banner viewing.

Figure 9.5

One showing of this Schick banner ad caused a dramatic brand benefit in the perceptions of those who saw it. (Data courtesy of Millward Brown Interactive and the Internet Advertising Bureau.)

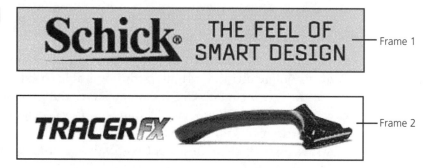

Frame 1

Frame 2

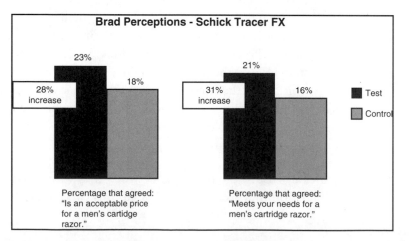

In the case of Schick's Tracer FX razor, members of the test group who were shown the banner ad were 31% more likely to agree that it "meets your need for a men's cartridge razor" compared to the control group. And the test group was 25% more inclined to believe that the product "is an acceptable price" compared to the control group.

Rex Briggs, the MBInteractive analyst who authored the report, had this to say about the responses to those two questions: "These shifts represent increases in perceived relevance and price performance—two critical dimensions for a packaged good."

In the case of the Toshiba Video Board ad banner, 11% of the test group felt the product was "better than other laptop computer accessories," versus 5% of the control group, a 120% increase in positive perception. Of those who saw Volvo's test banner, 11% had "a higher opinion of Volvo than other automobiles," versus 9% of the control group, a 44% increase. Those who viewed the Kenwood ad were 23% more inclined to agree that the brand "appeals to you more than other brands of home stereo systems."

MBinteractive crunches the numbers in myriad ways in the 88-page report, using a variety of complex, proprietary methodologies for quantifying "consumer loyalty," "brand awareness," and other generalized brand concepts. Their methods are carefully explained and based on strong assumptions, though, so the numbers can be taken at face value with relative confidence.

Among the 12 ads, average awareness of the brands increased 5%, from 61% to 64%, after just one additional exposure, the authors concluded. "Consumer loyalty" was up 26% for Volvo, 20% for Delta Business Class Air Travel, and more than 10% each for the Apple QuickTake digital camera, Deja News, and Toshiba.

The news wasn't all positive, though. The Strong Funds investment group lost more than 20% in consumer loyalty after one ad exposure, and two others also slipped slightly. But across all 12 test banners, consumer loyalty rose by an average of 4%.

The report's authors are cognizant of Mark Twain's warning about statistics: "People commonly use statistics like a drunk uses a lamppost: for support rather than for illumination." The IAB and MBinteractive both offer interpretations of the numbers and provide explanations for why the branding impact of a single ad banner appears to be so surprisingly high. (MBinteractive, using Millward Brown's proprietary "FORCE" measure for balancing across different media, goes so far as to argue that Web ad banners are more effective for branding than television commercials.)

Up Close and Personal

The most salient argument in favor of the Web's branding power, which many had made even before the IAB/MBinteractive study, is that Web users are deeply engrossed in the medium and sit only inches from the monitor, unlike TV viewers who lounge halfway across the room and take bathroom breaks and snack runs during most commercials.

In fact, it's little wonder that banners get our attention as much as they do. They're often the only animation on otherwise static pages, and often the first elements to load. While a viewer waits for a page to finish downloading, she has little choice but to watch as the banner fills the top position of the page and runs through its animated message.

Figure 9.6

RealAudio's ad on this CBS SportsLine page has the user's undivided attention as other page elements gradually load.

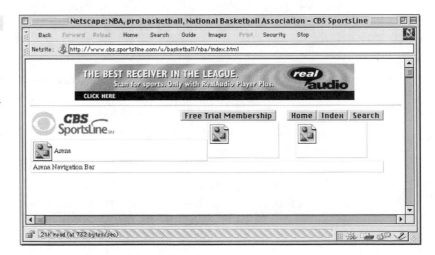

For some broad consumer brands, it may make more sense to devote budgetary resources to branding through banners than to try to drive traffic to a large destination Web site at all. In a March 1997 report titled "What Advertising Works," Forrester Research suggested, "Instead of building a big site, a brand like P&G's Tide should be looking for a way to sponsor the online schedules of every Little League in the country." (When we spoke to Tide's **Clothesline.com** site designers later that summer, they hadn't yet heard Forrester's suggestion, although they admitted it was interesting.)

For destination sites that use banners primarily to acquire visitors, branding still should not be overlooked.

"Even when a site is trying to drive traffic with its banners, there is a branding value there for them," said USWeb's Mr. Hill. "I can see a banner once and not click on it, but it sets the agenda in my mind for me to click on it later. I haven't forgotten it. If I know the brand and occasionally visit the site, the exposure reinforces my behavior. It tells me I'm right. If I haven't been to the site before, at least it puts it in my mind for the next time I have a free moment and am interested in that category of site."

Because the Web is as new as it is, Mr. Hill makes the point that having an online presence at all continues to have its own branding cachet.

"In the offline world, you can choose from among more than a dozen different brands of jeans," he said. "Online, Levi's has got a big presence. I go to their site or see one of their ads and I happen to be wearing Levi's, and it's a strong positive reinforcement. I think, 'They're the online jeans brand, and I'm an online kind of a guy. It's hip to wear Levi's.'"

MBinteractive's study supports this point. Sixty-three percent of respondents agreed with the statement, "Brands that advertise on the Web are more forward-thinking than other brands."

Figure 9.7

Levi's uses Web advertising to reinforce its hip, free-spirited image to the upscale digerati audience.

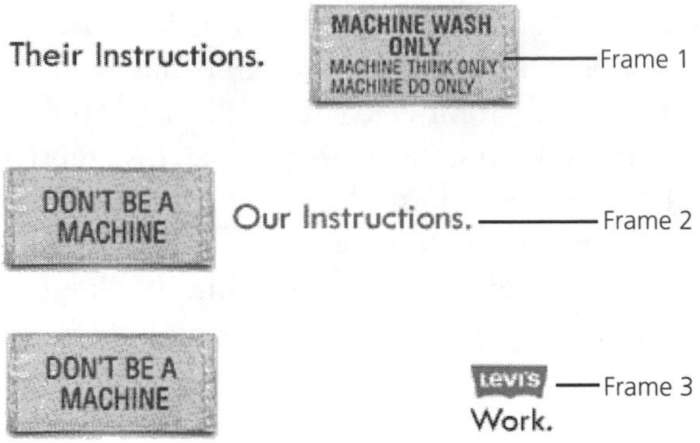

Another obvious benefit of online branding is the superb demographics of Web users. The latest data from the Web's largest demographic survey, conducted by the Georgia Institute of Technology, indicates that as more of the general population comes online, the average user's income and education levels are coming down while the average age goes up. But it's still the upper end of society leading the way.

In the eighth survey, conducted in October and November of 1997, the mean average household income was $53,000 a year, dropping from $58,000 in the seventh survey six months earlier. That's still far above the U.S. median annual household income, which was $35,500 in 1996 according to the U.S. Census Bureau. Forty-seven percent of respondents to the eighth survey had basic college degrees or higher, which is down from 54% in the seventh survey but still more than double than the 1995 U.S. national average of 23%.

The point as regards branding is clear: Although companies may not yet be able to reach the majority of their consumer audience online, they can reach the potentially most lucrative segment of that audience.

Direct Response

One way to view the online advertising objectives of branding versus direct response is in terms of long-term versus short-term rewards. Although branding may translate into sales eventually, it's generally not an immediate cause and effect. When you want to take advantage of the Web's capacity for instant results, clicks are what count.

Online advertising offers direct marketers substantial advantages over traditional telemarketing and mailing campaigns, chiefly in terms of keen targeting and cost savings.

As we'll discuss in more detail later in the chapter, you can increasingly target banner ads to Web surfers by using the same demographic data used in traditional direct marketing—ZIP code, age, gender, income, and education, as well as shopping history and other known factors. You can further layer other targeting criteria on top of these demographics, such as editorial affiliation, time of day, and immediate user behaviors (for example, intercepting users as they search topical keywords or browse shopping directories).

Internet Shopping Network: Big Savings Direct Marketing Online

"The cost of generating a lead on the Internet for us is substantially cheaper than it would be in the offline world," said Ken Neibaur, VP of marketing at the Internet Shopping Network (ISN). Owned by the Home Shopping Network cable TV marketing company, ISN has two online properties—the Computer Super Store, online since 1994 and claiming to be the Web's first commerce site, and First Auction, which began conducting real-time auctions of merchandise in 1997. According to Mr. Neibaur, the two stores combined were doing $2 million a month in sales by the beginning of 1998, with revenues rising by 15–20% a month.

The savings from direct marketing online versus the traditional approach are numerous, he explains, including dramatically lower expenses for acquiring customers, virtually nonexistent costs for repeat email marketing to existing customers, and great savings in campaign testing. Before joining ISN, Mr. Neibaur held management positions at several telemarketing and direct mail ventures, including as a VP at Lintas: Marketing Communications.

"Offline direct-mailing lists cost $60 to $125 per thousand names. The average CPM on banner ads is around $30," he said, noting that a direct-mail envelope is fairly comparable to a banner ad. Most direct-mail recipients throw away the envelopes unopened, and similarly most Web surfers won't click on banners to learn more about their offers.

"But the cost of buying the list is just one aspect of direct marketing costs offline. You've got postage, creative, printing, mailing services, so you're way up there just to acquire your customer base," he said.

On the Web, however, there are virtually no similar production and distribution expenses. Once customers have gone to ISN's online stores the first time and registered as members, ISN adds them to an email marketing list with their permission. A custom software program then automatically generates email messages with new promotions to send to them.

"It costs almost nothing to send to that list twice a week, and we will get anywhere from a 10% to 25% response," Mr. Neibaur continued. "I've never seen an offline direct mail house list get anything above a 10% response, I don't care what it is. And if I were offline and I had to send out direct mail or do telemarketing calls to keep those customers interested, it would cost me a lot of money" in terms of paper, postage, and phone expenses.

Online savings are even greater for direct marketing in terms of testing campaigns, he said.

"In the offline world, you have a tremendous amount of fixed costs going into testing. If you're doing broadcast, you have to produce a commercial and buy a certain amount of media time. For print advertising, you have to buy the creative [that is, ad industry jargon for the art and written copy] and get the insertions. And if you're doing direct mail, it's even worse because you have to print a lot of stuff and mail it. If you buy the wrong list, if your creative doesn't work, if your product is priced wrong, or whatever, you won't recoup that investment. If you spent a dollar on a mail package, which is very common, you're out of luck.

"On the Internet, you can put a test program out for a couple of days or an hour using some models. You can put out five or eight different ad banners in the same media buy and find out that afternoon or the next morning what isn't working and pull it back before you're exposed. On the Web, the up-front cost is basically you, the media buyer, and an art director. That's obviously not the case in the offline world," Mr. Neibaur said.

Figure 9.8

The Internet Shopping Network's First Auction site, together with its sister site the Computer Super Store, is bringing in $2 million a month and growing fast. ISN's marketers calculate their customer acquisition costs from advertising down to the penny, and they know they're getting a bargain.

Quantifying Clicks

More and more sites are giving in to pressure to charge for advertising not only on a CPM basis of impressions shown to visitors but also on a cost-per-click or cost-per-transaction basis. Our favorite jargon for this type of pricing, be it cost-per-click, cost-per-lead, or cost-per-sale, is *CPW*: cost-per-whatever.

Publishers are frequently reluctant to fix the pricing of a banner to its performance, which is understandable. They argue that many factors that might impact the CTR are out of their control, such as the quality of the banner's design and copy writing or the promotion on offer. It's a bit like a department store paying a newspaper for advertising based on how many sales the ad generates.

The dark secret, however, is that few Web sites are actually selling anywhere near their total inventory of available impressions. House ads, barter, and freebies frequently fill up the majority of ad impressions served at all but the top handful of sites. For this reason, many sites will negotiate CPW ad deals (although most try to keep the availability of

> ### THE MATH:
>
> 2% CTR of 1,000 impressions = 20 visitors.
>
> 20 visitors divided by the expense of $20 per thousand ad impressions = $1 per visitor.
>
> 5% of those visitors spend $50 a year.
>
> 5%, or 1 in 20 = $20 acquisition cost.
>
> Bottom line = $30 net revenue per acquisition.

such pricing models quiet, as they may be perceived to weaken the site's ability to ask high CPM rates).

Ad-supported sites ultimately recognize that getting something for that excess ad inventory (even if at fire-sale prices) is better than nothing. A few networks have recently introduced performance-based pricing over the table, including DoubleClick Direct, Petry, and PointCast Direct.

Do the Math for CPW

When you're measuring the success of advertising by a CTR or other CPW criteria, it is critical to do the math on the bottom-line worth of the "whatever" in "cost per whatever" in order to calculate the return on the investment of marketing expenses.

An online commerce site, for example, may be paying the equivalent of $1 per clickthrough, either on a straight CPW basis or as $20 CPM with a 2% CTR. By tracking visitors over time with cookies, the site may calculate that, on average, 5% of those who hit the homepage make a purchase worth $50 within a year. That means it costs the site $20 to acquire a $50 purchase. Considering that the customer may become a regular shopper, and balancing that against other overhead, marketers at such a site may decide that's a profitable acquisition cost.

It may be harder to make the same argument for using banner ads if a site survives off ad revenue. Using the same $1-per-clickthrough ad cost, a site would spend $10,000 to attract 10,000 visitors. If it sold its own banner spaces at the $20-per-thousand rate, it would immediately earn back only $200 in ad sales from those initial clickthroughs. (A site

THE MATH:

2% CTR of 1,000 impressions = 20 visitors.

20 visitors divided by the expense of $20 per thousand ad impressions = $1 per visitor.

$10,000 spent divided by $1 per visitor = 10,000 visitors.

$20 CPM earned = $0.02 per impression.

10,000 initial homepage impressions × $0.02 per impression = $200 earned.

$10,000 recouped divided by $0.02 per impression = 500,000 impressions must be shown.

500,000 impressions divided by 10,000 visitors = 50 impressions per visitor.

Bottom line = *Every last visitor* of the 2% who originally click through the ad banner must eventually view another 49 banners at the destination site for site to break even on the ad expense.

charging $20 CPM effectively earns 2 cents per banner shown.) In order for the site to break even on its advertising expenses, every one of those 10,000 visitors would have to click an additional 49 pages beyond the homepage to earn back the cost of the original ad campaign.

For many sites, justifying this math may be a tall order. Put yourself in the Web surfer's place: When you click on a banner, how likely are you to become a loyal user of that site and to visit it again 50 times over the course of several months? Probably not that likely. Most of the time you click a banner, take a quick look at the homepage it leads to, decide you're not interested, and never go back again. Right?

The One-Two Punch

Of course, the preceding equation oversimplifies matters. Although the $20 CPM and 2% CTR may be typical, lots of sites are doing 10% CTR and more, and some are paying $10 CPM or less, at which point the acquisition cost gets much more favorable. However, at $30 CPM and 1.5% CTR, the pendulum swings the other way. The main point is that advertisers who measure success by clickthrough need to do this math.

Figure 9.9

A picture may be worth a thousand words, but is it worth the price of CPM when generating traffic is the goal? Marketers who are measuring results by clickthroughs had better do the math.

On the other hand, this purely direct-response measure of success also ignores the inherent branding benefit of banners discussed earlier in the chapter. Recall Mr. Hill's argument that although a visitor might not click a banner the first time he sees it, he may recall the URL and visit later. With this in mind, the acquisition costs seem somewhat more reasonable.

But this works only when advertisers anticipate the latent branding benefit and promote the brand.

"It astounds me how many ad banners don't even have a company's name on them," said Kent Valandra, executive VP and director of New Media at Western International Media. An online advertising veteran, Mr. Valandra started working with Prodigy's ad department in the late '80s, before which he had spent 20 years in the print magazine world.

"It's obvious that banners have a branding value," he continued. "A salesman from *Time* magazine doesn't say to an advertiser, 'I can give you 50 million readers, of whom maybe 3 million are going to care about your ad.' If it's worth money for someone to put their name on a basketball court or a rodeo fence or the side of a bus, it's worth putting a name on a Web banner. You never see a billboard for cigarettes at a rodeo without the name of the cigarette."

The IAB/MBinteractive study further makes the point that a CTR is not an effective measure of the branding power of an ad. On average there was a less than 1% difference between people who did *not* click on an ad but who still recalled its message (43.7%) and those who had seen the ad, *including* those who had clicked on it, and who recalled its message (44.1%).

In the case of the Schick razor ad, a single exposure of the ad banner boosted by 31% the number of people who agreed that it "meets your needs for a men's cartridge razor." Yet the ad had a lowly 0.5% CTR. Clearly, the CTR alone is a poor measure of that ad's branding success.

The moral of the story is that although a cryptic banner that doesn't reveal the name of the company or product may marginally raise the CTR, the sacrifice of branding is usually a net loss. As Forrester Research noted in its report "What Advertising Works," MCI's memorable "Shop Naked!" banner campaign for its online shopping mall generated a lot of clicks, but not many shoppers. The mall is now defunct. (You might wonder what a telecommunications company was doing in the consumer-product retail business in the first place, but that's a different question.)

Stimulating Clicks

In cases where clickthroughs are an important and well-considered objective, there are a few rules of thumb for design and ad management, in addition to the most critical factor of targeting the right audience:

- Bold colors

- Top of page placement

- Animation

- Call to action (for example, "click here," "buy one, get one free," or even the standard blue hyperlink border around the banner)

- Limited frequency of exposures

Most of these fall in line with the classic direct-marketing mnemonic of *AIDA*: A promotion should grab **attention**, rouse **interest**, stimulate **desire**, and call to **action**.

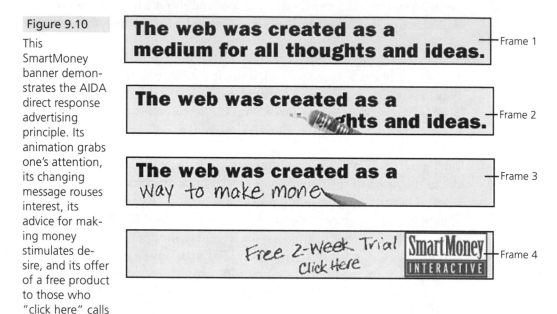

Figure 9.10

This SmartMoney banner demonstrates the AIDA direct response advertising principle. Its animation grabs one's attention, its changing message rouses interest, its advice for making money stimulates desire, and its offer of a free product to those who "click here" calls to action.

The one online-specific rule of thumb worth elaborating on is the last one: limited frequency of exposures. Contrary to the accepted wisdom in traditional brand advertising, that a prospective customer becomes more likely to buy a product the more he's exposed to the same advertisement (ideally somewhere around 7–10 viewings), the law of diminishing returns seems to apply more quickly on the Web.

In mid-1996, the DoubleClick network conducted an oft-cited study regarding the effects of ad frequency on CTRs. It concluded that after a typical Web surfer had seen the same ad more than three times, the likelihood he would click on it dropped below 1%. DoubleClick dubbed this phenomenon "banner burnout."

As a result, many sites use cookies to track how many times any given Web surfer sees the same ad. Of course, even if individual sites control the frequency of specific ad exposures, Web surfers may encounter the same ads running on other sites. Therefore, advertisers are advised to creatively change their banners often.

Types of Online Ads

Because the Internet is an amalgamation of several media experiences—text, images, sound, video, 3D, chat, and so on—online ads also come in many varieties. Other than scratch-and-sniff magazine ads, advertising on the Web can come close to matching the experience of promotions in every other media, and then some.

Within the Banner

Before we get "beyond the banner," an almost meaningless buzz phrase so many online advertisers love to talk about (but seemingly rarely act upon), there is much for you to consider within the realm of those lovable, ubiquitous hyperlinked rectangles.

When HotWired introduced the first ad banner for AT&T in 1994, it was simply a static graphic image fixed at the top of the page. No particular targeting, no rotation, no animation, nada. Pretty crude by today's standards. Now banners do more than act as static, two-dimensional logos fixed on every page. In addition to advanced technical targeting techniques discussed later in the chapter, banners have become dramatically more flashy and functional, thanks to Shockwave, Java, compressed audio and video formats, and other hot technologies.

Animation

One drawback to using the "rich-media" formats (that is, anything much more exciting than static graphics) in ad banners is that some users and even more sites don't support them. The news for end users is more encouraging. According to the browser statistics survey maintained by University of Illinois student Ed Kubaitis, discussed in Chapter 3, "Design Optimization," as of December 1997 more than 80% of Internet users surfed on version 3.0 or higher of Netscape and Microsoft's browsers, which support Java by default and accept the more sophisticated multimedia plug-ins, such as Shockwave.

Less encouraging for advertisers were the sites themselves. AdKnowledge, an advertising services company that maintains a database of the 1,000 or so top Internet publishers, reported in August 1997 that only 17% of sites they track support Java in ads, and 14% support Shockwave. Although Java is by now a fairly reliable technology on most browsers, Shockwave animations are limited by whether Web surfers have downloaded and installed the required plug-in.

The most common type of banner animation uses the GIF89 technique. Its popularly stems from its near-universal browser support (including the 2.0 versions of the "big two" browsers), smaller file sizes than other animation types, and the relative simplicity of creating the animations. The name derives from a 1989 adaptation of the graphic interchange format (GIF) that CompuServe developed a few years earlier.

Basically, GIF89s aren't much different than the penny-arcade mutoscopes that so charmed folks 100 years ago: a series of images that flip past each other in quick succession. Most of the banner ads that endlessly cycle through the same four frames of clever text ending in "Click Here!" are GIF89s.

A technology named for the year 1989 is ancient history in Web terms, of course, and innovative companies have since introduced more compelling animation techniques. A company called InterVU, for example, has developed a technology to put video in ad banners for such clients as Budweiser, Warner Bros., and Volvo. InterVU claims that 90% of Web surfers can view video clips with its technology, which first figures out which video format a Web surfer can support, be it MPEG, Vivo, QuickTime, or plain old GIF89, and then serves the appropriate one.

Figure 9.11

InterVU's video banner technology has brought ads like Budweiser's "Frank and Louie" series to life on the Web.

USWeb worked with Silicon Graphics's virtual reality division, Cosmo, to distribute the first *virtual reality modeling language (VRML)* ad banner on the Web. During the media hype surrounding NASA's Mars probe in the summer of 1997, Silicon Grahpics developed an ad banner for Pepsi Cola that featured the Sojourner buggy driving around a 3D simulation of the Martian surface and bumping into a giant can of Pepsi. At the time, relatively few Web surfers had a VRML extension installed on their browsers to experience the ad properly, but it made quite a sensation in cutting-edge circles and was a powerful proof of the concept. Silicon Graphics Cosmo Player is now a standard component of the Netscape 4.0 browser, so VRML ads may well become more common in the near future.

Figure 9.12

It's just not the same in print. The first 3D Web banner, promoting Pepsi during the Mars Sojourner hype, using Silicon Graphics's Cosmo VRML technology.

Interactivity

Realizing that about 98% of the time Web surfers don't want to click ad banners because they're happy with the site they're on, some marketers have begun creating ads in which Web surfers can perform functions within the banner without needing to click through to another destination.

Narrative Enlivens Ad Interactions

A company called Narrative Communications makes Enliven, a software product that specializes in interactive banners. The ads are Java files, so they don't require any special plug-ins on standard browsers, yet they deliver smooth animation and sound effects sure to grab a Web surfer's attention. Using streaming technology, the ads download additional data from the server only when the user interacts, creating an experience of seemingly endless new content without excessive delays.

Figure 9.13

Hewlett-Packard's sensational Pong banner, designed by Red Sky Interactive with Shockwave technology, set new standards for creativity in banner design. The banner let netizens relive the '70s by playing the world's first video game again.

Figure 9.14

This banner for Diamond Multimedia uses Narrative's Enliven technology to rousing effect. The ad starts with a baseball bat swinging at a ball and making an audible crack, followed by a crowd's cheers. It then offers some true/false questions and a chance to win prizes.

The result is a more powerful ad experience than possible on TV or in print. The user truly interacts with the brand as she clicks on icons, selects choices from pull-down menus, drags and drops items across the screen, and otherwise immerses herself in the ad. Although still a novelty, the ads are fun and can typically absorb users for five minutes or more.

Advertisers such as Citibank, New Balance, and L.L. Bean have used Enliven in ads to demonstrate product features, collect sweepstakes entries, provide useful consumer information, and more, all within standard-size banner ads.

"Our advertisers regularly see anywhere between 16% and 35% of users interacting with the ads," said Jamie Bertasi, director of business development at Narrative. "Our server, meanwhile, collects a tremendous amount of data about all the users' interactions, down to how long they hold their mouse over a particular item, whether more surfers click on the left or the right side, and so on. It gives the advertisers a tremendous amount of information to work with to redesign their ads more effectively, change the promotion, whatever."

A competitor, Thinking Media, makes a similar product with an advantage to publishers in that it doesn't require them to purchase a special server for the streaming effect, as Narrative's Enliven does. Which company, if either, will become the standard for interactive ads is anyone's guess at this point.

Another company, First Virtual, which specializes in secure transaction technology, has developed a type of ad banner in which Web surfers can actually make secure purchases within the banner (in addition to a newer, unrelated line of software for email commerce). Customers of the banner technology, called VirtualTAG, include PC Zone, Casio, and the U.S. Post Office, who have used it to sell computers, watches, and stamps.

Ms. Bertasi says that in 1998 Narrative plans to enhance Enliven so it can also transact secure commerce within banners.

Figure 9.15

First Virtual used its VirtualTAG electronic-commerce banner technology to create this ad where a user can donate money to the United Cerebral Palsy charity in an animated, interactive game-like environment.

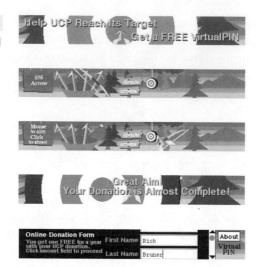

One downside to interactive banners is that many users have become wary of clicking on them due to the trend of faux interactive ads. These deceptive ads invite the user to click on a search field or scrollbar within the banner, only to find that it's a static graphic that automatically transfers the user to a new page.

Porno sites, always at the vanguard of new techniques to attract users, favor this ruse. Try searching on the word "butt" on Yahoo!, Excite, or another search engine. The resulting banners for hardcore porno sites frequently indicate that they're in the process of automatically downloading a video clip to your desktop. They prominently feature a Cancel button, but when you press it, it merely takes you to the site you're trying to avoid. The search engines are unapologetic about displaying these all-round unsavory ads.

Figure 9.16

What appears to be the first search box on this AltaVista page is actually a fake interactive ad banner that loads DoubleClick's site when clicked. A few experiences like that and Web surfers may be conditioned against trying real interactive ads.

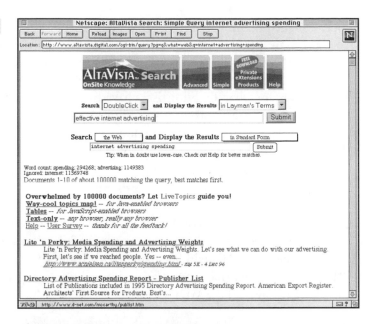

Figure 9.17

Searching Yahoo! for "butt" brings up this banner. Although it's really just a GIF89 animation, users may believe they're downloading a porno video. Hitting the Cancel button calls up a smut site.

Interstitials

If ever a piece of computer jargon deserved to be hung up by its thumbs, it has to be the abominable *interstitials*. These are the full-screen ads that occasionally pop up between pages on cutting-edge sites. Unfortunately, *interstitial* is indeed a genuine, if somewhat obscure dictionary word meaning "situated in the space that intervenes between things."

Interstitials are what TV advertisers have been waiting for on the Web. They get in your face, take up the full browser screen, and don't go away until you click on them or they're done with their animation. The term has been applied to *splash screen* ads, which are simply static ad pages that the user has to click to go to the next page, but we prefer to think of true interstitials as animated ones lasting 5–15 seconds.

"Until now, online advertising has lacked the kind of impact possible with TV commercials, where a well-made AT&T ad can make viewers weepy," said Evan Neufeld, an analyst with Jupiter Communications. "You just can't get that from a banner. Interstitials, however, promise to bring that power to the Web."

In a June 1997 report titled "Banners and Beyond," Jupiter analysts predicted that by the year 2001, a quarter of all online ad spending would go to interstitials. We certainly hope that doesn't mean a quarter of all *ads* will be interstitials, or anywhere close. The same report notes that although Net users haven't objected to the still-uncommon phenomenon of interstitials, if they became so widespread that Web-surfing meant constant 10-second interruptions by animated commercials, users would almost certainly revolt.

In addition to users' annoyance at having their machines hijacked by intrusive ads they can't avoid—flying in the face of the innate freedom the Web offers users—there's also the matter of delays while the interstitials download.

The "interstitial" aspect of the ads is that they appear between Web pages. Theoretically, while the user views page A, the interstitial file should download in the background, ready to run instantly when the user clicks to go to page B. But anyone who has waited for a 15-second Shockwave animation to download can guess that the experience might not be so seamless.

Figure 9.18

Berkeley Systems' frenetic online trivia game, You Don't Know Jack, makes great use of interstitial ads. Three times during play, the game pauses for a pair of full-screen animated ads. Here, James Bond walks through his classic logo to promote a marathon 007 week on TBS.

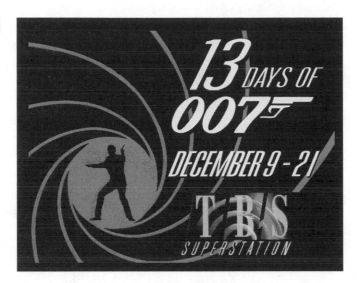

PointCast: Interstitial Expertise

A pioneer of interstitial-style animated ads is the push-technology leader PointCast. Using Macromedia Director (the same application used to design Shockwave animations), ad agencies have created hundreds of animated PointCast ads for companies including Toyota, Birds Eye, and MCI. Because it's a push application (see Chapter 7 for more discussion on *push*), PointCast gets around the delay of downloading large animation files. Its users are generally connected to the Web through corporate T1 lines, so the server can feed the files to the desktop without waiting for users to "pull" the data off a Web site, as browsers must do. As a result, the animations are preloaded for instant play while the user is on the phone, writing memos, or otherwise occupied.

Pulling off this smooth effect on a Web site is more challenging. One software company with interstitial technology, Adletts, has attempted to work around the problem by keeping its Java animations files very small, around 15KB. Instead of taking over the entire browser screen, the Adletts files open a small window where the quick animations run in the foreground and cannot be canceled until they're finished.

Because interstitials are still in the early stages, it remains to be seen whether they'll have the impact some analysts predict without being condemned by users as an annoyance, scaring sites away from using them.

Sponsorships

In addition to Jupiter's prediction that interstitials will make up a quarter of all ad spending by 2001, the analyst group thinks that half of all ad spending will remain with banners, particularly interactive ones. The remaining quarter, they believe, will be applied to sponsorships.

We suspect that sponsorships will end up with a larger piece of the pie than interstitials.

Already, sponsorships are popular across the Web in a variety of forms. With the boundaries between online editorial and marketing still maturing, it's frequently difficult to tell where the content ends and the advertising begins. Regardless, a lot of marketers are feeling confident in exploring sponsorships.

"There is definitely a potential danger there for both sites and advertisers that users may feel cheated, that what they thought was editorial content they later realize is paid advertising," said Christopher Theodoros, VP and director of creative sponsorship strategies at DoubleClick. "When approached carefully, however, sponsorships can be an extremely powerful form of advertising online. It's a question of preserving the credibility of the content while enhancing it with the brand association."

Although in most forms of sponsorship Web surfers are encouraged to click through to the sponsor's site, the goal of this model is principally brand-building. Advertisers and publishers are still playing with the definitions of sponsorship on the Web, and so far the results have taken many different forms. In our view, based on current trends, there are five basic types of sponsorships:

- Branded content

- Event promotions

- Advertorials

- Microsites

- Portals

Branded Content

Branded content most closely follows the "brought to you by" model of early television and today's public television. Think of yesteryear's "Mutual of Omaha's Wild Kingdom."

In the branded content model, the advertiser has no hand in creating or shaping the content. Editorial control is left entirely to the publisher, while the brand benefits from the association with the quality content. These kinds of deals are frequently negotiated as long-term contracts, normally in an exclusive arrangement so that no other advertiser, particularly a competitor, is associated with the content.

In such cases an advertiser may sponsor a regular section of a site, or the entire site in some cases. Oldsmobile's sponsorship of CBS SportsLine's Auto Racing section is an example of a site section sponsorship. The relationship has lasted more than a year, precluding any other auto brand from being associated with this editorial positioning. Toyota, meanwhile, has gone a step further and underwritten the entire ad budget of Time Warner's Cars and Culture site.

Figure 9.19

CBS SportsLine's Auto Racing section is "presented by Aurora from Oldsmobile," a branded content sponsorship that has lasted more than a year.

Event Promotions

Event promotions involve a closer integration of publisher and advertiser content. These promotions last only a short period, normally from one to several weeks, and highlight a special offer, contest, or event. They're frequently given great prominence by the publisher, such as at the top of the homepage.

Yahoo! seems to run this type of contest sponsorship perpetually, with the promotion frequently integrated into the Yahoo! logo. The Dilbert contest discussed in Chapter 7 is an example of this type of sponsorship, in which both United Media and Nynex's Big Yellow business directory were promoted. Later Yahoo! hosted a virtual road rally contest sponsored by Volvo, with a grand prize of a trip to Scandinavia.

Figure 9.20

Yahoo! regularly hosts event promotions, such as this contest sponsored by Volvo.

Movies frequently engage in this type of sponsorship. For the U.S. launch of the film *Mr. Bean*, Rowan Atkinson's goofy character was spotted loping incongruously across HotWired's pages. Disney, meanwhile, commemorated the opening of *101 Dalmatians* by adding black spots to the backgrounds of several prominent sites.

Advertorials

Further blurring the line between ad and editorial content online are *advertorials*. They're a familiar tradition in print journalism, where publishers normally make it abundantly clear that they're paid advertisements. Typically they do this by setting the type in a distinct font, surrounding the item in a border, and prominently labeling it "Paid Advertisement." Web publishers aren't always so fastidious.

Many smaller publishers struggling to stay afloat are willing to cut corners on such formalities and will display material in whatever way makes advertisers happy. Surprisingly, even established media companies have shown a willingness to blur this line in their online ventures.

For example, one wonders whether *Forbes* is the "capitalist tool" or merely the tool of capitalists. The magazine's Web site was quick to embrace the advertorial model, sharing columns evenly in its various content sections, with staff articles on the left and advertiser text on the right. In the first year or so, the site did label this sponsorship "advertisement" in bold type at the top. More recently, however, that label has disappeared, replaced by a small disclaimer at the bottom of the column.

Figure 9.21

The whole right-hand column of this page is an advertorial, although Forbes doesn't make this clear until the bottom of the column.

Microsites

Microsites expand the idea of the advertorial to multiple ad/content pages, along the lines of special ad supplements to magazines and newspapers. Rather than drawing the visitor away from the editorial site to the advertiser's corporate site, these microsites usually maintain a thematic congruity with the publisher's content while allowing the advertiser to immerse the visitor in the brand. For users, microsites can be an attractive way to explore a brand without a complete shift of context and the annoyance of waiting for a whole new set of server connections to load a new site in the browser.

A good example of a microsite is Levi's "They Go On" section within **NBC.com**. The ad feature was highlighted prominently on NBC's homepage alongside microsites for the *Homicide* series, Jay Leno's *Tonight Show*, and other network programming, as if "They Go On" were one of NBC's shows. However, the microsite turns out to be an enigmatic, artsy account of a young couple's cross-country road trip in the impressionistic style of Levi's striking "They Go On" television commercials.

Figure 9.22

It's hard to tell whether this microsite for Levi's on **NBC.com** is advertising or content. On dozens of stylish pages, it recounts the travels of a young couple around the country and includes discussion forums for visitors. At heart, however, it's an ad in the hip, youthful cinematic style of Levi's "They Go On" TV commercials.

Portals

What we refer to as *portals* are the murkiest category of sponsorship. Here, the distinctions between advertising and syndication and revenue-sharing and other online promotional and money-making strategies begin to meld completely.

A portal sponsorship, by our definition, is where one site agrees to integrate the content of another site as a service to Web surfers and a branding value to the content provider. Examples include a news site incorporating the functions of a leading search engine, or a content aggregator like AOL linking to only one shopping site in a particular category, or a business magazine offering up-to-the-minute stock quotes from a specialized stock service.

Amazon.com and Barnes and Noble have been in pitched battle to secure exclusive linking arrangements with leading sites as the preferred online bookstore. Amazon.com Associates Program encourages smaller sites to post an Amazon.com logo with recommendations of specific books, rewarding the sites with up to a 15% revenue share on any subsequent sales via the link. Is that an ad or a sales commission? The distinction probably doesn't matter to the sites getting paid to host the link. Amazon.com wins either way, getting free branding even if the link generates no sales.

In many portal arrangements, no money ever changes hands. **ABCNews.com**, for example, links to Mr. Showbiz for its entertainment news, and likewise Mr. Showbiz links to **ABCNews.com** on its homepage. Because both sites are properties of ABC, it's a pure cross-promotion deal.

USA Today's site features several portals to content from other publishers, such as investment advice from the Motley Fool. One suspects that *USA Today* gets the content for free from Motley Fool in exchange for the great brand exposure. When asked, executives from both *USA Today* and Motley Fool declined to explain the terms of the arrangement, citing a confidentiality agreement. However, *USA Today* marketing director Allegra Young acknowledged that the site does indeed get content for free from some partners in exchange for the publicity it offers them.

Figure 9.23

DLJdirect pays the *New York Times* for the publicity it receives on **NYTimes.com** and provides the news giant with a stock quote service for free. A classic portal sponsorship.

Non-Web Advertising

Although the Web generally gets star billing among Internet media, there are of course other platforms, such as email, push technology, and chat, each with significant numbers of users and advertising possibilities.

One advantage these services have over Web advertising is that they provide strong demographic targeting opportunities. Chat, push, and email subscription services generally break through the Web's barrier of anonymity by offering users personalized services that require them to define their age, gender, geographic location, and other demographic data, along with hobbies and other special interests. Whereas many Web sites encounter reluctance from users to fill out registration forms, these alternative platforms can often entice valuable demographics from users in exchange for value-added services.

Email

Electronic mail or email is used by significantly more people worldwide than the Web. And although unsolicited commercial emails, called *spam*, will likely remain a brand-damaging anathema to most Internet users indefinitely, there are several viable channels available for email advertising.

Services such as Juno, Hotmail, and RocketMail have signed up millions who have agreed to receive ads in exchange for free email service. Juno supplies users with its own software that dials directly to a local access number for the email account, thereby eliminating the need for users to have their own Internet access.

Hotmail and RocketMail, on the other hand, offer email via the Web, raising the seeming contradiction that users must first have access to the Internet and the Web before they can get free email. Yet these services have found a sizable, if diverse, base of users, including students and others with limited institutional Web access, library surfers, business travelers who may find Web access on the road, users seeking secondary private email accounts to avoid snooping bosses or conduct secret romances, and employees in risky start-up companies who want a consistent online address in case their corporate handle vanishes in bankruptcy.

Juno lets advertisers send direct email promotions to users, in addition to serving banner ads within its proprietary email software. Hotmail and RocketMail serve only traditional Web banner ads when users log on to those Web sites to check their email.

Figure 9.24

Hotmail gives users email for free on the Web in exchange for banner ads, such as this one for Visa.

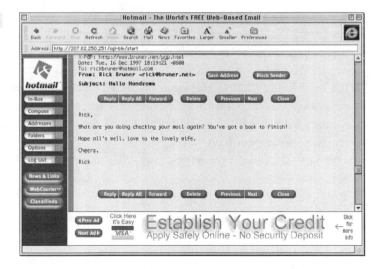

BonusMail presents another email advertising model. Users agree to receive direct email ads in exchange for points they accumulate, redeemable for free gifts at a variety of participating sponsors. To collect points, users must demonstrate that they have read the ads by replying to the messages with code words embedded in the ads. When they act on special promotional offers in the ads, they receive additional credits. Bonus-Mail has targeted users of HTML-enhanced email software packages for its service, so nearly 70% of subscribers get graphics, hyperlinks, and specially formatted text in the direct email ad messages.

BonusMail's 27-year-old president and CEO, Steven Markowitz, described the opportunity he envisioned in founding the company: "When I came up with the idea, I saw it as a way to solve a problem direct marketers faced online. On the one hand, spam has a terrible reputation and is still damaging for the image of advertisers who engage in it. On the other hand, there is a tremendous appeal in correlating the simplicity of email with computer-managed consumer demographics. The answer, as I saw it, was to give users an incentive to agree to receive ad messages, while making sure those messages were closely targeted to their interests. After all, the difference in perception between what is junk mail and what is valuable information depends entirely on how interesting the offer is to the recipient."

Chat

Real-time chat is one of the fastest-growing applications in online culture. Since the early popularization of cyberspace, netizens on commercial services like CompuServe and AOL, as well as those on the geekier Internet Relay Chat (IRC) protocol, have enjoyed the magical connectedness of typing text into their computer screens and seeing instant responses from others who are hundreds or thousands of miles away. More recently, businesses have begun to embrace chat for use in customer service, virtual business meetings, and other applications. The driving force behind the medium, however, remains flirtation and other social interaction.

In early 1997, AOL led the charge in chat advertising, enabling marketers to display ads to the millions of users of its more than 15,000 chat rooms. In the same year Web-based chat software hit its stride, and now many sites offer chat communities as exclusive site services or as enhancements to other content.

WebChat Broadcasting, for example, one of the largest Internet chat communities, has integrated graphics into its chat software, allowing members to append pictures of themselves to their posts. The same technology allows ads to float amidst the scrolling chat text, in addition to ads fixed elsewhere in the page frames.

Figure 9.25

In WebChat Broadcast's forum on pro football, Atlanta Internet Bank's banner gets some great exposure amidst sports fans' chat about getting drunk.

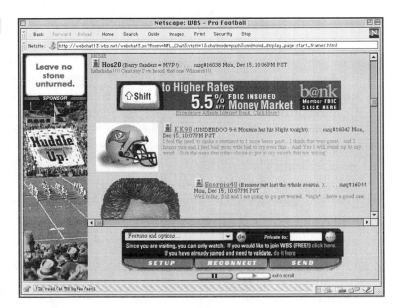

A hopeful software firm, Blaxxun (formerly known as Black Sun), has created a product called Community Server that allows advertisers to create robot advertisements that draw users into private chats about products. The chatting ads can be sent into action when users type key phrases during public chat sessions.

The company went so far as to develop a 3D version of the software for the small-but-growing world of VRML chat rooms. As a proof of concept, it developed a character named Dusty, a chatting vacuum cleaner, to promote Black & Decker's Dustbuster product. When visitors wandered into a 3D world on Blaxxun's site and happened to use a word such as "dirt" or "housework" during a chat (or even if they just hung around in the virtual plaza long enough), they were approached by the 3D likeness of a handheld vacuum cleaner with Groucho Marx glasses, a mustache, and bushy eyebrows. This *avatar* (VRML-speak for a 3D virtual character), Dusty, politely invited them into a preprogrammed conversation about the virtues of the Dustbuster. As far as we know, this 3D ad robot technology never found paying customers, and Blaxxun, a Munich-based company, has humbly closed its U.S. offices and kept a low profile about the product since its launch.

Chat presents both benefits and liabilities for advertisers. On the upside, the audience is generally very loyal, checking back with the same communities frequently and staying logged in to the services longer than visitors to typical Web sites, which presents opportunities for strong brand associations. Also, most chat sites collect basic demographic information about users that can be used in ad targeting.

On the downside, chat doesn't generally drive much traffic because users come for the conversation, not for ideas on where to surf next. Also, although specific chat rooms may have narrow themes, such as professional hockey, mountain climbing, or Jimi Hendrix, there's no telling what path the actual conversations will take. Brands may end up being positioned next to off-color or otherwise inappropriate discussions, possibly even bashing of the advertiser in question.

Push

As we discussed in Chapter 7 push technology has yet to come close to the Internet-rocking impact promised in the hype of early 1997. As of this writing, it's too early to tell whether the release of Netscape's Netcaster and Microsoft's Active Desktop push platforms, bundled with the 4.0 versions of their browsers, will revitalize this trend.

Jupiter, in its June 1997 report "Beyond the Browser," certainly believed it will, predicting that "push technology solutions will become ubiquitous among leading Web sites, and that a significant portion of publishers' revenue will be derived from these services." We remain to be convinced.

Meanwhile, PointCast, the granddaddy of push applications, does give some indication of the powerful potential of push advertising. Since its launch in early 1996, PointCast claims to have attracted more than 2 million loyal users. The service began targeting mainly office workers in the high-tech industry who have fast, constant connections to the Internet. Using proprietary end-user software, the service kicks in as a screen saver when users' computers are idle, scrolling news stories and animated ads.

Building on its immediate success with users, PointCast has signed syndication arrangements with more than 1,000 content providers. It has also introduced targeted news services including a Canadian edition, a college network, and specialized vertical professional news networks serving such niche industries as banking, health care, law, real estate, and state and federal government agencies.

Figure 9.26

PointCast's Business Network channel, supported by advertisers like MCI, reaches the valuable demographic of corporate workers with fast Internet connections.

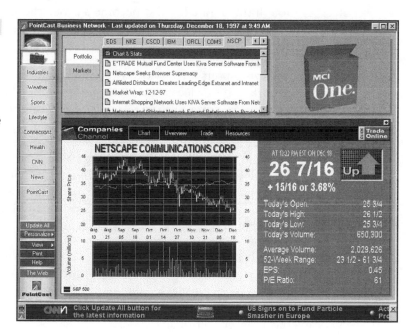

Anna Zornosa, senior vice president of advertising and affiliate development at PointCast, explained that in late 1995, selling advertisers on the idea of TV-like animated ads on the Internet wasn't a piece of cake.

"Everyone's initial reaction was, 'Oh, come on, how are you going to make an ad impression with a screen saver?' None of the clients or ad agencies had ever made a 30-second animated computer commercial before.

"In the magazine industry, a typical ad sales call lasts about 40 minutes. Our early sales calls lasted 3-4 hours. An hour into the meeting, we would mention you can click on the ad. They were amazed. Until then, they hadn't realized these were interactive ads we were talking about."

Since those early days, the network has proved its worth to many of the dozens of advertisers who've taken advantage of it, including Polaroid, Oldsmobile, and Procter & Gamble.

Targeting

The battle cry of Internet marketing has long been "one-to-one marketing." Although the phrase has fast become a cyber-cliche, the message behind it is real. In the world of online advertising, the operative word is *targeting*.

Imagine if television sets were two-way communication devices that could stare back at their viewers and relay information about them to the broadcast station. For example, one TV set could see that its viewer was a woman in her mid-40s. In fact, it knew her name was Mary Wilson. She was fairly affluent, judging by the furnishings in her living room, yet she was single. According to her viewing habits, the TV surmised that she was interested in sports, cooking, and celebrity entertainment news. It knew that Mary lived on the lower-east side of Manhattan. And it also had a sense of self, aware that it was a six-year-old Sony and that soon she would be in the market for a replacement.

The TV dutifully sent all this information back to the broadcaster, who accordingly targeted her with ads suited just for her: running shoes, New York singles bars, cooking classes, and new TVs. Her neighbor in the apartment next door watched the same shows at the same time, but saw a completely different set of ads.

It sounds like an Orwellian nightmare. But this scenario isn't far off from what's taking place on the Web today, whether the majority of netizens realize it or not.

Rotating advertising is no mean feat for any site, and targeting those ads to individual users based on their unique characteristics, all within a fraction of a second, seems impossibly complicated. Yet more than a dozen specialized companies provide software packages and services to do exactly that, including Accipiter, AdKnowledge, AdSmart, Aptex, ATG,

Autonomy, BellCore, DoubleClick, FlyCast, Imgis, Intelligent Interactions, MatchLogic, Narrowline, Nestor, NetGravity, Real Media, and others.

Although these companies take care of the under-the-hood technical aspects of ad targeting, it behooves you to understand the general strategies for audience segmentation online. These include content, technographic, demographic, geographic, and psychographic targeting.

Content

The most basic form of online ad targeting, and also one of the most effective, is content affiliation. Just as a running shoe manufacturer would advertise in *Sports Illustrated* magazine and an investment service would advertise in *Money* magazine, advertisers online generally seek their target audiences according to the editorial themes of specialized sites. In fact, the vast majority of ad targeting on the Web today is done this way.

Content targeting generally doesn't necessarily exploit much technical sophistication. Rather, it's done through familiar, manual means: Media buyers analyze which sites are suitable venues for their marketing objectives, and the ads are then placed in general rotation across the site or within particular site sections.

One of the advantages (and difficulties) of targeting by content is the incredible breadth and diversity of Web sites out there. Most of the more than 1 million sites on the Web are run by hobbyists or institutions that don't run any ads. Most of them would probably be more than willing to do so if the opportunity presented itself, though. For advertisers in search of niche markets, no other medium comes close to the Web's minute categorization.

The challenge for the marketer is in qualifying what's available. The Web doesn't yet have the kinds of established directories that ad agencies use to reference media properties in TV, radio, newspapers, and magazines. The few services that come close, notably AdKnowledge's MarketMatch database, include only a few hundred sites among the thousands of potential ad venues.

Even the more professional sites have wildly divergent rate cards and reporting standards, making it sometimes maddening for advertisers to be clear about what they're paying for.

LINKEXCHANGE: KING OF NICHE AND REACH

For advertisers who want to consolidate large ad buys in a single package, there are several advertising networks that represent dozens or even hundreds of large and medium sites, including DoubleClick, Zulu Media, 24/7 Media, Real Media, AdSmart, and FlyCast.

One network stands out as very different, with the unique value propositions of incredible *reach* (that is, a large distribution to many Web surfers) and extraordinary niche targeting: the LinkExchange network.

The brainchild of a couple of 23-year-old Harvard computer graduates, Sanjay Madan and Tony Hsieh, LinkExchange brilliantly embodies the original "information wants to be free" spirit of the Internet community. Because of this, many marketers neglected to take the network seriously, assuming the founders were just starry-eyed kids who'd get real jobs eventually. The investment specialists at Sequoia Capital looked a bit deeper and saw the network's financial promise, however, banking the company for $3 million in mid-1997. At that point, many analysts and advertisers finally started to catch on to the distinctive power of this network.

In a nutshell, LinkExchange offers small sites free advertising on a 2:1 basis—for every two ads a member displays on its own site, it gets one ad to promote itself on other member sites. Because each member site displays twice as many ads as it's given to promote itself, the LinkExchange company ends up with a huge available inventory of unused ad credits.

That's where the money comes in: LinkExchange can sell all those excess ads to non-members—that is, paying advertisers.

The idea has spawned many imitators, but none comes remotely close to LinkExchange's reach. The network has caught on like wildfire, counting more than 200,000 members by the end of 1997, less than two years after it launched. To put it in perspective, more than 10% of all sites on the Web belong to the LinkExchange network. The network shows more than five million ads a day, and, according to the Media Metrix research group, its combined sites are seen by more Web surfers than any other Web services except Yahoo! and America Online.

The appeal to advertisers is twofold. First, no other service rivals LinkExchange's impact in making a massive impression across the whole Web.

Consider the case of Universal Studios' promotion of its celebrity chat for *The Lost World: Jurassic Park*. Like many film studios, Universal regularly schedules chats to coincide with its movie releases. According to LinkExchange's executives, Universal came to them in a panic two days before the premiere of the film. In all the work the moviemakers did to get ready for the blockbuster's debut, they'd overlooked their usual means of promoting the celebrity chat, and now there was no time left to pursue those avenues. Not expecting much, Universal asked LinkExchange to do what it could to get the word out.

Universal's celebrity chats typically had been attracting around 2,000–3,000 participants. After LinkExchange blanketed more than 100,000 sites (the size of the network at the time) for a day, a record 12,000 chatters showed up to type along with stars Jeff Goldblum and Julianne Moore. Universal was impressed enough about setting an Internet chat record to put out a press release.

Second, LinkExchange can deliver incredible content targeting by every imaginable niche topic. It has categorized its member sites into 1,600 different topic affiliations.

Figure 9.27

Surf Point, LinkExchange's member directory, lists 433 sites in the real estate category alone.

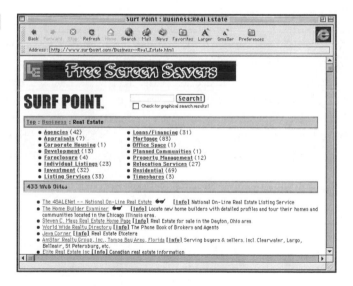

Imagine an advertiser who's interested in targeting football players and fans with a football trivia game. He may go predictably to ESPN SportsZone and CBS SportsLine, as well as the NFL site and perhaps a handful of other top sports sites. LinkExchange, meanwhile, has nearly 10,000 sports sites, including 250 sites devoted to professional football, 100 on college football, 75 on fantasy football, 20 on football trading cards, 10 on high school football, and another 100 or so in six other football categories.

In addition to other major sports categories, LinkExchange's section "Other Ball Sports" includes further subcategories for sites dedicated to billiards and snooker, bowling, cricket, Australian football, handball, lacrosse, racquetball, squash, rugby, table tennis, badminton, volleyball, and more.

"Some advertisers think they should stick to sites with known brands," said Ali Partovi, VP of business development for LinkExchange. "But think of advertising on radio. No advertiser tells their ad agency that they want their ads to run during a certain DJ's show on a particular station in Seattle, or immediately after a specific song on a station in Dallas. They say, 'Get me broad reach during drive-time on top 40 stations,' and it's the media buyer's job at the ad agency to know which stations fit the bill. LinkExchange provides that same alternative on the Web."

Technographic

Also called *environmental* targeting, aiming ads to users according to the technographic information volunteered by every browser is the most basic form of dynamic ad targeting. In the back-and-forth chatting of the HTTP Web protocol, the browser gives the server various information about the Web surfer's computer and network, such as what kind of browser and operating system he uses, his ISP, what URL he linked to your site from, what time of day he visited, and other data.

With the appropriate server software, sites can target ads to individual users based on all these criteria. Many sites that brag about being able to target ads to users "dynamically" or in "real-time" are targeting according to such technographic variables, mainly because it's the easiest data about users to collect.

Unfortunately, technographic targeting is of limited benefit to most non-technology advertisers. If you're selling beer, mutual funds, or cars, it probably doesn't make much difference whether Web surfers use Netscape or Microsoft browsers on Macs or PCs.

Figure 9.28

Was it an amazing coincidence that I'm one of the precious few remaining Macintosh users, and I saw this same ad for the Mac version of Internet Explorer all across the Web one week?? No. The sites sniffed out my OS before serving the ad.

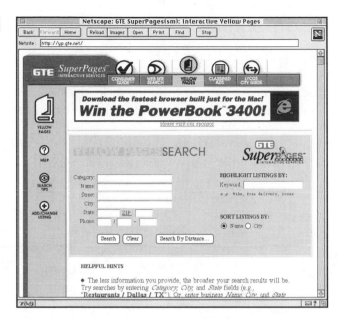

Perhaps a product particularly geared towards students could target according to .edu domains. Or you could target Web surfers with AOL accounts on the broad assumption that they represent typical Middle American consumers (and presuming there's some advantage to targeting them on a particular Web site instead of directly within AOL's network).

Time of day is another data point that sites extol as a target for advertisers. They cite examples such as a TV program that's promoted an hour before showtime or a snack maker that runs banners around lunch time. The problem with targeting by time, however, is time zones. Although it may be TV primetime according to the site's California-based servers, it would already be pushing midnight for a New York Web surfer. Judging the users' geographical location by technographic information is a much trickier proposition, as we'll discuss shortly.

On the balance, although technographics can be very important for software vendors and other technological companies, non-tech advertisers need to scrutinize the purported benefits of this kind of ad targeting.

Demographic

Demographic targeting is "the beef" of the "one-to-one marketing" hype. Demographics weed out the pimple-faced teenage burger-flippers surfing in mom's basement from the males aged 35–45 in the Bay Area who earn over $100,000 a year and are interested in fast cars.

Thankfully, from a privacy standpoint, it's still rather difficult to distinguish the two groups from their browsers alone. Most demographic information valuable to marketers must be gleaned from Web surfers directly. This generally means requesting visitors to fill out site registration data.

Figure 9.29

Hotmail's free email service relies on users to fill out a brief demographic survey, allowing the site to target ads more effectively to them.

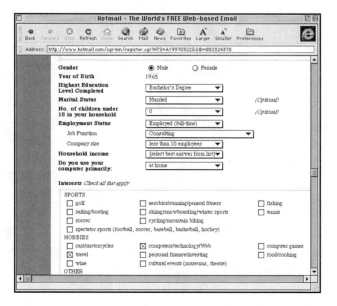

The problem for advertisers is that few sites truly implement demographic targeting effectively. There are two main reasons for this. First, many users won't fill out such forms, either due to privacy concerns or because it's a pain in the posterior to keep entering the same data about themselves at site after site. Second, even when sites do manage to collect lots of user information, managing that data is no mean feat for a site with thousands or millions of visitors.

Nonetheless, there are sites out there that manage to do so, offering advertisers powerfully advanced targeting abilities. The *New York Times* is one of the few sites that has succeeded in demanding that all users register to gain access. Due to its superb content, this is a tradeoff that more than two million registered users have been willing to make. As a result, the *Times* can target ads to the demographic "golden triangle" of *ZAG (ZIP code, age, and gender)*, plus income brackets.

Bruce Judson, executive VP and chief marketing officer at CellularVision, a New York-based high-speed wireless ISP, praised the *New York Times'* demographic targeting as the most effective advertising vehicle in any media that CellularVision has used to promote its services. Mr. Judson, who is the former general manager of Time Inc. New Media and cofounder of Time's Pathfinder site, explained that initially CellularVision wanted to broadly target New York state residents due to geographic licensing restrictions. However, the company soon found that it got significantly higher direct sales results the more it customized the ads to highly local regions.

"After some initial tests with the *Times,* we started to customize within geographic areas, which was made possible by their unique ZIP code capabilities," he said. "We literally said, 'Hey Brooklyn!' in an ad, or 'Hey Chelsea!' People coming to the site really knew, 'Oh, this is for me! I live in Brooklyn,' or 'I live in Chelsea.' We found that this kind of personalization led to a dramatic lift in responses. More importantly, we also found that the kind of audience that we brought in converted very well to customers."

A company called Imgis, which outsources the technical infrastructure involved in serving ads for sites and networks, has announced its intention to take demographic ad targeting to the next level by matching Web surfers against their offline shopping histories. The company has arranged to use demographic information from MetroMail, a 50-year-old giant in the direct marketing business with extensive consumer information on millions of Americans, and match that against the customer lists from ISPs and other sources. This way Imgis could let advertisers target netizens who bought luxury cars five years ago, for example, or those with appetites for expensive electronic gadgets.

Figure 9.30

CellularVision used the *New York Times'* ZIP code demographic to target ads to users in particular New York neighborhoods, such as the fashionable downtown Chelsea district. Acquisition rates outperformed the company's ads in all other media on a cost basis.

Not surprisingly, privacy advocates have jumped all over Imgis for its plan. Company officials insist that privacy will be respected to a very high degree. No names, phone numbers, or even email addresses will be available to advertisers or even Imgis employees, due to a method of cross-referencing anonymous serial numbers through a trusted third party.

Nonetheless, even the fact that direct marketers in the offline world regularly use these same sorts of consumer histories for target marketing doesn't ease the anxieties of many Internet users. Netizens hold the new online media to a higher standard of privacy protection, as was discussed in Chapter 2, "Web Value Propositions."

COOKIES AND OPS

Probably the most misunderstood, maligned, and punned-upon Internet technology is the so-called *cookie* file.

Originally dubbed *magic cookie* by its inventors at Netscape, a cookie is nothing more than a text file that resides on the user's hard drive, into which sites can record a short string of data about the user for future reference. Without cookies, the HTTP protocol of the Web doesn't provide any easy way to recognize the same user from one click to the next.

Typically, a site will use a cookie to assign a serial number to an individual user, against which it can cross-reference data stored on the site's own database regarding the user's previous interactions with the site.

Common uses for cookies include the following: enabling a user of a commerce site to carry a virtual shopping basket from page to page, so the site can keep track of what items the user selected for purchase on earlier pages; recognizing a registered member at the homepage so he doesn't have to always enter his password and ID; tracking how many times a Web surfer has seen a particular ad banner to avoid showing him the same one too many times; and matching a user to his demographic profile.

Despite hysterical media reports, cookies cannot "learn" anything about Web surfers. They're simply repositories for data, not agents that sniff anything out. They most certainly can't determine a visitor's email address, bank account number, or any other personal information, unless he has already volunteered that information to the site in the first place. In that case, the cookie simply allows the site to cross-reference the ID of the browser against the user's personal information in the site's database.

Because sites don't actually store much more than a serial number on the user's hard drive, an unrelated site can't use the cookie to gain access to any personal information that the user may have divulged. If sites belong to the same network, however, the network can cross-reference the share data about individual users from one site in the network to the next through cookies.

For example, most of the ad networks, such as DoubleClick, Real Media, and MatchLogic, use cookies to track users across sites within their networks. When a visitor shows up at Site A, the network serves him an ad, slipping him a cookie marker when doing so. When the same user shows up at Site B in the network, the network recognizes him and manages its ad targeting accordingly.

The idea of third-party cookies bothered some privacy advocates, who in mid-1997 succeeded in lobbying a leading Internet standards body, the Internet Engineering Task Force (IETF), to propose a new set of standards that would do away with third-party cookies.

The online advertising community, which hadn't paid attention to the drafting process of the new standards, woke up in a panic and lobbied Microsoft and Netscape to ignore the proposed standards. Because the IETF only recommends standards without any power to enforce them, the Big Two browser makers sided with the advertising community. They ignored the IETF's recommendations in the release of their 4.0 browsers, leaving cookie management pretty much the same as it had been. Eliminating third-party cookies would have badly shaken the ability of many advertisers to target effectively.

As a compromise, Netscape, Microsoft, and a slew of other companies endorsed a new proposed technology known as the *Open Profiling Standard (OPS)*. Details of the initiative have been scant since its announcement in the summer of 1997, but committees are at work drafting a form of it likely to be adopted with the 5.0 versions of the main browsers.

Basically, OPS would allow users to configure their browsers at setup with a wide range of personal demographic data. This would include most of the information requested on registration forms, such as name, email address, gender, and so on, and even such sensitive information as credit card numbers.

The information would be stored securely within the browser so that snooping colleagues or other users couldn't access it without a password. Then, when the Web surfer encountered a site that asked for personal data, he could release only the amount of data he wanted on a site-by-site basis, and without having to retype it over and over.

Presuming it does come to pass, OPS sounds like it would solve several sticky problems of personal data management, ad targeting, and privacy on the Web.

Geographic

Many marketers are realizing that the World Wide Web can be used effectively for very local marketing. Local Web services, from city entertainment listings such as Microsoft's Sidewalk to small- and medium-sized businesses who want to market regionally, are a fast-growing Web trend. And as CellularVision found on the *New York Times* site, targeting ads to users by neighborhood can be highly effective.

So how can you target geographically? The most reliable way is, again, demographic data supplied by the users. As we've seen, however, relatively few sites are prepared to deliver *real* demographics. Fortunately, there are several alternative ways you can target by geography.

One method that's not always reliable is known as *reverse IP look-up*. Sites and networks attempt to recognize visitors by their assigned IP address—a unique string of numbers assigned to every host computer connected to the Internet—and determine where that computer resides physically. This works with many corporate Internet users, whose desktop computers are constantly online and are assigned fixed IP addresses that never change.

The drawback is that the majority of Internet users are connecting from home through ISPs that assign different IP addresses to users each time they connect. The problem is particularly acute with AOL's 10 million-plus users, who are all routed through a handful of external gateways to the Internet. So according to their IP addresses, they almost all appear to be residents of Vienna, Virginia. The same may be true of employees of large national corporations, all of whose IP addresses may be routed through one gateway.

At most, sites may be able to geographically locate 10–20% of their traffic within a general region by using the reverse IP look-up method. The technique certainly cannot promise the kind of neighborhood pinpointing that ZIP code–based targeting provides.

A more obvious alternative is to advertise on locally oriented sites, such as a regional newspaper's online service.

Furthermore, many sites can deduce a Web surfer's geographical location through her use of specialized services such as weather or mapping. Why else would someone check the weather in San Francisco unless she lived there or had some intimate interest in the region?

Figure 9.31

The Weather Channel's site shows a copy of a BayInsider ad to surfers who search on San Francisco weather conditions.

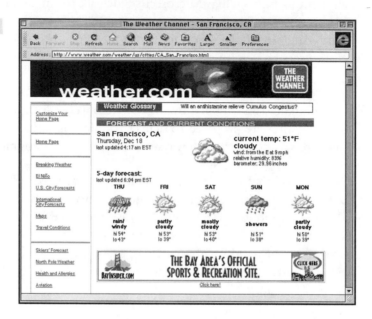

Many sites provide localized service to Web surfers by asking for their ZIP codes and no other demographic data. *TV Guide's* site, for example, provides local TV listings based on users' ZIP codes. **MovieFinder.com** does the same for local cinema showtimes.

Advertisers who are determined to target ads geographically need only hunt around a bit to discover many sites that can provide this valuable data point.

Psychographic

Arguably the most promising means of ad targeting is based on reading people's behavior. Psychologists and market researchers agree that in order to reliably predict what people will do in the future, you should pay less attention to what they *say* they'll do than to what they're already *doing*.

Already among the most valuable kinds of ad targeting is catching Web surfers as they're searching for somewhere to go. The most obvious form of this is through keywords on search engines. The search engines sell banner ads that come up on the results pages in response to surfers searching on popular keywords. Most prime words associated with big-ticket items, such as "travel," "cars," and "computers," are sold out months or years in advance on the leading search engines.

"We see 25% clickthrough rates on our ads tied to the search word 'airline,'" said Anouk Snyder, advertising and promotion manager at Preview Travel. "We buy on Infoseek, Yahoo!, AltaVista, Hotbot, and Excite. There's nothing so remarkable about the creative design of our ads. It's the keywords that do it. It's hard to buy good keywords."

Keywords fetch an even higher premium on "yellow pages" directories, where it's taken for granted that Web surfers are in shopping mode as they search for product categories.

The recent emergence of *neural networking* technology on the Web is likely to have an important impact on ad targeting in the near future. Aptex, Autonomy, and Nestor are three leading vendors of neural networking software, originally designed for military use in pattern recognition, such as the modus operandi of terrorists. The same software is already providing remarkable results on the Web, recognizing patterns in how users interact with Web pages and serving ads accordingly. In short order, the software can get the gist of what kind of content a Web surfer is browsing and anticipate which ad would best catch his attention.

The Infoseek search engine has gotten rave reviews from advertisers for its Ultramatch service, which is based on Aptex's SelectCast software.

"We've seen clickthrough rates double for clients that have advertised on sites using SelectCast," said Brent Hall, senior media buyer at Anderson Lembke, an ad agency that's active in Web advertising.

Mike Lynch, CEO of Autonomy, describes how analyzing a user's behavior and forming a psychographic profile can be a more accurate predictor of behavior than mere demographic measures.

"Say you knew that I was 40-year-old male, living in Silicon Valley, married, and earning $150,000 a year," he said. "You'd think the ads best suited for me would be for a red sports car or a cell phone or a top-of-the-line hi-fi system. What you don't know, however, is that I hate my job, my marriage is falling apart, and I'm dreaming of backpacking in Nepal. If you could read the pages I'm looking at online, however, like our software can, you'd have a better idea and could target me with ads for graduate schools, travel packages, marriage counselors, or dating services."

Miles Walsh, CEO of the FlyCast ad network, is also convinced that neural networks have a big role in the future of online advertising. He plans to buy one of the neural networking products for his ad network in the coming months. "The combination of editable cookies, along the lines of the proposed Open Profile Standard, and neural networks are going to be huge," he said. "They promise the best of both worlds. Editable cookies will let the user give you the demographic information he wants you to know about him, and the neural networks will let you observe what he's doing and make strong predictions about what he's really looking for. Using the two together is going to take direct marketing online to the next level."

Stay tuned. It promises to be a wild ride.

Resources

Also see the Appendix, "Internet Resources," for more online resources related to Web advertising.

Associations

The Internet Advertising Bureau (IAB)

http://www.iab.net/

The IAB is the leading association for companies concerned with Web advertising, whose members include leading online publishers, advertisers, software makers, ad agencies, and others. The site of a wealth of free resources and even more to paying members.

The Coalition for Advertising Supported Information and Entertainment (CASIE)

http://www.casie.org/

Best known by its acronym, CASIE represents mostly ad agencies. The site offers some useful resources.

The Direct Marketing Association

http://www.the-dma.org/

The Direct Marketing Association doesn't have a particularly strong Web site yet, but it's a leading association for direct marketing in the real world, so maybe it will become a better resource with time.

American Association of Advertising Agencies (AAAA)

http://www.aaaa.org/

"The Four As," as it's known, is a leading association in the traditional advertising world. Drill down a bit, and the site offers many useful links and services.

Audit Bureau of Circulations (ABC)

http://www.accessabc.com/

The ABC, the reigning body for monitoring publications' circulation figures in the world of print, has branched into Web measurements as well. The site features some useful services.

Online Advertising News

Advertising Age

http://www.adage.com/

Ad Age, the bible of the real world ad trade, was quick to get hip to the Net, both with its own site and a dedicated section covering Internet advertising (to which your author is a regular contributor). The Interaction section of the site is a bookmark for most who follow online advertising.

Adweek

http://www.adweek.com/

Adweek, *Ad Age's* historic rival, also has a site featuring online ad news.

ClickZ

http://www.clickz.com/

This regularly updated site features descriptions of many of the players in the online advertising space and other resources.

ChannelSeven

http://www.channelseven.com/

The site reviews online ad campaigns and offers other sevices.

Internet Advertising Report

http://www.internetnews.com/iar/

One of the many properties of Mecklermedia's **Internet.com** site, the Internet Advertising Report also covers the online industry closely.

Iconocast

http://www.iconocast.com/

This email newsletter is a valuable insider report of behind-the-scenes deals in the online ad space. It is written with wit by Michael Tchong, founder of MacWEEK magazine and former executive at the Chiat/Day ad agency. The Web site provides subscription information and archives.

Microscope

http://www.microsope.com/

Purchased by ClickZ in late 1997, Microscope reviews ad campaigns and invites media buyers to write about their experiences.

Discussion Groups

The Online Advertising Discussion List

http://www.o-a.com/

The Online Ads email list is generally thought of as the best forum for the wide range of companies trying to make a buck or promote a product with Web advertising. Newbies and old hands are in equal measure. Sign-up is easy at the site. The free list also features the weekly AdBytes digest of many of the week's most important stories about online advertising, with links to complete coverage by other media.

Internet Advertising Discussion List

http://www.exposure-usa.com/i-advertising

This is a near facsimile of the Online Ads list. We prefer Online Ads, though, when we have time to follow only one.

WWW Artists Consortium Advertising SIG List

http://wwwac.org/docs/listserv.html

You can find another fair-quality ad list discussion here.

LE-Digest

http://www.le-digest.com/

This list forum is specifically for members of the LinkExchange ad network, but is open to anyone.

Other Resources

The Online Advertising Forum

http://www.olaf.net/

This site is a collection of lots of good online ad-related links and content.

Advertising Online from The Mining Company

http://adsonline.miningco.com/

Here you can find a strong set of links, including current news titles from other sites, and other online ad resources.

Internet Advertising Bureau/Millward Brown Interactive's 1997 Advertising Effectiveness Study

http://www.mbinteractive.com/site/iab/study.html

This URL is a direct link to the free, excellent study described in detail earlier in the chapter.

SRDS

http://www.srds.com/

This service is a staple in traditional advertising for providing data on ad outlets ranging from consumer magazines and newspaper to direct marketing lists, radio, and TV. Like everyone else, it's moving online. Although its best services are available only to subscribers, the site does have an excellent list of other online advertising and marketing resources.

Direct E-Mail List Source

http://www.copywriter.com/lists

This page gives thousands of email lists that accept paying advertising, letting advertisers leverage email without spamming.

DoubleClick Resource Center

http://www.doubleclick.net/nf/general/resouset.htm

The leading ad network offers lots of advice on this page, including its tips for effective banners and the "Banner Burnout" study mentioned earlier in the chapter.

Four Corners Effective Banners

http://www.whitepalm.com//

An oddly branded site itself, seemingly the side project of an online real estate service (White Palm), this page has extensive listings to advice, original and collected, about effective banner campaigns.

Yahoo! on Web Advertising

http://www.yahoo.com/Computers_and_Internet/Internet/
Business_and_Economics/
Advertising_on_Web_and_Internet/

This page links to lots more sites covering the topic of online advertising.

Internet Resources

Disclaimer

The following URLs aren't meant as endorsements of any products or services, nor are they meant to be comprehensive lists of the services in any categories. They're either useful resources or examples that were cited in this book.

Internet Guides, Histories, and Glossaries

Business Netiquette International

http://www.wp.com/fredfish/Netiq.html

Creative Good Web Guide

http://www.creativegood.com/help/

The Internet TourBus

http://csbh.mhv.net/~bobrankin/tourbus/

Intro to Usenet (newsgroups addresses, not Web URLs)

news.newusers.questions

news.announce.newusers

news.answers

Learn the Net

http://www.learnthenet.com/

Netscape on Netiquette

home.netscape.com/menu/netet/

WhatIs (Internet guide and glossary)

http://whatis.com/

Yahoo! on Internet Beginners Guides

http://www.yahoo.com/Computers_and_Internet/Internet/
Information_and_Documentation/Beginner_s_Guides/

PC Webopaedia

http://www.pcwebopaedia.com/

Web Words

http://www.webwords.net/

Yahoo! on Jargon

http://www.yahoo.com/Computers_and_Internet/
Information_and_Documentation/
Computing_Dictionaries/

and

http://www.yahoo.com/Computers_and_Internet/Internet/
Information_and_Documentation/Internet_Glossaries/

Intenet Society on Internet History

http://www.isoc.org/internet-history/

Yahoo! on Internet History

http://www.yahoo.com/Computers_and_Internet/Internet/
History/

"As We May Think" by Vannevar Bush (important 1945 technology article)

http://www.bush.or.at/

Online Research Reports

ABC Interactive Audit Reports

http://www.accessabvs.com/webaudit/reports.html

BrowserWatch Statistics

http://browserwatch.internet.com/stats.html

CommerceNet/Nielsen Internet Demographics Survey

http://www.commerce.net/nielsen/

CyberAtlas

http://www.cyberatlas.com/

E-Land E-Stats

http://www.e-land.com/e-stat_pages/

Georgia Tech GVU's WWW User Survey

http://www-survey.cc.gatech.edu/

Growth and Usage of the Web and Internet

http://www.mit.edu/people/mkgray/net/

Hermes Research Project

http://www-personal.umich.edu/~sgupta/hermes/

Internet Advertising Bureau/Millward Brown Interactive Advertising Effectiveness Study

http://www.mbinteractive.com/site/iab/study.html

The Internet Index

http://www.openmarket.com/intindex/

Mediamark Research, Inc

http://www.mediamark.com/

Morgan Stanley Internet Advertising Report

http://www.ms.com/misc/inetad/index.html

NUA Internet Surveys

http://www.nua.ie/surveys/

Netcraft Web Server Survey

http://www.netcraft.com/survey/

Network Wizards Internet Domain Surveys

http://www.nw.com/zone/WWW/top.html

Project2000

http://www2000.ogsm.vanderbilt.edu/

TRUSTe/Boston Consulting Group Privacy Survey

http://www.truste.org/webpublishers/studies_BCG.html

University of Illinois Browser Statistics Survey

http://www.cen.uiuc.edu/bstats/latest.html

USA Data

http://www.usadata.com/

ViaWeb Search Engine Study

http://www.viaweb.com/vw/search.html

WebCensus

http://www.webcensus.com

WebReference Banner Ad Placement Study

http://www.webreference.com/dev/banners/topbot.html

Yahoo! on Net statistics

http://www.yahoo.com/Computers_and_Internet/Internet/
World_Wide_Web/Statistics_and_Demographics/

Ziff-Davis InternetTrack

http://www.ziffdavis.com/marketresearch/
internettrak.htm

Search, Directory, and Listing Services

Unless otherwise noted, the following services are general Web search tools.

AltaVisa

http://www.altavista.digital.com/

AOL NetFind

http://www.aol.com/netfind/

Beatrice's Web Guide

http://www.bguide.com

Beth's Sweepstakes

http://rapidnet.com/~tiger/sweeps.htm

BigBook (business directory)

http://www.bigbook.com/

BigYellow (business directory)

http://www.bigyellow.com/

Brian's Free Stuff Home Page

http://come.to/freestuff/

CataList (mailing lists)

http://www.lsoft.com/lists/listref.html

Cyber InterCaptive (cyber-cafes)

http://www.clearlight.com/~kireau/cafe.shtml

CyberiaCafe (cyber-cafes)

http://www.cyberiacafe.net/

Deja News (search engine for Usenet newsgroups)

http://www.dejanews.com/

Excite

http://www.excite.com/

Four11 (people search)

http://www.four11.com/

Global Computing Cyber Cafes

http://www.globalcomputing.com/cafes.html

HotBot

http://www.hotbot.com/

Huron Online (sweepstakes listings)

http://www.huronline.com/

Infoseek

http://www.infoseek.com/

Liszt (mailing lists search)

http://www.liszt.com

LookSmart

http://www.looksmart.com/

Lycos

http://www.lycos.com/

MetaCrawler

http://www.metacrawler.com/

Netguide (online events)

http://www.netguide.com/Happenings/

Northern Light

http://www.northernlight.com/

Search.com

http://www.search.com/

SuperPages (business directory)

http://www.superpages.com/

SurfPoint (LinkExchange member search)

http://www.surfpoint.com

Volition (listing of Net giveaways)

http://www.volition.com

WebCrawler

http://www.webcrawler.com

WebTaxi

http://www.webtaxi.com/

WhoWhere (people search)

http://www.whowhere.com

WorldPages (business directory)

http://www.worldpages.com/

Yack (chat event guide)

http://www.yack.com/

Yahoo Net Events

http://events.yahoo.com/

Yahoo!

http://www.yahoo.com/

Yahoo! on Contest Indices

http://www.yahoo.com/Entertainment/
Contests__Surveys__Polls/

Yahoo!'s on Cyber-Cafes

http://www.yahoo.com/Society_and_Culture/Cyberculture/
Internet_Cafes/

Official Internet Bodies and Lobby Groups

Center for Democracy and Technology

http://www.cdt.org/

Citizens Internet Empowerment Coalition

http://www.ciec.org/

Electronic Frontier Foundation

http://www.eff.org/

Internet Engineering Task Force

http://www.ietf.org/

Internet Society

http://info.isoc.org/

InterNIC

http://www.internic.net/

InterNIC "WhoIs" domain registration

http://rs.internic.net/cgi-bin/whois

Policy Oversight Committee (Generic Top Level Domain Memorandum of Understanding)

http://www.gtld-mou.org/

World Wide Web Consortium

http://www.w3.org/

Online Marketing Resources

Ad/Vantage Pawluk

http://www.pawluk.com/

AdSpend

http://www.jup.com/adspend/publishers.shtml

Advertising Law Internet Site

http://www.webcom.com:80/~lewrose/home.html

Advertising Media Internet Central

http://www.amic.com/

Advertising Research Foundation

http://www.amic.com/arf

Advertising World (University of Texas)

http://advweb.cocomm.utexas.edu/world/

American Marketing Association

http://www.ama.org/

American Advertising Federation

http://www.aaf.org/

American Association of Advertising Agencies (AAAA)

http://www.aaaa.org/

American Association of Domain Names

http://www.domains.org/

American Demographics

http://www.demographics.com/

American Journalism Review NewsLink

http://www.ajr.org/

Association of Direct Marketing Agencies

http://www.cyberdirect.com/ADMA/

Association for Interactive Media

http://www.interactivehq.org/

Association of Internet Professionals

http://www.isip.org/ and http://www.association.org/

Audit Bureau of Circulations

http://www.accessabc.com/

BPA International

http://www.bpai.com/

Bruce Clay

http://www.bruceclay.com/

Bruner Communications

http://www.bruner.net/

Business Marketing Association

http://www.marketing.org/

Businesswire

http://www.businesswire.com/

Coalition for Advertising Supported Information and Entertainment (CASIE)

http://www.casie.org/

CommerceNet

http://www.commerce.net/

CommercePark

http://www.commercepark.com/

Contest Central Sites

http://www.contestworld.com/advertise/free.html

Copywriter.com

http://www.copywriter.com/

CyberPulse

http://www.webcom.com/impulse/

Direct Email List Source

http://www.copywriter.com/lists/

Direct Marketing Association

http://www.the-dma.org/

Direct Marketing Club of Southern California

http://www.dmcsc.com/

Direct Marketing Plaza

http://www.dmplaza.com/

Direct Marketing World

http://www.dmworld.com/

The Domain Name Right's Coalition

http://www.domain-name.org/

DoubleClick Resource Center

http://www.doubleclick.net/nf/general/resouset.htm

E-Land

http://www.e-land.com/

Electronic Frontier Foundation on Domain Disputes

http://www.eff.org/pub/Intellectual_property/
Internet_address_disputes/
and

http://www.eff.org/pub/GII_NII/DNS_control/
eff_dns_19970428.statement

FlyCast Community Resource Center

http://www.flycast.com/ResourceCenter.htm

Four Corners (White Palm)

http://www.whitepalm.com/fourcorners/

Georgetown Law Center's What's in A Name?

http://www.law.georgetown.edu/lc/internic/domain1.html

Ideas For Business

http://www.ideasiteforbusiness.com/

Info Scavenger

http://www.infoscavenger.com/

InfoQuest

http://www.teleport.com/~tbchad/

International Newspaper Marketing Association

http://www.inma.org./

International WebCaster Organization

http://www.webcasters.org/

Internet Advertising Association

http://www.internet-association.org/

Internet Advertising Bureau

http://www.iab.net/

Internet Advertising Discussion List

http://www.exposure-usa.com/i-advertising

Internet Press Guild

http://www.netpress.org/

Internet Services Association

http://www.isa.net/

John Marshall Law School Index of Cyber Legal Issues:

http://www.jmls.edu/cyber/index/

JunkBusters

http://www.junkbusters.com/

LE-Digest

http://www.ledigest.com/

LinkExchange Resource Center

http://www.linkexchange.com/members/resources.html

Magazinedata

http://www.magazinedata.com/

Marketing Research Association

http://www.mra-net.org/

Media Literacy Online Project

http://interact.uoregon.edu/MediaLit/HomePage

MediaSource

http://www.mediasource.com/

Mining Company Online Advertising

http://adsonline.miningco.com/

MouseTracks

http://nsns.com/MouseTracks/

Multimedia Development Group

http://www.mdg.org/

NetPost

http://www.netpost.com/

New York New Media Association

http://www.nynma.org/

The Online Advertising Discussion List

http://www.o-a.com/

Online Advertising Forum (OLAF)

http://www.olaf.net/

Oppedahl & Larson

http://www.patents.com/

PR Newswire

http://www.prnewswire.com/

Publicity.com

http://www.publicity.com/

Push Concepts

http://www.pushconcepts.com/

Ragan's Interactive Public Relations

http://www.ragan.com/

SearchEngineWatch

http://www. searchenginewatch.com/

Sharrow.com

http://www.sharrow.com/

Spam Abuse

http://spam.abuse.net/

SRDS

http://www.srds.com/

Tenagra Marketing Resources

http://marketing.tenagra.com/

Thomson & Thomson

http://www.thomson-thomson.com/

Thunder Lizard Download Handouts

http://www.thunderlizard.com/dwnld_handout.html

TRUSTe

http://www.truste.org/

URLwire

http://www.urlwire.com/

USWeb's Resource Center

http://www.usweb.com/solutions/res_lib/whitepapers.html

Web Grrls

http://www.webgrrls.com/

WebCasting Special Interest Group

http://wcslg.org/

WilsonWeb

http://www.wilsonweb.com/

World Wide Web Artists Consortium

http://www.wwwac.org/

Yahoo! on Best of the Web Directories

www.yahoo.com/Computers_and_Internet/Internet/
World_Wide_Web/Best_of_the_Web/

Yahoo! on Domain Brokers

http://www.yahoo.com/Business_and_Economy/Companies/Internet_Services/Domain_Registration/Brokerages/

Yahoo! on Domain Controversies

http://www.yahoo.com/Computers_and_Internet/Internet/Domain_Registration/Domain_Name_Controversies/

Yahoo! on Spam

http://www.yahoo.com/Computers_and_Internet/Internet/Policies/Abuse/

Yahoo! on Specialized Search Services

http://www.yahoo.com/Computers_and_Internet/Internet/World_Wide_Web/Searching_the_Web/

Yahoo! on Web Advertising

http://www.yahoo.com/Computers_and_Internet/Internet/Business_and_Economics/Advertising_on_Web_and_Internet/

Internet and Online Marketing News

@NY-Newsletter

http://www.news-ny.com/

A Clue

http://tbass.com/clue/

Advertising Age

http://www.adage.com

AdTalks

http://www.adtalk.com/

AdWeek

http://www.adweek.com/

American City Business Journals—High Tech

http://www.amcity.com/journals/high_tech/

American Demographic/Marketing Tools Bookstore

http://www.marketingtools.com/

BackChannel

http://www.commercepark.com/AAAA/bc/

BoardWatch

http://www.boardwatch.com/

Browsers.com

http://www.browsers.com/

ChannelSeven

http://www.channelseven.com/

ClickZ

http://www.clickz.com/

CMPnet

http://www. cmpnet.com/

CNET

http://www. cnet.com/

Colloquy

http://www.colloquy.org/

CyberTimes (New York Times publication)

http://www.nytimes.com/yr/mo/day/cyber/

Direct Marketing News

http://www.dmnews.com/

Fast Company

http://www.fastcompany.com/

Forbes Digital Tool

http://www.forbes.com/

HotWired

http://www.hotwired.com/

Iconocast

http://www.iconocast.com/

InfoWeek

http://www.infoweek.com

Internet Advertising Report

http://www.internetnews.com/iar/

Internet Industry Standard

http://www.thestandard.net/

Internet SourceBook

http://www.internetsourcebook.com/

Internet.com

http://www.internet.com/

Marketing Computers

http://www.marketingcomputers.com/

MarketsResearch.Com

http://www.marketsresearch.com/

MediaCentral (Direct Marketing News)

http://www.mediacentral.com/

Microscope

http://www.microscope.com/

NetMarketing

http://netb2b.com/

News.com

http://www.news.com/

NewsHub

http://www.newshub.com/

NewsLinx

http://www.newslinx.com/

NewsPage

http://www.newspage.com/

Red Herring

http://www.redherring.com/

Sales and Marketing Management

http://www.smmmag.com/

The Scene

http://www.news-ny.com/scene.htm

Silicon Alley Reporter

http://www.siliconalleyreporter.com/

Skywriting

http://www.erspros.com/irc/skywrite/main.html

Suck.com

http://www.suck.com

Target Marketing Online

http://www.napco.com/tm/tmcover.html

TechWeb

http://www.techweb.com/

Upside

http://www.upside.com/

Web Digest For Marketers

http://www.wdfm.com/

WebWeek

http://www.webweek.com

Who's Marketing Online

http://www.wmo.com/

Wired News

http://www.wirednews.com/

ZDNet

http://www.zdnet.com/

ZDNet's NetPolitics

http://www.zdnet.com/products/netpolitics.html

Software and Online Service Companies

Aaddzz

http://www.aaddzz.com/

Accipiter

http://www.accipiter.com/

Accrue Software

http://www.accrue.com/

AdKnowledge

http://www.adknowledge.com/

Adletts

http://www.adletts.com/

AdSmart

http://www.adsmart.net/

AdVenture

http://www.ad-venture.com/

Andromedia

http://www.andromedia.com/

Apple Computer

http://www.apple.com/

Aptex

http://www.aptex.com/

Art Technology Group

http://www.atg.com/

Autonomy

http://www.agentware.com/

BackWeb Technologies

http://www.backweb.com/

Bare Bones Software

http://www.barebones.com/

Be Free

http://www.befree.com/

BellCore

http://www.bellcore.com/

Blaxxun

http://www.blaxxun.com/

Broadvision

http://www.broadvision.com/

CKS

http://www.cks.com/

Poppe Tyson

http://www.poppe.com/

Business Evolution

http://www.businessevolution.com/

CellularVision

http://www.cellularvision.com/

Clarify

http://www.clarify.com/

Cisco Systems

http://cisco.com/

Cosmo Software

http://www.cosmo.sgi.com/

Diamond Multimedia

http://www.diamondmm.com/

Documentum

http://www.documentum.com/

DoubleClick Network

http://www.doubleclick.net/

Equilibrium

http://www.equilibrium.com/

Firefly

http://www.firefly.net/

First Floor

http://www.firstfloor.com/

First Virtual

http://www.firstvirtual.com/

FlyCast

http://www.flycast.com/

Hotmail

http://www.hotmail.com/

ichat

http://www.ichat.com/

Imgis

http://www.imgis.com/

inCommon

http://www.incommon.com/

Individual

http://www.individual.com/

Intelligent Interactions

http://www.ipe.com/

InterMind

http://www.intermind.com/

Internet Profiles (I/PRO)

http://www.ipro.com/

InterVU

http://www.intervu.com/

JavaSoft

http://www.javasoft.com/

Juno Online

http://www.juno.com/

LinkExchange

http://www.linkexchange.com/

Macromedia

http://www.macromedia.com/

Marimba

http://www.marimba.com/

MatchLogic

http://www.matchlogic.com/

The MBone Information Web

http://www.mbone.com/

Microsoft Corporation

http://www.microsoft.com/

Modem Media

http://www.modemmedia.com/

Narrative Communications

http://www.narrative.com/

Narrowline

http://www.narrowline.com/

Nestor

http://www.nestor.com/

Net Perceptions

http://www.netperceptions.com/

Netcentives

http://www.netcentives.com/

NetDelivery

http://www.netdelivery.com/

NetGravity

http://www.netgravity.com/

Netiva

http://www.netiva.com/

Netscape Communications Corporation

http://www.netscape.com/

Network Solutions

http://www.netsol.com/

Niehaus Ryan Group, Public Relations

http://www.nrgpr.com/

Organic Online

http://www.organic.com/

Qualcomm

http://www.qualcomm.com/

Real Media

http://www.realmedia.com/

Real Networks

http://www.real.com/

Red Sky Interactive

http://www.redsky.com/

RevNet

http://www.revnet.com/

RocketMail

http://www.rocketmail.com/

Silicon Graphics

http://www.sgi.com/

Silknet Software

http://www.silknet.com/

Sofres IMR

http://www.sofresimr.com/

Smart Technologies

http://smartdna.com/

StarPoint

http://www.starpt.com/

Sun Microsystems

http://www.sun.com/

Thinking Media

http://www.thethinkingmedia.com/

24/7 Media

http://www.247media.com/

USWeb

http://www.usweb.com/

Vantive

http://www.vantive.com/

Vignette

http://www.vignette.com/

Visibility Index

http://www.visibilityindex.com/

Wayfarer Communications

http://www.wayfarer.com/

Western International Media

http://www.wimc.com/

WorldNIC

http://www.worldnic.com/

Zulu Media

http://www.zulumedia.com/

General News, Business, Entertainment, and Culture

ABC.com

http://www.abc.com/

ABCNews

http://www.abcnews.com/

America Online

http://www.aol.com/

Cars and Culture

http://www.carsandculture.com/

CBS.com

http://www.cbs.com/

CBS SportsLine

http://www.cbs.sportsline.com/

CNN Interactive

http://www.cnn.com/

CNNfn

http://www.cnnfn.com/

CompuServe

http://www.compuserve.com/The Dilbert Zone

http://www.unitedmedia.com/comics/dilbert/

Disney

http://www.disney.com/

DLJdirect

http://www.dljdirect.com/

E!Online

http://www.eonline.com/

ESPN SportZone

http://espn.sportszone.com/

GeoCities

http://www.geocities.com/

MapQuest

http://www.mapquest.com/

Microsoft Network

http://www.msn.com/

Motley Fool

http://www.fool.com/

MovieFinder

http://www.moviefinder.com/

Mr. Showbiz

http://www.mrshowbiz.com/

MSNBC

http://www.msnbc.com/

MTV

http://www.mtv.com/

NBC.com

http://www.nbc.com/

New York Times

http://www.nytimes.com/

Open 24

http://www.open24.com/

PathFinder

http://www.pathfinder.com/

PointCast

http://www.pointcast.com/

Prodigy

http://www.prodigy.com/

Quote.com

http://www.quote.com/

SF Gate

http://www.sfgate.com/

Sidewalk

http://www.sidewalk.com/

Snap!

http://www.snap.com/

The Station (Sony)

http://www.station.sony.com/

Ticketmaster

http://www.ticketmaster.com/

TotalNews

http://www.totalnews.com/

Tripod

http://www.tripod.com

USA Today

http://www.usatoday.com/

Wall Street Journal

http://www.wsj.com/

Weather Channel, The

http://www.weather.com/

WebChat Broadcasting

http://www.wbs.net/

Women's Wire

http://women.com/guide/

You Don't Know Jack

http://www.bezerk.com/netshow/

Yoyodyne

http://www.yoyo.com/

Examples of Marketing and E-Commerce Sites

Amazon.com

http://www.amazon.com/

American Airlines NetSAAVers

http://www.americanair.com/aa_home/net_saavers.htm

Andy's Garage Sale

http://www.andysgarage.com/

Avon

http://www.avon.com/

Barnes & Noble

http://www.barnesandnoble.com/

Best Diamond Value

http://www.jeweler.com

BonusMail

http://www.bonusmail.com/

Burger King

http://www.burgerking.com/

Charles Schwab & Co.—SchwabNOW!

http://www.schwab.com/

Coca-Cola

http://www.coke.com/

Cosmopolitan

http://www.cosmomag.com/

Crest

http://www.pg.com/docYourhome/docCrest/

Direct Value to You

http://www.dv2u.com/

Federal Express

http://www.fedex.com/

Fingerhut Companies

http://www.fingerhut.com/

First Auction

http://www.firstauction.com/

Ford Motor Company

http://www.ford.com/

Fragrance Counter

http://www.fragrancecounter.com/

General Motors

http://www.gm.com/

Good Guys, The

http://www.thegoodguys.com/

Harley Davidson

http://www.harley-davidson.com/

Home Depot

http://www.homedepot.com/

I Can't Believe It's Not Butter

http://www.icbinb.com/

Internet Shopping Network

http://www.isn.com/

JC Penney

http://www.jcpenney.com/

JM Lexus

http://www.jmlexus.com/

Joe Boxer

http://www.joeboxer.com/

Kotex

http://www.kotex.com/

KPIX TV

http://www.kpix.com/

L'Eggs Store

http://www.pantyhose.com

L.L. Bean

http://www.llbean.com/

LandsEnd

http://www.landsend.com/

Levi Strauss

http://www.levi.com/

McDonald's

http://www.mcdonalds.com/

Minolta Printers

http://www.minoltaprinters.com/

Nike

http://www.nike.com/

1-800 Flowers

http://www.1800flowers.com/

Pampers

http://www.pampers.com/

Peapod

http://www.peapod.com/

Pepsi-Cola

http://www.pepsi.com/

Preview Travel

http://www.previewtravel.com/

Ragu

http://www.ragu.com/

REI

http://www.rei.com/

Saturn

http://www.saturn.com/

Sears Roebuck

http://www.sears.com/

SFBay Matchmaker

http://www.sfbaymatchmaker.com/

Software.net

http://www.software.net/

Spam (Hormel)

http://www.spam.com/

Staples

http://www.staples.com/

Taco Bell

http://www.tacobell.com/

Tide ClothesLine

http://www.clothesline.com/

Tower Records

http://www.towerrecords.com/

Toyota

http://www.toyota.com/

TV Guide

http://www.tvguide.com/

Virtual Vineyards

http://www.virtualvin.com/

Web Fuel

http://www.webfuel.com/

The X-Files (official site)

http://www.thex-files.com/

Internet Market Research Groups

Burke

http://www.burke.com/

Cowles/Simba

http://www.simbanet.com/

CyberDialogue

http://www.cyberdialogue.com/

Find/SVP

http://www.findsvp.com/

Forrester Research

http://www.forrester.com/

Gartner Group

http://www.gartner.com/

IntelliQuest Information Group

http://www.intelliquest.com/

Jupiter Communications

http://www.jup.com/

Media Metrix (formerly PC Meter)

http://www.mediametrix.com/

Millward Brown

http://www.millwardbrown.com/

NetRatings

http://www.netratings.com/

Nielsen Media Research

http://www.nielsenmedia.com/

Relevant Knowledge

http://www.relevantknowledge.com/

YankeeGroup

http://www.yankeegroup.com/

Design and Navigation Aids

Builder.com

http://www.builder.com

Developer.com

http://www.developer.com/

High Five

http://www.highfive.com

JavaScript.com

http://www.javascripts.com/

WebCoder

http://www.webcoder.com/

WebMonkey

http://www.hotwired.com/webmonkey/

Wed Designers and Developers Association

http://www.wdda.org/

Yahoo! on Design Guides

http://www.yahoo.com/Computers_and_Internet/Internet/
World_Wide_Web/Page_Design_and_Layout/

Index